THE SOUTH AND THE CARIBBEAN

The South and the Caribbean

Essays and Commentaries by
BONHAM C. RICHARDSON
CHARLES JOYNER
STANLEY L. ENGERMAN
ALINE HELG
DANIEL C. LITTLEFIELD
ROGER D. ABRAHAMS
KENNETH BILBY
RALPH LEE WOODWARD, JR.
DAVID ELTIS
MILTON JAMAIL

Edited by
DOUGLASS SULLIVAN-GONZÁLEZ
and CHARLES REAGAN WILSON

UNIVERSITY PRESS OF MISSISSIPPI
Jackson

www.upress.state.ms.us

Copyright © 2001 by University Press of Mississippi
All rights reserved
Manufactured in the United States of America

09 08 07 06 05 04 03 02 01   4 3 2 1
∞

Library of Congress Cataloging-in-Publication Data

The South and the Caribbean : essays and commentaries / by Bonham
C. Richardson . . . [et al.] ; edited by Douglass Sullivan-González and
Charles Reagan Wilson.
     p.   cm.
     Papers from the 22nd Annual Chancellor Porter L. Fortune, Jr.,
Symposium on Southern History, held in Oxford, Mississippi in
October 1996.
     Includes bibliographical references and index.
     ISBN 1-57806-312-4 (alk. paper)
     1. Southern States—Civilization—Congresses.   2. Caribbean
Area—Civilization—Congresses.   3. Southern States—
Relations—Caribbean Area—Congresses.   4. Caribbean Area—
Relations—Southern States—Congresses.   5. Regionalism—
Southern States—Congresses.   6. Regionalism—Caribbean
Area—Congress.   7. Culture diffusion—Southern States—
Congresses.   8. Culture diffusion—Caribbean Area—Congresses.
I. Richardson,   Bonham C., 1939–   II. Sullivan-González,
Douglass, 1956–   III. Wilson, Charles Reagan.   IV. Chancellor
Porter L. Fortune, Jr., Symposium on Southern History (22nd :
1996 : University of Mississippi)
F209 .S695   2001
975—dc21   00-032056

British Library Cataloging-in-Publication Data available

Contents

Acknowledgments   vii

Introduction   ix

The South and the Caribbean: A Regional Perspective   3
BONHAM C. RICHARDSON

Comparative Slavery: African Culture in the South and the
     Caribbean   21
CHARLES JOYNER   Commentary: Stanley L. Engerman

The Problem of Race in Cuba and the United States   49
ALINE HELG   Commentary: Daniel C. Littlefield

Afro-Caribbean Culture and the South: Music with
     Movement   97
ROGER D. ABRAHAMS   Commentary: Kenneth Bilby

The Political Economy of the Caribbean   127
RALPH LEE WOODWARD, JR.   Commentary: David Eltis

Baseball in Southern Culture, American Culture, and the
     Caribbean   151
MILTON JAMAIL

Notes   167

Contributors   199

Index   201

Acknowledgments

The Porter L. Fortune Jr. History Symposium dates its origins to 1975, when historians met at the University of Mississippi to consider the latest scholarship on slavery. It quickly became an annual event, which in recent years has focused on such issues as the basis of a southern political tradition, gender and its effect in reconceptualizing political study in the South, recent regionalist approaches, and the role of ideas in the Civil Rights Movement. The twenty-second symposia met at Oxford, Mississippi, in October 1996, to explore the relationship between the Caribbean and the American South. Presenters of major papers included Bonham C. Richardson, Charles Joyner, Aline Helg, Roger D. Abrahams, Ralph Lee Woodward Jr., and Milton Jamail. Commentators were Stanley L. Engerman, Daniel C. Littlefield, Kenneth Bilby, and David Eltis.

The editors are grateful to many people for their support of the symposium. Dale Abadie, dean of Liberal Arts and professor of History, welcomed the participants to the meeting. Robert Haws, chair of the Department of History, coordinated much of the logistical work of the symposium from his office and generally encouraged us to undertake this topic. The faculty, graduate students, and secretaries of the Department of History and the Center for the Study of Southern Culture assisted in numerous ways with participants and in enlivening the discussions related to the symposium. Joanna Holland was key in coordinating the details of the meeting. We would like to thank Betty Harness and Susan Glisson for their role in preparing the manuscript for publication. The editors especially want to acknowledge the support of Maribel Sullivan-González and Marie Antoon, in their encouragement of us in planning this symposium and in our general work as historians.

Introduction

Fernand Braudel's 1947 thesis, *The Mediterranean*, forced historians to transcend political boundaries and to examine the cultural and social linkages that grew out of a common geography.
Braudel successfully reshaped historic debate on the impact of
Philip the II and his sixteenth-century expeditions into neighboring lands and seas. Historians no longer locked their analytical
eyes on Castile and Tripoli and Portugal and Italy. Now, scholars
questioned the society that emerged out of the Mediterranean.

The 1996 Porter L. Fortune Jr. Symposium at the University
of Mississippi sought to refocus similar linkages given a common
geography. The broad spanse of water known as the Caribbean
circumscribed what would become known as the South with the
trade of sugar and rum and African slaves in the group of islands
that form a perimeter around the Gulf of Mexico. Today concise
political boundaries separate the coasts of the American South
from the multicultural worlds that dominate the islands. Yet all
anecdotal evidence suggests far greater ties. Listen to the reggae
in the streets of New Orleans or the rhumba in Atlanta. Note the
moans of the blues in the cafes of Veracruz. Watch the major
leagues and witness how young Dominicans hurl lightning-fast
balls to become national heroes on a small island beset by political and economic woes.

What then is the South? Do these real human linkages suggest
a greater regionalism than previously studied? *The South and the
Caribbean* explores these connections, and this volume represents an effort to come to terms with the fluctuating boundaries
that separate and bond our people. Bonham C. Richardson, Professor of Geography at Virginia Polytechnic Institute and State
University, opened the conference with these and other queries.

Richardson proposed a cultural region "with Little Rock at the
northwest corner and French Guiana at the southeast that also

includes the eastern rim of Central America as well as the Bahamas." Geographical proximity and climatic conditions set the parameters of development. A political economy based on slavery
and monocrop production, Richardson asserted, gave birth to a
common history. African peoples brought to work the fields interacted with their masters and produced a multicultural heritage
in the post-colonial world. A "notable devotion" toward the home
and village marks this Caribbean region combined with a peculiar cultural insularity designed to protect the newly-created
identity. Today, however, given the technological advances in
transportation and communication, we witness a vigorous cultural and economic interaction between the Caribbean and the
South. The Atlanta-based "CNNization" of the Caribbean world
and the Caribbeanization of American music and baseball culti-
vates a new identity for both regions. How both the South and
the Caribbean preserve their uniqueness and transform under
the power of these overwhelming forces remains to be seen.

Three presenters spoke of the creative cultures unleashed
when a brutal European economy enslaved Africans for labor. A
shared language, common political aspirations, and a vivacious
song and dance characterize the South in the Caribbean. Charles
Joyner, Burroughs Distinguished Professor of Southern History
and Culture at Coastal Carolina University, examined the creolization of African culture in South Carolina and the Caribbean.
Joyner pointed to the common language of Creole, "the shared
property" of the descendants of the African slaves that became
the primary vehicle to maintain and reassert the creative African
heritage. African Americans gave birth to a new culture through
this common language that found expression in a common music
and poetry that transcends political boundaries. Aline Helg, Associate Professor of History at the University of Texas at Austin,
looked at how the historic patterns of slavery found new form
in the national periods. Comparing Cuba and the South, Helg
concluded that both Cuban and southern elites developed new
relations to justify continued domination of blacks. Whereas

blacks in the South gained political equality in the 1960s, socio-economic dependence upon whites reinforced the inherited racism. Blacks in Cuba confront a rhetoric of socialist equality that prevents them from protesting racism.

Roger Abrahams, Professor of Folklore and Folklife at the University of Pennsylvania, traces the roots of common beliefs and practices, in which people "organize the energies to the call of the spirit." These flash moments that do not follow dominant patterns indicate, Abrahams asserts, "the existence of counter-hegemonic forces constantly emerging from within such dislocated and dispossessed communities." Abrahams thus sees historic patterns of styles in current song and dance that give further proof of the dynamic cultural movement between, first, the plantation owner and slave and, now, between white and black hip hop and rap culture.

Lastly, the economic linkages that connect these two political regions have created lasting legacies. The two final presenters, Professors Ralph Lee Woodward, Jr., and Milton Jamail, looked at what the two worlds bequeathed to us today—a legacy of the plantation and a great love for baseball. Woodward, Professor of History at Tulane University, examined how agricultural exploitation of the Caribbean region helped fuel the industrial revolution. Revenues from the blood and sweat of laborers became an essential component of the world system that evolved in the North Atlantic. Jamail, lecturer at the University of Texas at Austin and guest columnist for *USA Today Baseball Weekly*, looked at four Latino players who came to the United States and ultimately received recognition as great players of the game while enduring the hardships of a segregated society. Cubans carried the love of the game to their Caribbean neighbors and to the adjoining coastal areas of Mexico. Baseball quickly transcended class and rooted itself in the lives of very common folk in this great region. Legends like Vic Power, Felipe Alou, Juan Marichal, and Ruben Amaro have been instrumental in creating strong cultural bonds between the two regions.

The South and the Caribbean flow into each other culturally, economically, and socially. These papers and their commentaries suggest that future study of the South and the Caribbean will have to deal with both regions in order to understand either. Thus the merging of the regions through song, dance, language, game, and political aspiration serves to give birth to a New South and a New Caribbean.

August 1999

Charles Reagan Wilson   Douglass Sullivan-González
Director, Center for the Study of   Assistant Professor of
   Southern Culture and   History
Professor of History

THE SOUTH AND THE CARIBBEAN

The South and the Caribbean: A Regional Perspective

BONHAM C. RICHARDSON

President Ronald Reagan's visit to Barbados early in 1982 provided an important lesson in small-island economics. Barbados had suffered a listless tourist season, a disappointment vaguely attributed to economic recession in the United States. But Reagan's brief visit in April filled Bridgetown area hotels for two weeks with State Department officials, security personnel, and newspaper reporters so as to change the entire 1981–82 Barbadian tourist winter into a marginal success.

The event also highlighted American ignorance about the Caribbean. The purpose of Reagan's visit was to inaugurate the Caribbean Basin Initiative, designed in part to isolate economically Cuba, Nicaragua, and Grenada from pro-American states in the region and to thwart leftist sentiment in El Salvador. In a memorable interview televised in Barbados, an American commentator—with Central America on her mind—interviewed the Cambridge-educated Barbadian Prime Minister, Tom Adams. Shortly into the discussion, in which she was querying Adams about foreign aid, insurgency, and anti-American sentiment, Adams politely informed her that nothing she was asking made any sense whatever for Barbados because it differs from most of Central America culturally, historically, economically, and in nearly every other way.

Scholars of the Caribbean can appreciate Adams' polite impatience because we are often viewed by colleagues, administrators, and area studies devotees as those who study a minor, offbeat appendage of Latin America and whose courses might offer students a pleasing respite of scenery, baseball, and calypso from

3

the more important analyses of latifundismo, globalism, and urban popular discontent. My guess is that scholars of the United States South—especially those at non-southern universities—have had similar experiences. I can imagine that, more than once, academic planners have enthused about the possibilities for American Studies programs with curricula emphasizing such salient American characteristics as the ethnic melting pot or the rise of nineteenth century industry and then, as an afterthought, suggesting that they also must not forget the South.

My point is not to emphasize regional distinctions for either the South or the Caribbean but to follow the lead implied by our symposium's title; perhaps neither region need be a stepchild if we redefine and consolidate them within different boundaries. Consider a broad culture region with Little Rock at the northwest corner and French Guiana at the southeast that also includes the eastern rim of Central America as well as the Bahamas. At least two geographers have posited this kind of arrangement: Donald Meinig of Syracuse University has identified a broad subtropical, or Afro-North, America realm in his multi-volume historical geography of North America; and Terry Jordan of the University of Texas has suggested that a low-lying "Creole Coast" runs from Chesapeake Bay to Corpus Christi underpinned by a so-called "Romano-Caribbean ethnicity" blending cultural and material traits from both the South and the Caribbean.[1]

On reflection, the two regions have been, are, and will be fused profoundly. The French/Haitian influences on New Orleans, Charleston, and other southern ports in the early 1800s were followed by a geography of what might have been with the Ostend Manifesto, the filibusters, and Knights of the Golden Circle during the Confederacy, followed by President Ulysses Grant's designs on the Samaná Bay of northeastern Hispaniola. Then the Spanish-American War, Panama Canal, and gunboat diplomacy tied the Caribbean irrevocably to the United States. Today at the geographical center of our hypothesized region are juxtaposed some of the richest and poorest localities in the hemisphere, their nearness inspiring recurring impulses of human migration from the Greater Antilles to southern Florida. Once Fidel is gone, hundreds of thousands of Miami Cubans will invade their homeland with money, ideas, and advice. That we cannot predict the particular trajectory or reactions that this invasion will create diminishes neither its importance nor its inevitability.

None of these points is new. And I feel certain that academic specialists of the U.S. South, like those of us working in the Caribbean, have, on more than one occasion, sensed common ground, causing us to gaze longingly at one another across the Gulf of Mexico. We share interests in histories of harsh plantation regimes supported by oppressive political systems. We appreciate the comparative studies contrasting labor systems imposed by different subtropical staple crops. We thrill at learning that family ties and geographical localities are intertwined in coastal Guyana just as they are in the Mississippi Delta. And we are emboldened by the comparative research of our most talented colleagues who have illustrated the rewards of cross-regional perspectives, whether they be Sidney Mintz and Richard Price dealing with the origins of Afro-American culture, Eugene Genovese comparing slave resistance and revolts, or Rebecca Scott assessing historical variations in the cultivation of sugar cane.[2]

But before being swept away in a tide of cross-regional enthusiasm, we must understand far more about the other area we are studying. Despite my own boyhood in Texas and Oklahoma and the bulk of my academic career spent in western Virginia plus a frantic reading effort in the last several months, I confess a woeful ignorance about the South. Still, this paper attempts to elucidate some of the Caribbean's principal geographical characteristics in light of the salient features of the South as I understand them.

In his book written sixty years ago about the *Human Geography of the South* (1935), the sociologist Rupert Vance asserted that the South's climate was "regarded by many as the region's *raison d'etre*." Vance's chapters about climate include a debunking of the reigning climatic determinism of the day and are well done by today's standards. The special report about the U.S. South in *The Economist* in 1994 emphasized a point others have made, that much of the recent economic success is owed to the now-widespread use of modern air conditioning. And Carl Degler asserts that a key feature of the South is the climate because it "is the only section of the country that comes close to a tropical climate—and in some parts it comes very close."[3]

Within the parameters of the crucial frost-free character of the Caribbean, spatial and seasonal climatic variety influences the human occupation of its islands and rimlands. Caribbean planters never worried about a 200-day growing season boundary as in the cotton South, but they learned early that seasonal coolness on the northern sides of the Greater Antilles inhibited cultivation of the most temperature-sensitive tropical crops. More common throughout the Caribbean is drought that has always threatened the low-lying islands such as Antigua and Barbados. Downward-moving air masses off northern Venezuela help explain the anomalous low-latitude deserts that are Aruba, Bonaire, and Curaçao. And on every tiny and therefore drought-prone island of the Eastern Caribbean, hillside dwellings—often given names for the migration destinations where money was earned to build them—feature concrete catchment and cistern complexes to store water in the event of prolonged aridity.

Drought and flooding can each affect a given Caribbean locale in a short period. Grenada suffered damaging aridity for most of 1894. Then heavy September rains destroyed bridges and roads, fickle and perverse extremes that could be recounted for other times and other Caribbean places. Where islands are sufficiently large, Windward and Leeward are important contrasts. The differences between rainy northern Puerto Rico and the arid south coast are dramatized within a short span of the high-speed highway that bisects the island's center. Residents of Port-of-Spain, Trinidad, swelter on the Leeward side of the island and seek the cooling easterly breezes of Maraccas Bay, a few miles across the mountains.

Year-round warmth is, of course, the Caribbean's attraction and selling point in tourist brochures. But the region's residents are wary of the same climate because of the autumn hurricane threat. The U.S. South is not unaware of the hurricane season, and the associated autumn rains mark the southern cotton boundary inland from the Gulf Coast. In the islands, in contrast, every late summer and autumn day includes the possibility that a new Atlantic storm has been spotted, its route thereafter a potential menace. Hurricane tracks are unpredictable beyond describing their vaguely curving southeast to northeast trajectories. And the back to back blows dealt to the Leeward Caribbean by Luís followed by Marilyn in August and September of 1995 are obvious reminders that hurricanes can follow one another in relentless succession.

Different from the climatological contrasts of the South and the Caribbean is the perverse similarity with which climate has been used to justify slavery and oppression in both areas. The common wisdom that blacks were biologically suited for field labor from dawn until dusk under a broiling sun and whites genetically adapted to shaded supervisory roles was far more than cocktail conversation in the Caribbean. When Thomas Carlyle wrote his vitriolic essay about Quashee and the pumpkins in 1849, critics attacked the essay's blatant racism; unquestioned was his facile climatic determinism about the bounteous tropical climate and the inferiority of peoples who had evolved in lower latitudes without the benefits of bracing seasonality that had led to European thrift and responsibility. Rather, these and similar points underpinned much of the British Caribbean development dogma even into this century and justified harsh rules and laws that curbed public expenditures for even the most meager public help for the poor. Rupert Vance and others note that the South's climate provided a similar justification for slavery.[4]

Geophysicists tell us that the fractured crustal opening that eventually became the Caribbean Sea appeared only eighty to one hundred million years ago when Africa, South America, and

North America split apart from a common landmass. The immediate question that estimate raises is, of course, from which continent was the dinosaur DNA carried by that mosquito entombed in Dominican amber in the cinematic version of *Jurassic Park?* In a less frivolous vein, the seismic activity of the Caribbean region is important historically. Many will recall from David McCullough's book about the Panama Canal that the eruption of Mt. Pelée in Martinique in 1902 influenced the U.S. Senate that Panama, rather than presumably more earthquake-prone Nicaragua, was the more suitable canal route.[5]

Today the arc of the Lesser Antilles from St. Martin south to Trinidad marks the intersection of two of the earth's crustal plates. Montserrat is only the most recent island to experience volcanic tremors and eruptions. Throughout the Eastern Caribbean older men and women recall earthquakes that sent a neighboring village or two sliding into the sea, events not always confirmed by conventional archival records but real enough in people's minds to shape attitudes about living on particular islands. In a broader sense, noting volcanic instability underscores the fragmented insularity of the entire region.

In identifying what distinguishes the Caribbean from all other world regions, the late Gordon K. Lewis asserted that "The first of those features, and that from which everything else flows, is . . . that the European colonial powers created Caribbean colonies *de novo* . . . once . . . the original . . . Indian stocks had been reduced . . ." Geographers might add a commonsensical corollary to Lewis's observation, specifying that the Caribbean's core is— first and foremost—a series of discrete particles of land surrounded by ocean water, earth features known to non-academics as islands. If this point appears overly obvious, allow me to discuss what I hope will appear as the subtleties of Caribbean insularity or islandness.[6]

On his second voyage, Columbus headed northwest to Hispaniola from his landfall at Dominica. "(A)nd so to each one I gave a new name . . . ," he noted of the islands he passed, christened, and thereby added semantically to a European orbit. In the decades thereafter, the complete accessibility that individual Caribbean islands afforded European-based sailing vessels allowed them to be colonized and ecologically transformed by Europeans and their African slaves, changes occurring at very early dates.[7]

How early? African slaves were introduced into what is now the Dominican Republic by 1505; upon arrival, some escaped into the hills, thereby establishing a free black identity in the Western Hemisphere more than a century before either Plymouth Rock or Jamestown. In 1817, the year Mississippi achieved statehood, slaves in St. Kitts, Barbados, and Guadeloupe had been producing raw sugar for European markets for nearly two centuries, on Hispaniola for more than three.[8]

No Indian Removal Act was necessary for Caribbean planters and officials. Different from the Cherokees in Georgia and the Choctaws in Mississippi, the Caribs of the Lesser Antilles and the Taino Arawaks of the Greater Antilles usually died off so quickly that their initial presence did little to inhibit European takeovers. To be sure, introduced pathogens—as Alfred Crosby, Kenneth Kiple, and others have written about so capably— probably accounted for more deaths than did European cruelty. But small places provided few buffers for indigenous subsistence systems when Europeans competed relentlessly for the only arable lands. Unlike the mainland Maya, for example, Caribbean Indians had no extensive interiors providing physical subsistence or symbolic refuge with which to blunt and mediate European demands.[9]

Nor did small Caribbean islands have extensive zones of piney woods, sandy barrens, or otherwise marginal areas that could support a numerous and transitory populace of poor whites. The earliest non-aboriginal farmers of the Eastern Caribbean were indeed white indentured workers. But when sugar cane arrived via Brazil in the early 1600s, a massive number of slaves soon appeared as well, in effect sweeping away most small-scale white cultivators. Post-emancipation Jamaica considered importing

white yeoman farmers to occupy the mountainous interior, and
the Spanish-speaking Greater Antilles each contained small-scale
cultivators who played important local roles in the late nineteenth century, but most of the islands had starkly polarized plantation cultures characterized by a small number of whites on the
one hand and a large number of African slaves on the other.

This oversimplified demographic model varied from one island
to another, yet its salient attributes help to throw light on differences in race relations between the South and the Caribbean.
With few white women in the colonial Caribbean, it seems inevitable that a brown-skinned, mulatto group would emerge
throughout the region. Their status and socioeconomic identities
varied from place to place. Perhaps the best-known were the cel-
ebrated *gens de couleur* of St. Domingue, the offspring of French
planters and slave women, people often recognized by their
fathers, formally educated and wielding power and authority in
pre-revolution Haiti. One century later in the British Caribbean,
as the Colonial Office sought political solutions for the problem
posed by its once-profitable but now-antiquated sugar colonies,
brown-skinned people were often more capable than were the
white officials sent from Britain.[10]

Differences abound between St. Domingue in the late eighteenth century and the British islands in the late nineteenth, and
color and caste vary widely elsewhere in the region—not least
because of the considerable Asian influence owing to the inden-
ture system. Yet these differences cannot obscure the fact that
the term "black" is neither common nor appropriate for mixed
blood peoples of the Caribbean as it is understood in the U.S.
South. The point is best exemplified by individual experience.
Writing in *The New Yorker* in 1996, Malcolm Gladwell explained
that, although many of his brown-skinned friends and relatives of
Jamaican heritage have emigrated to the greater New York area,
most do not consider themselves black at all in the United States
sense. Elaborating the point, Gladwell offers: "This question of

who West Indians are and how they define themselves may seem
trivial, like racial hairsplitting. But it is not trivial."[11]

That Afro-Caribbean peoples—whether or not they are of
mixed blood—see themselves as different from African Americans is not trivial either. In the early twentieth century tens of
thousands of West Indians immigrated to the eastern seaboard, a
substantial number coming to Boston's Roxbury district. In the
following decades Boston's West Indian community—though not
oblivious to racism outside their own district—kept mainly to
themselves, taking pride in their relative prosperity, their own
churches, and their devotion to friends and family. Louis Walcott,
among the most gifted of this transplanted West Indian community, was an intensely religious young man, a brilliant student, a
gifted musician, and a champion sprinter. When he ventured
south in 1950 to accept a track and field scholarship in North
Carolina, he encountered the hostility and racism he thought
were reserved only for United States blacks. This painful experience represented for young Louis Walcott a sea change, influ-
encing him to change his name to Louis Farrakhan, at once an
individual response to racism and an event with far wider implications.[12]

Caribbean peoples possess a storehouse of similar anecdotes.
According to them, gradations in skin color, language, occupation, and much else serving to differentiate individuals at home
are ignored in favor of an oversimplified black-white dichotomy
when they come north. Rob Ruck's *The Tropic of Baseball* tells
of when the Milwaukee (later Atlanta) Braves' slugger Rico Carty
first came to spring practice in Florida in 1960. After learning
that Carty, born in St. Martin and more recently from the Dominican Republic, had eaten at a reputed whites-only establishment
near the ballpark, friends warned him, "Man, you lucky they
didn't lynch you over there. . . . Black people can't eat over
there!" Carty's response was, "I'm not black, I'm Spanish."[13]

Eating and insularity also were interrelated in the days of Caribbean slavery, helping account for the well-known demo-

graphic contrasts between Caribbean slaves and those in the South, differences often attributed to sugar cane's arduous labor regime. The islands' best lands were devoted to cash crops, with food often imported from eastern North America. The food-deficits that still characterize most of the Caribbean's island states today can thus be interpreted as a colonial legacy. More important in the life, and often death, of Caribbean slaves, shipping could be disrupted by external events including war or weather. While colonial Caribbean planters complained of external complications that plagued the orderly flow of business, their slaves—who often grew thin and sickly during the so-called "starving time" when autumn weather curtailed shipping—had their lives at stake.

The legendary environmental destruction, principally soil erosion, that laid waste to so much of the cotton South was, if anything, worse in the Caribbean. The transformation of multi-species insular ecosystems to monocrop production units began in the Eastern Caribbean in the seventeenth century and has been dubbed the era of "The Great Clearing" by the historians Carl and Roberta Bridenbaugh.[14] Stripping islandwide forest covers to provide building materials, fuel, and sugar cane acreage meant that summer and autumn rainstorms no longer nurtured subtropical forests but instead were pounding erosive agents. To be sure, mature cane anchored the soil, but after harvest and before the next crop shaded the ground, serious erosion occurred. The clearing of the natural vegetation also intensified local droughts and dried up streams, especially on the smaller islands.

Physical environmental challenges and high slave population densities were perversely interrelated on Caribbean sugar cane islands. Annual slave death rates ran as high as twenty-five percent in the decades when slave gangs removed forest covers. In 1732 Governor William Mathew of the British Leeward Islands noted that St. Kitts's arable land had by then been cleared up to the mountainsides. He further suggested that, as local soil fertility decreased, a denser slave population would be necessary. In

other words, importing more slaves and forcing them to drive the
land harder could compensate for environmental deterioration,
at least in Mathew's view. Conditions were even worse along the
mudflats of coastal Guyana. The late Guyanese historian Walter
Rodney estimated that their transformation to a sea-level plantation zone criss-crossed with canals and protected by earthen
dams "meant," in his words, "that slaves moved 100 million tons
of heavy, waterlogged clay with shovel in hand, while enduring
conditions of perpetual mud and water."[15]

Given the overall colonial strategy of meeting these and other
challenges with a nearly inexhaustible supply of imported slave
labor, it is little wonder that the Caribbean has been considered
overpopulated for as long as that term has been around. The region's introduced overpopulation became particularly obvious
with the wrenching economic changes of the nineteenth century.
Steam milling of cane sugar extended the overhead cost of factory
construction over thousands of new acres in Brazil, Cuba, Mauritius, Natal, and Fiji, and the associated rise of mid-latitude beet
sugar in Western Europe and the United States was even more
damaging to the traditional Caribbean sugar cane economies.
The "old islands" (as much of the Eastern Caribbean came to be
described in official British correspondence) were becoming, by
the time of the U.S. Civil War, economic anachronisms with
eroded landscapes and dense human populations.

Slave emancipation throughout the century—in the British
possessions in the 1830s, the French and Danish in 1848, the
Dutch in 1863, Puerto Rico in 1873, and Cuba not until 1886—
freed people and sometimes land. Sidney Mintz's term "reconsti-
tuted peasantries" describes the many ways in which small cultivators emerged from Caribbean slavery, farming hillside plots as
freeholders in some places or as renters or sharecroppers in others, participating in local markets, creating new identities with
what little was at hand, and establishing true independence by
resisting ongoing planter oppression.[16]

But where land was withheld from freed slaves, insularity imposed formidable constraints on those attempting to assert their independence from local plantocracies. Upon emancipation in the 1830s, hundreds of men and women from some of the "old islands" of the Eastern Caribbean overcame these constraints by traveling away to Trinidad and British Guyana for higher wages. Their movements defied local vagrancy laws, rode on dangerously small sailing vessels, and usually were not one way. In sailing away and returning home, these individuals extended their livelihood patterns through extraordinary personal effort, established themselves as leaders in their home communities, and realized the freedom that had been formally granted.[17]

Such are the origins of Caribbean migration, an enduring demographic and cultural trait well-known to metropolitan TV viewers today as a current event associated with illegal immigration to the United States, the so-called "coloured problem" in Britain, or varying levels of xenophobia in France, the Netherlands, and even Canada. To be sure, migration from the South, mainly by black Americans, has been momentous and, according to some historians, ranks among the most important human movements in all of history. Yet human migration from and within the Caribbean is fundamental to the region, and today some of the smaller island economies would collapse without it.

Since emancipation, Caribbean peoples have migrated temporarily and permanently, movements that cannot be easily classified. They migrate to get ahead, support loved ones left behind, escape drought or economic depression, or simply do what everyone else is doing. In this century, every major economic event in the circum-Caribbean has attracted peoples from the islands and rimlands, migrants who in earlier days were almost exclusively men but whose ranks have been augmented more and more by women. The establishment of banana plantations in eastern Central America, the Panama Canal construction, the building of oil derricks in Venezuela's Lake Maracaibo and the associated refineries in Aruba and Curaçao, sugar cane harvesting in Cuba and the Dominican Republic, work on U.S. bases in World War II, hotel construction in the U.S. Virgin Islands, and more have been carried out by Caribbean migrants.

Not surprisingly, migration and return has imprinted local cultures throughout the region. In some places, young men are considered suitable marriage partners only after working abroad. When young adults are away, home islands are skewed demographically between grandparents and small children. In the smallest places, money that purchases taxis, houses, and fishing boats invariably comes from remittances sent or brought back from abroad. Everyone in Barbados has a relative or friend living in New York. The term "Nuyorican" in Puerto Rico can indicate admiration for success or disdain for false pretense, depending on how it is used. And you will find many of these same points in Carol Stack's new book about black migrants returning to the Carolinas from east coast urban centers.[18]

The recent movements of hundreds of thousands of Caribbean peoples to New York and other North Atlantic metropoles have extended Caribbean migrations importance far beyond the Caribbean itself. These newcomers have altered the fabrics of their host societies by introducing their own foods, clothing, music, celebrations, sensibilities, and work ethics. And the somewhat sudden presence of large concentrations of Caribbean peoples in North Atlantic metropoles provide the basis for, among other things, serious self-reflection. For Americans who pride themselves on their assimilation of peoples from throughout the world, the immigration of Caribbean peoples represents at once a test of our ability truly to welcome and assimilate as well as an extension of a more numerous African American presence that is centuries old. For Europeans, Caribbean migration represents a geographic reversal of an issue as old as empire itself: the associations between rulers and ruled, abstractions formerly confined to far corners of the globe, are now local European issues of immediate significance.

Despite the worldly outlook that migration has produced, a notable devotion toward home, village, and local lands exists on

every Caribbean island. Anthologies of Caribbean literature testify, in the region's several languages, to the writers' fierce identi-
fications with native landscapes. The late Jamaican economist
George Beckford proclaimed an idea applicable throughout the
Caribbean: "The story of the Jamaican people is essentially the
story of a struggle for land." In both the Caribbean and the South,
land is a buffer against the demands by entrenched powerhold-
ers. In his book about growing up black in rural Mississippi,
Chalmers Archer enthused about the land his parents bought in
1939 with what he referred to as "a great appreciation of ownership and pride. We were not sharecroppers or renters any longer.
We were landowners!" Archer's exuberance is similar but less
direct than was the eighty-year-old tailor in Barbados's St. Peter
parish when I asked him fifteen years ago why the small land plot
his father bought in 1925 was so important. His answer: "We
could then tell the plantation to go to hell!"[19]

Caribbean tenacity about land is most obvious in the tiniest
islands where reverence about place is bound up with love of
family, a feeling intensified in small island populations with a
limited number of surnames. One result is defensiveness and
stereotyping of outsiders, especially those from nearby islands.
Residents of miniscule La Désirade, east of Guadeloupe, consider people from the larger island irresponsible spendthrifts
whose only interests are in drinking and dancing, whereas Gua-
deloupéens say that residents of La Désirade are clannish, secre-
tive, and behind the times. These mutual stereotypes, not inci-
dentally, are precisely what you will hear from Trinidadians about
Tobagonians and vice versa, and they hold for virtually all of the
multi-island states of the English-speaking Caribbean such as
Antigua-Barbuda, St. Kitts-Nevis, and St. Vincent and the Grenadines.

Caribbean insularity and associated dense human populations
have led to a kind of cultural compression. Many people from,
literally, all over the world have arrived in a variety of circumstances for centuries, their juxtaposition forcing familiarity with

others and compelling a coping with the unusual. The Trinidadian historian Kusha Haraksingh speaks of "collapsing space" that has led to what he calls cultural confusion among his own Indian forefathers who came from throughout the subcontinent to Trinidad, an island one-tenth of one percent the size of India. Haraksingh asserts that different ways of displaying prayer flags, celebrating holy days, and conducting daily tasks have frustrated the Indo-Trinidadian population with an unwieldy heterogeneity. The Jamaican-born Harvard sociologist/historian Orlando Patterson finds in this compressed social atmosphere a possible key to understanding the resilience of Caribbean peoples and captures the idea with his elegant term "creative nonadaptation."[20]

Whatever the origins, the creativity and dynamism among Caribbean peoples extend well beyond the Caribbean itself to influence the U.S. South and other places. Colin Powell, of Jamaican heritage, is doubtless today's best-known political figure from the region, but recall that Alexander Hamilton was born on Nevis and that congresswoman and presidential candidate Shirley Chisholm was of Barbadian extraction. Further, Louis Farrakhan is only the most recent and best-known black activist with a Caribbean background: Malcolm X's mother came from Grenada; W. E. B. Du Bois claimed Haitian ancestry; Marcus Garvey was Jamaican. In the creative and performing arts, Harry Belafonte, Jamaica Kincaid, V.S. Naipaul, Sidney Poitier, and Derek Walcott are known everywhere today. Yet they were preceded in the 1920s by Caribbean writers and artists who played significant roles in the Harlem Renaissance.[21] Today Caribbean sights and sounds are ingrained in American life. Reggae from Jamaica and rap music from Trinidad are packaged and rebroadcast as American exports. The contingent of Dominicans on every major league baseball team has helped redefine our so-called national pastime.

Whereas cultural impulses heading north from the Caribbean are pervasive and lasting, those moving in the other direction are of an entirely different magnitude. For more than a century,

academics and journalists have competed for catchwords and slo-
gans in attempts to capture the profound influences of the United
States upon Caribbean societies that have affected individuals
and families, altered the fabrics of local societies, and changed
the ways people regard themselves and each other. Today these
influences are instantaneous because television signals from Atlanta and elsewhere penetrate hotel lobbies, storefronts, and hillside villages throughout the Caribbean, so much so that fretful
parents and local leaders from Belize to Barbados to the Bahamas
agonize over what might be called the CNNization of their societies.

These cultural transmissions underlie tangible changes emanating from North America, variously dubbed "modernization,"
"development," or "globalization," that continue to transform the
Caribbean as in the past. Early in the twentieth century American capital carved banana enclaves from tropical forests on the
eastern rim of Central America, and in the Greater Antilles en-
croachment by American-financed sugar cane obliterated entire
villages. Today new golf courses, tourist hotels, and controlled
access highways on Caribbean islands have much the same effect.

The transforming ability of modern technology aided by the
speed with which capital is transferred and focused is without
precedent. Combine this synergy with small island vulnerability,
and one can begin to understand why today some island cultures
are not simply changing or adapting but disappearing altogether.
Tiny Petit St. Vincent in the English-speaking Grenadines, not
long ago an islet with a few houses and goat herders, is now an
islandwide getaway for rich Americans. Much the same can be
said for Les Saintes, really a French tropical resort rather than
its formal identity as a dependency of Guadeloupe. St. Martin—
jointly affiliated with France and the Netherlands—is, because of
the proliferation of condominiums, traffic jams, and high crime
rates, unrecognizable from what it was three decades ago. The
posh hotels on Anguilla and Nevis charge more for a single

night's lodging than the average annual monetary income for one of the islands' residents, a financial discrepancy with wrenching cultural implications.

Contemplating insularity again affords perspective about these unprecedented changes. In his new book on island biogeography, the nature writer David Quammen tells how very special islands are and why. "Geographical isolation" writes Quammen "is the flywheel of evolution" because unpredictable changes and adaptations, such as organisms taking on bizarre and resplendent forms, can run quickly through tiny, self-contained populations. Might we add by extension an economic corollary and suggest that a single visit by a U.S. President can revive an entire island's economy? Even if we can, the darker side of island biogeography, according to Quammen and others, is that islands offer little to buffer externally-introduced dangers such as disease, the arrival of humans, or regional drought. And it takes neither imagination nor blind faith in reductionism to equate what Quammen sees as the potential dangers in island biogeography with the transformations occurring today in the Caribbean.[22]

From an entirely different perspective, hear the same grim message from the Caribbean's Nobel laureate Derek Walcott on the possible future of the region about which he has written so eloquently:

> How quickly it could all disappear! And how it is beginning to drive us further into where we hope are impenetrable places, green secrets at the end of bad roads, headlands where the next view is not of a hotel but of some long beach without a figure and the hanging question of some fisherman's smoke at its far end. The Caribbean is not an idyll, not to its natives. They draw their working strength from it organically, like trees, like the sea almond or the spice laurel of the heights. Its peasantry and its fishermen are not there to be loved or even photographed; they are trees who sweat, and whose bark is filmed with salt, but every day on some island, rootless trees

in suits are signing favourable tax breaks with entrepreneurs, poisoning the sea almond and the spice laurel of the mountains to their roots. A morning could come in which governments might ask what happened not merely to the forests and the bays but to a whole people.[23]

In conclusion, I must emphasize that gloomy forecasts of the Caribbean's imminent demise have a lengthy pedigree. Such predictions have recurred for as long and with a similar frequency as have proclamations about the New South. Caribbean peoples emerged from conditions of physical and human violence. And they have weathered a history of recurring assaults. In adapting to external demands for a half millenium, these peoples have developed remarkable survival skills, traits that are probably now enduring their sternest test.

Comparative Slavery: African Culture in the South and the Caribbean

CHARLES JOYNER

In the summer of 1991 I was presenting a paper on slave culture to a joint meeting of the Association of Caribbean Studies and the Southern Conference of Afro-American studies in Dakar, Senegal. There, some highly educated African and African-American intellectuals questioned whether studies of slavery are not *inherently* demeaning. What is needed, some of them insisted, are "positive images." But where can we find more positive images than the enslaved Africans who overcame their subjection to "horrors unbefitting even to wild animals." The people who resisted and overcame such horrors deserve recognition as something more than mere victims. Theirs is an epic story of brave men and women who not only endured almost unimaginable conditions, but who left their mark on history in ways that are still meaningful (or should be) to the present generation—and to the future.

Slavery "was an economic institution of the first importance," as Eric Williams pointed out a half-century ago. The ancient world was built on slavery. The economies of Greece and Rome had been based on slavery. Perhaps the economic importance of New World slavery in the modern world is best demonstrated in Williams' memorable comment that the slaves "were stolen in Africa to work the lands stolen from the Indians in America." Slaves grew the cotton that clothed the modern world. Slaves grew the rice that filled the plates of the modern world. Slaves grew the tobacco that filled the pipes and cigars of the modern world. Slaves grew the coffee that filled the cups of the modern world and the sugar that sweetened them. Brazil, the Caribbean islands, and the Old South all rose on the backs of slave laborers.[1]

The ancestors brought Africa with them in their heads. Perhaps the most significant links between Africa and the New World are to be found in culture. Culture is a process. Among slaves in the New World, culture was an interaction between an African past and an American present.[2] On the slave plantations of the New World, linguistic diversity and ethnic rivalries made it difficult for the Africans to join forces against their outnumbered masters. Africans were drawn from different parts of the African continent. They spoke different and mutually unintelligible languages. And they came from various ethnic groups and from various kinds of societies. Africans in the New World were much more ethnically heterogeneous than were the Europeans, who jumbled Africans as much as possible in order to prevent a concentration of large numbers of slaves of a common ethnic identity or common language on the same plantation. The slave population might be as mixed on any given plantation as the slave population in general.[3]

But slaves, like all human beings, sought identity with their fellows, identity with family, kin, tribe, or language. Slaves from the same ethnic and linguistic groups tended to band together on their own initiative, producing a high degree of solidarity among them and making possible the survival of African cultural patterns in the New World. Links with Africa were revived with the arrival of each new slave ship carrying its cargo of human property. Many of the older slaves, Jamaican merchant Bryan Edwards wrote in 1793, "wished, like the patriarchs of old, to see their sons take to themselves wives from their own nation and kindred; and all of them, I presume, because, among other considerations, they expected to revive and retrace in the conversation of their new visitors, the remembrance and ideas of past pleasures and scenes of their youth."[4]

The memories and mythology of Brazil, Carolina, and the Caribbean were shaped by two *great* traditions, one in Europe and one in Africa. The slave plantations of the New World constituted a social crucible, where African and European cultures melted, fused, and transformed themselves. Out of elements of both "great traditions," the slaves created a unique and magnificent culture that has achieved worldwide recognition as an indigenous "great tradition" in its own right—including such internationally famed cultural forms as spirituals, blues, jazz, and the various permuations of rock in the American South; carioca, samba, and bossa nova in Brazil; and calypso, mambo, mento, steel bands, ska, rocksteady, reggae, and dub poetry in the Caribbean. After such an outpouring of creativity who could remain unaware of the slaves' contribution to the culture of the Americas or doubt its enduring value?[5]

The slaves used their cultural creativity as a form of resistance. It has become stylish in some quarters to see almost any form of independent behavior on the part of the slaves as a form of resistance. Sidney Mintz cogently questions the value of dividing slave actions into categories of "accommodation" and "resistance," as though the lines between such categories were always clear. "Some acts with consequences that can be read as resistance did not originate with resistance," he notes. "Some acts with consequences that can be read as accommodation did not originate with accommodation." And some forms of slave behavior, in his opinion, may be read as both accommodation and resistance simultaneously. "We must try," he says, "to understand how the slaves coped as whole persons with their condition."[6]

The transformation of diverse African cultures into an African-American culture is one of the most far-reaching examples of culture change in human history. In the New World, a variety of African cultures converged and modified one another. African men and women of various ethnic and linguistic groups mixed— culturally and physically—in ways that rarely occurred in Africa. There were Fula, Fulani, Mandinka, Mende. There were Coromantees from the Gold Coast, considered to be ferocious and unforgiving, but hardy and favored as field hands. There were also Congos and Angolas, said to be docile and handsome, but weak and predisposed to run away. And there were Ibos from the Niger Delta, alleged to be sickly, melancholy, and suicidal. Among these diverse Africans were also Muslims from the Guinea highlands. On any given morning in a Caribbean sugar field or a Carolina rice field an enslaved African could meet more Africans from more ethnic or linguistic groups than he or she would likely encounter in a lifetime in Africa. The varied African cultures were fused increasingly in combinations that did not exist in Africa. A new culture, predominantly African in origin, but different from any particular African culture, began to take shape.[7]

Through language people not only communicate with and entertain one another but link themselves into a community, give shape to a common culture, and hand down that culture to their posterity. Africa was linguistically diverse. The earliest slaves spoke hundreds of different languages, languages that were often mutually unintelligible.[8] Linguists call the complex process by which two or more languages converge to form a new native tongue "creolization." By varied combinations of sound and syntax, semantics and lexicon, gestures and intonation, enslaved Africans in the Caribbean and in the lowcountry mixed elements of their several African languages with elements of either English, Spanish, French, Dutch, or Portuguese to develop common creole languages. A creole language is neither an African "survival" nor an example of "borrowing" from a European language but a new language that occupied a central position in the slaves' intellectual and cultural life. In developing a creole language the slaves did something more than simply retain their native African language or adopt a European one. Creation is a greater cultural achievement than retention or adoption. Although thousands of African words were incorporated into the new language, the vocabulary of the creole languages was mainly English. But the grammatical rules of the creole languages were not the rules of English at all, they were the shared rules of many African lan-

guages. The creole languages of the slaves continued to develop—both in inner form and in outer use—in a situation of
linguistic contact. There was reciprocal influence of European
and African features upon both the creole and the local standard.
The European contribution was principally lexical; the African
contribution was principally grammatical. To acknowledge the
convergence of African and European elements in African-American culture is not to imply that Europe and Africa always converged in relatively equal proportions. In the demographic imbalance of the Caribbean and the lowcountry of South Carolina
and Georgia, African cultural influences significantly outweighed
European ones.[9]

African-English creoles developed not only along the coast of
South Carolina and Georgia, but also in Barbados, Antigua, Guyana, Jamaica, and Surinam. Similarly, African-Portuguese creoles
developed in Brazil and Curacao. African-Spanish creoles developed in Cuba, Puerto Rico, and Colombia. African-French creoles developed in French Guiana, Grenada, Guadeloupe, Haiti,
and Louisiana. And African-Dutch creoles-"Creolsk"-developed
in the Virgin Islands, as well as in in the Dutch Leeward Islands of Aruba, Bonaire, and Curaçao, which also developed an
African-Spanish/Portuguese creole. Grammatically these various
New World creole languages showed striking similarities, clearly
pointing to African origins and a continuing presence Africaine.
But variation among them in lexicon, in phonology, and in semantics suggest that the varying linguistic components of the immediate environment played a major role in the way each creole
language developed.[10]

Language was, of course, only one element of the transformation from African to African-American culture. But the process of
linguistic change provides a model for explaining other elements
of culture change. What might be called the creolization of culture involves the unconscious grammatical principles of culture-
the deep structure that generates specific cultural patterns. Such
grammatical principles survived the middle passage and gov-

erned the selective adaptation of elements of both African and European culture.[11]

To underestimate the Africanity of African-American culture is to rob the slaves of their heritage. But to overestimate the Africanity of African-American culture is to rob the slaves of their creativity. Africans were creative in Africa; they did not cease to be creative as involuntary settlers in America. To overemphasize the "survival" of African culture is to minimize the power of African creativity when removed from the African context and to disparage the cultural achievement of African-American slaves. African inheritances constituted a residual culture that helped to guide enslaved Africans in interpreting and shaping encountered cultural elements in the New World. Cultural innovations, if they are to be accepted, must operate within an accepted intellectual framework. But in interpreting and shaping their world, African-Americans were informed not only by a residual culture but also by an emergent culture, a culture growing out of their experience as plantation slaves, a culture that served to unify a slave community divided as much as unified by their diverse African languages. On the slave plantations of Brazil, Carolina, and the Caribbean, both residual and emergent elements interacted in a broad process of culture change. Herded together with others with whom they shared only a common condition of servitude and some degree of cultural overlap, enslaved Africans were compelled to create a new language, a new religion, and a precarious new lifestyle.[12]

Consider a parallel New World example: the creolization of African-American religion. Christianity is a universal religion and not, strictly speaking, a white one. Nevertheless, most enslaved Africans encountered Christianity through white missionaries. Two main considerations seem to have prompted slaveholders' support (or toleration) of efforts to convert slaves to Christianity. First, making Christians of so-called "heathens" would afford the slaves a means of salvation, while at the same time providing the masters with a moral justification for having enslaved them.

Second, making Christians of so-called "heathens" would uplift their allegedly "licentious" morals and the putative "instability" of their family life, while at the same time removing an impediment to the "natural" increase of the slaveholders' human property. The motives were perhaps as much social as spiritual. After all, St. Paul's charge of cheerful obedience would promote not only salvation in the hereafter but a docile and obedient labor force in the here and now. Christianity would teach the slaves to be contented and happy in their present condition.[13]

In the French and Spanish Caribbean Roman Catholics could baptize their slaves into the church without requiring extensive preparation from the initiates. In Cuba and in Saint-Domingue the law prescribed that all slaves be baptized in the Catholic religion. But Quakers were the first religious group in the English Caribbean to proselytize their slaves. Barbados authorities adamantly opposed the Quakers' taking their slaves to meeting and levied thousands of pounds in fines against them. The earliest missionaries to work among the slaves on Barbados were sent by the Moravians, arriving in 1765. Methodists began their own Barbados slave missions in 1788; but their missionaries were disliked by the established church and were suspected of promoting insubordination among the slaves. Methodist services were frequently harassed and disrupted by planters and other whites on Barbados. Methodists enjoyed greater success on Grenada and St. Kitts. By assiduously avoiding criticism of white behavior in the islands Moravians escaped the hostility visited upon the Methodists. As a result their mission to the slaves enjoyed greater success. In the Danish West Indies the Moravians were first and largest, followed by Roman Catholics, Anglicans, Dutch Reformed, Methodist, and eventually Lutheran. At first the Church of England profoundly disapproved of Christianizing the slaves. The Anglicans did ultimately establish stations of the Church Missionary Society in Jamaica, Trinidad, and Guiana, but serious missions to the slaves did not begin on Barbados until 1823, when a few Anglican priests and planters attempted to further the religious instruction of the slaves.[14]

Despite John Wesley's praise for the Africans' singing and his encouragement of psalm and hymn singing as a means of evangelism, neither Methodists, Moravians, nor Anglicans had much respect for the native belief systems and cultures of the African past. They considered the slaves' Christianity to be "very superficial." They complained to their superiors in London about what they considered the immorality of the slaves, and expressed an almost paranoid apprehension of all evidences of such surviving "heathen superstitions" as Obeah and Myalism. Their efforts to stamp out the slaves' drumming and dancing were frustrating. If the slaves were to become fully converted, the missionaries believed, they would have to abandon their African "heathenism" completely. Nevertheless, the dissonance between the slaveholders' vision of a social order based on the enslavement of some human beings by other human beings and the vision of Christian brotherhood held up by missionaries insured that some kind of confrontation would be inevitable.[15]

Christianity enjoyed no monopoly among enslaved Africans and their descendants in the New World. Christianity had to compete in a religiously diverse environment. African-born slaves, for instance, often maintained their traditional religious outlooks. "At the time I first went to Carolina, there were a great many African slaves in the country," recalled self-emancipated slave Charles Ball. "Many of them believed there were several gods; some of whom were good, and others evil." Other African-born slaves continued to embrace Islam. "I knew several who must have been, from what I have since learned, Mohammedans [sic]," Ball noted. "There was one man on this plantation who prayed five times every day, always turning his face to the east." Given the dominance of Islam among the Fulani, Mandinka, and Wolof of the Senegambian area from which Carolina rice planters imported the largest number of their slaves, it would have been surprising had there not been a strong Islamic presence on the

coastal plantations of South Carolina. Rice plantation journals indicate that rations of beef instead of pork were issued to Muslim
slaves at hog-killing time, but precisely how strong their presence was is unknown and is likely to remain so. Considerably
more evidence survives of a strong and continuing Islamic presence among plantation slaves in coastal Georgia. And there is also
evidence that literate Muslims met to discuss and transmit the
sacred teachings of the Koran in some areas of the Caribbean as
well. Muslims were especially numerous in Cuba, which—like
South Carolina—imported large numbers of Fulani, Mandinka,
and Wolof.[16]

In the New World, elements from African religious beliefs and
elements from Christian religious beliefs were filtered through
the mentality, sentiments, and affective needs of the slaves and
synthesized into something *sui generis*, an African-American
mode of religious expression rather than an African one, yet one
that still preserved something of traditional African religion. African deities were transubstantiated into Catholic or Anglican
Saints. As Monica Schuler describes it, slaves tended to adopt
from Christianity "familiar elements which paralleled their own
beliefs, placing the borrowed symbols, ideas, and practices within
an essentially African context." When they danced before a
Christian altar, they were worshipping the Christian God in precisely the manner in which mighty divinities were worshipped in
many African societies.[17]

The diversity of African religious forms was not incompatible
with a broadly shared cosmology that included beliefs that deities
(at least most of them) were involved in human actions, that the
dead intervened in the lives of the living, as well as with certain
broadly shared basic assumptions about the nature of causation,
the relationship between illness or other misfortune and social
conflict, and the role of sorcery in revealing particular causes.
While specific forms might vary from one ethnic group to another
in Africa, religion typically encompassed the people's entire existence.[18]

If we apply the test of creolization, we can see that, at the
vocabulary level—that is, in its theology—Afro-Christianity
would seem to be a prime example of cultural borrowing. There
do appear to be some differences in emphasis between black
Christians and white Christians, with a greater emphasis among
whites on sin and the fear of damnation, contrasted with a greater
emphasis among blacks on salvation and deliverance from bond-
age in a symbolic Egypt. The contrast may be exaggerated, and
at most it is a difference of emphasis rather than of kind. At the
grammatical level, however—that is at the level of how the theology (the vocabulary) of Christianity was used to generate meaning, to worship God—the differences between black Christians
and white Christians are so profound that typically each thinks
nothing very religious is going on in the worship services of the
other. Black Christians often suppose that white Christians go to
church to hear a lecture. (In that supposition they are not, of
course, altogether mistaken.) White Christians often suppose that
black Christians go to church to have a good time. The concept
of "having a good time in the name of the Lord" is not normally
a doctrine of white Christianity. White worship services feature
a performer-audience relationship, with a performer in the pulpit
addressing a passive audience in the pews. Black services, on the
other hand, feature a mutual performance of worship.[19]

African-Americans did not simply adopt the God and the faith
of the white missionaries. In establishing a spiritual life for themselves, they reinterpreted the elements of Christianity in terms
of deep-rooted African "grammatical" orientations—mental rules
governing appropriate behavior—that profoundly affected their
adoption, adaptation, and application of Christianity. Far from
the African context of their sacred world, black Christians
blended the heritage of Africa with the European version of
Christianity to create a unique hybrid. African-American worship
services were characterized by spirit possession and a kinetic behavior known as "shouting" in the South Carolina and Georgia
lowcountry. Shouting was often described as "dancing" by white

observers, but not by Gullah Christians, who regarded dancing as sinful. Black Christians "shouted" with great enthusiasm, however, to the accompaniment of polyrhythmic hand-clapping and foot-stomping. In Jamaica Moravian missionary John Lang noted in his diary that "during the sermon, a heathen woman began to twist her body about, and make all manner of Grimaces. . . . When the service was over, I inquired what ailed her, and was told, that it was a usual thing with the negroes on M. estate, and called by them *Conviction*."[20] The Rev. Lang might well have been describing the same kinetic phenomenon that black Carolinians called "shouting."

Slave religious services were especially marked by music. Whether they slipped away into the woods on Sunday evenings, dodging the overseers, or had prayer meetings on Wednesday nights in their cabins, slaves would often turn a wash pot upside down "so de sound of our voices would go under de pot." Then they "would have a good time shouting, singing, and praying just like we pleased." Deeply expressive of African-American life, the spirituals rank among the world's classic folk expressions. Ostensibly concerned with a better life after death in a literal heaven with the troubles of this world left behind, the spirituals offered African-Americans struggling for spiritual survival on the slave plantations not only a musical escape from bitter reality but also a transcendent meaning for life. The spirituals expressed both a reaffirmation of their human dignity and a ringing condemnation of the wicked ways of the world. Singlehandedly the spirituals debunk the stereotype that enslaved Africans brought no culture with them to the New World, that African-Americans were cultural beggars waiting for a few crumbs of culture to be given to them, that the slave plantations were "schools for civilizing savages." African-Americans were not merely receivers of European culture, they were also donors of African culture. Thus they rank among the principal creators of the culture of the New World.[21]

The hauntingly beautiful spirituals of the slaves drew their inspiration from the Bible. A favorite theme was the suffering of the Jews of the Old Testament, enslaved in Egypt. Such spirituals provided the slaves' with a means of expressing belief in their own ultimate deliverance from slavery. Whether in Carolina or Caribbean spirituals or in Brazilian condomble rituals, the slaves sang in the traditional African call-and-response style. The song leader would sing out,

> The tallest tree in Paradise!
> And the congregation would sing in response,
> > Oh, yes, it is Jesus, my Lord!
> Once again the leader would sing out,
> > Christian call it tree ob life!
> And once again the chorus would respond,
> > Oh, yes, it is Jesus, my Lord!
> And again the leader,
> > Run along Moses, don't get late
> And again the chorus,
> > Oh, yes, it is Jesus, my Lord!
> And once again the leader,
> > Before Lord Jesus shut de gate!
> And once again the response,
> > Oh, yes, it is Jesus, my Lord!

In African-American worship services, such antiphonal singing and the soaring rhetoric of prayers combined with ecstatic shouts to provide a release from the travails of slavery.[22]

Some African-Americans embraced supernatural folk beliefs that were part of neither Islam or Christianity, but persisted in a kind of parallel stream. In the South Carolina and Georgia low-country, haunts were spirits of the dead who had returned to harass the living: a modified Afro-Carolinian version of the Congo zumbi or the Haitian zombi. Hags—the disembodied spirits of witches who leave their skins behind—were believed able to fly through the air in order to "ride" humans, that is, to give them nightmares. Even more fearsome were plat-eyes—evil spirits who changed shapes at will in order to lure victims into danger and rob them of their sanity. Such beliefs were neither abandoned by black Christians nor quite incorporated into African-American Christianity. Hags, haunts, and plat-eyes persisted in a parallel stream of belief.[23]

Many features of African-American religion either converged or coexisted with Christianity, but a third stream of African cosmology maintained a subterranean existence outside of and inimical to African-American Christianity. This element of slave religion continues to be both largely unknown and at least partly unknowable. African-American sorcery—whether known as Voodoo or hoodoo in South Carolina, or Shango or Obeah in the Caribbean—maintained a subterranean existence in opposition to African-American Christianity. Practiced clandestinely, such sorcery involved rituals in which "conjure doctors" used certain substances held to be magical for protective or malign purposes—to cure an illness, kill an enemy, or secure someone's love. Documentation of such sorcery is inevitably scanty, as such magical shamanism was practiced clandestinely. Still, sufficient evidence remains to testify to the existence of an underground stream of magical shamanism not only throughout the slavery period but beyond.[24]

The Jamaican planter M.G. ("Monk") Lewis said that his slaves were not religious, since they had no priest save the Obeahman. But there is evidence that slaves throughout the Caribbean were involved in a system of religious expression commonly known as Obeah. The Jamaican merchant Bryan Edwards claimed that Obeah was fundamentally African in orientation, and that its practitioners were "always" Africans. They were "consulted upon all occasions," he wrote, "in order to revenge injuries and insults, discover and punish thieves and adulterers, to predict the future, and for the conciliation of favour." Modern scholars such as Orlando Patterson and Sidney Mintz distinguish between Obeah and Myalism. Patterson relates the benign sorcery of Myalism to West African "good magic" and the malign sorcery of Obeah to West African "bad magic." But few masters made any such dis-

tinctions, and on the slave plantations of the Caribbean the two
were yoked together not only in the popular mind but also before
the law. To nineteenth-century whites neither Obeah nor Myalism were anything more than superstition and witchcraft. They
especially deplored the Obeahman for his alleged proficiency in
poisoning enemies, and they made numerous efforts to suppress
Obeah by legislation.[25]

To the slaves, however, the Obeahman (or woman) fulfilled the
functions of doctor, philosopher, and priest, providing both ritual
links with the spirit world and a mystical sense of continuity between the living, the dead, and the yet-unborn. On the slave
plantations of the Caribbean, as in the early Christian church,
healing was an act of faith. Obeah's rituals and fetishes could be
benign as well as malign. If Obeah were considered the source
of most misfortunes, Obeah practitioners were also held in high
esteem as healers. So long as the white man's medicine was regarded with suspicion, Obeah was assured of patients; moreover,
the positive role played by the Obeah in treating slave illnesses
demonstrates the role religion played in every aspect of the
slaves' existence. Obeah allowed the slaves an exalted feeling of
direct contact with the supernatural in attempting to cope with
their ailments. Depending upon their diagnosis, the Obeah practitioners might take a pharmaceutical approach to treatment:
their valued African pharmacopoeia had accompanied them to
the West Indies as part of their oral traditions. They found the
semitropical environment there sufficiently similar to that of
West Africa that their pharmaceutical knowledge was easily
adapted to somewhat new flora. But other ailments might call for
a sort of psychotherapy, as expressed in divination.[26]

The creolization of African-American music was as pro-
nounced as the creolization of African-American religion. Slaves
showed extraordinary ingenuity in adapting the richness of the
African musical legacy to the New World environment, making
old instruments from new materials and creating old sounds on
new instruments. Necessity was upon them to make their own

music, their own songs. They sang as they marched off to the
fields in the morning. They sang as they plowed and hoed under
the broiling sun. Most slaveholders liked for their slaves to sing
while working, and few could prevent it in any case. The slaves
sang as they marched home from the fields in the evening. They
entertained their children with play songs after the day's work
was done, and sang the children to sleep with lullabyes. At night
and on weekends they sang and played their hand-made musical
instruments. Charles Leslie described such a musical gathering
in Jamaica in 1740: "They have two musical Instruments, like
Kettle-Drums, for each Company of Dancers, with which they
make a very barbarous Melody. They have other musical Instruments, as a Banjil [or banjo], not unlike our Lute in any Thing
but the Musick, the Rookaw, which is two Sticks jagged [the
guerra], and a Jenkoving, which is a Way of clapping their Hands
on the Mouth of two Jars: These are all played together, accompanied with Voices, which make a very terrible Kind of Harmony."
Sylvester Hovey wrote of slaves dancing to the music of the banjo
during Christmas festivities on St. Croix. The British physician
Sir Hans Sloane must have been describing what Leslie called a
banjil when he wrote of his having seen in Jamaica instruments
"made of small Gourds fitted with Necks, strung with horse hairs,
or the peeled stalks of climbing Plants or Withs. These instruments are sometimes made of hollowed Timber covered with
Parchment or other skin wetted, having for its Neck the strings
ty'd or shorter, so as to alter the sounds." Other observers described something called the "Coromantee flute," made from the
branches of the trumpet tree, and such instruments as a musical
bow called a bender (said to produce a peculiarly haunting note),
goatskin-covered drums called goombay, their edges scraped
with a sharpened stick, and African-style drums and trumpets
made from hollow logs. Johan Lorentz Carstens described slaves
in the Danish Virgin Islands playing such instruments as "jaw-
bones of donkeys, strung with horse hairs and draped with color-
ful silk ribbons." Fanny Kemble, the wife of a Georgia slave-

holder, believed African Americans had a natural gift of music. She found the melodies of their rowing songs "wild and striking." She was especially taken with what was, to her, the unusual antiphonal structure of their songs: "The way in which the chorus strikes in with the burden, between each phrase of the melody chanted by a single voice, is very curious and effective, especially with the rhythm of the rowlocks for accompaniment." In Jamaica, after the sugar cane harvest, slave "musicianers" facilitated a form of creolization that went far beyond making music. According to Jamaican planter Alexander Barclay, the slaves would "assemble in their master's or manager's house, and, as a matter of course, take possession of the largest room, bringing with them a fiddle and tambourine. Here all authority and all distinction of colour ceases; black and white, overseer and book-keeper, mingle together in the dance."[27]

The drums were easily the most popular of the instruments. Beating on their white skins served the slaves as a release from the daily drudgery of slave life, especially during the sanctioned catharsis of holidays. The Rev. John Becker wrote in his diary, on Christmas day of 1812, that "scarcely was our worship closed, before the heathen negroes on the estate began to beat their drums, to dance, and to sing, in a most outrageous manner. The noise lasted all night, and prevented us from falling asleep." The Rev. Becker was hardly unique in such opinions. Most whites disliked the music made by slave "musicianers," which they regarded as a discordant and barbaric racket. But drumming was also considered potentially dangerous. It was known to build an infectious mood of excitement, sometimes working slaves up into a frenzy. Some whites suspected that the drums were also used as a form of communication among the slaves, perhaps used to signal revolts. Ordinances were passed banning the drums. And well they might be, for the drums helped to keep alive what Richard Price calls "bundles of rites or drums/ dances/songs/language, which had their origin in particular African ethnicities."[28]

African-American folktales provide another example of cultural creolization. In the New World, as in Africa, the most widely collected folktales were animal trickster stories. In the savannah areas of West Africa, as among the Bantu peoples generally, the trickster was a hare. Among the Yoruba he was a tortoise, and among the Limba and Luba he was an antelope. In the forested regions of the Ivory Coast, Ghana, and Sierra Leone, as among the Hausa, the Luo, and the Zande, the trickster was a spider. Among the Fante-Ashanti the spider trickster was the famous Anansi. The folk-hero of the New World slaves was such an animal trickster—typically the spider—Buh 'Nansi—in the Caribbean, Buh Rabbit in the Carolina lowcountry, although he was occasionally a partridge, a turtle, or a squirrel. In the New World there was also a cycle of human trickster tales. The human trickster was a slave, called John, John Henry, John the Conqueror, or High John among English-speaking narrators. In the French Caribbean he was known as Père Jean.[29]

African-American children in the New World delighted in the narratives of the tiny trickster's struggle for mastery with his more powerful but less intelligent adversaries. Slave storytellers—such as the one who promised Jamaican magistrate Richard Madden that he would reform and no longer "tell oder neger nancy stories all day long"—blended ancestral African elements with elements of the New World historical experience in tales of the audacious animal tricksters Anancy the spider-man and Buh Rabbit and of the no-less-audacious slave tricksters John and Père Jean. Many of the tales collected in the South Carolina and Georgia lowcountry are also widely known throughout the Caribbean, especially in Antigua, the Bahamas, Haiti, Jamaica, Montserrat, Nevis, St. Vincent, Trinidad, and Tobago. The trickster tales told by slave storytellers taught the children many lessons. One lesson was that the powerless must learn the ways of the powerful in order to survive. Another valuable lesson was that one must learn how to avoid a trick as well as how to perpetrate one. Hearing such stories, the young came to understand that existing power relations were not necessarily natural power relations. These stories, portraying the weak defeating the strong by using their wits, promoted the idea of freedom even within the confines of slavery. They were able to identify with Buh Rabbit, the trickster, while Buh Bear, the fool, seemed so much like "Ole Mossa"—the man who claimed to own them. The children learned that ethics appropriate in some situations might not be helpful in others. The obligations of friendship were expected within the slave community; but, when dealing with the master, one had much to gain and little to lose by adopting the ethics of the trickster.[30]

The importance of food to African-Americans in the New World is best revealed in two of their proverbs from the South Carolina lowcountry: "A full belly makes strong arms an' a willin' heart," but "hunger tame wild beast." The slaves supplemented the plantation rations, which might be limited to some yams and cornmeal, a pound or two of salt fish, and a bunch of plantains, by growing food in their own gardens and raising chickens and goats. Some foodstuffs were imported to the New World from Europe, others (such as okra, yams, and rice) were imported from Africa. Others (such as maize, or corn) were adopted from Native Americans. Such tropical fruits of the Caribbean as oranges, lemons, limes, guavas, mangos, muskmelons, papayas, pineapples, and watermelons were native to the New World. Barbadian merchant Richard Ligon declared pineapple juice to be "the Nector which the Gods drunk." According to him it was much better than the local rum, known as kill-devil, of which he wrote, "the people drink much of it, indeed too much, for it often layes them asleep on the ground, and that is accounted a very unwholesome lodging." Applying the test of creolization, we can say that much of the vocabulary—the material ingredients—were adopted, but the grammar—the way the food was prepared—was African. Blacks and whites alike ate the grains, fruits, vegetables, and meats grown in the plantation gardens. But slave cooks applied remembered recipes, African cooking methods, and ancestral preferences for spicier food to these material ingredients. Creole cookery combined African and European elements into new and distinctive Caribbean and lowcountry cuisines, perfected by slave cooks in the kitchens of the plantation Big Houses as well as in the open air and in the slave cabins.[31]

Behind the Big House, beyond the kitchens, barns, stables, carriage houses, and other plantation outbuildings, was "a small village," consisting of a row of little oblong huts, averaging "from fifteen to twenty feet in length, and divided into two apartments," according to Jamaican merchant Bryan Edwards, and were designed to accommodate "one Negro and his wife." The huts were constructed sticks, Guinea grass, and cane trash, and of "hard posts driven into the ground, and interlaced with wattles and plaister." The "natural earth, which is commonly dry enough," served as a floor; and the roof was "thatched with palm." The bedstead was a platform of boards, while the bed itself was simply a "mat, covered with with a blanket." In Barbados a few huts were built of stone, but most were built of "the strong reed or cane of the Guinea corn." Like the Jamaican huts, they were "all thatched with the cane-trash;" but unlike the Jamaican village, the Barbados huts "lie scattered about the hill." Slave houses in Demerara were built of "frail materials" and "enclosed with wattles plastered with mud." By the mid-1820s the old wattle-and-daub huts were being increasingly replaced by wooden houses. The South Carolina lowcountry manifested a particularly interesting form of architectural creolization: talented black builders fashioned houses with facades (the vocabulary level) that looked like Euro-American structures, marked by European notions of symmetry and control. But they concealed floor plans (the grammatical level) marked by African spatial orientations. Their facades looked like the British hall-and-parlor house type. The floor plans, however, reveal their great similarity to Yoruba two-room houses in Nigeria.[32]

The decades of plantation slavery constituted a crucial period during which the slaves of the New World imposed an African sensibility upon new materials in a new environment to create new material objects and a significant new material culture. African-American women often got together at night after a day's work in the fields to make warm and beautiful patchwork quilts, creating beautiful designs from numerous patches of cloth. Although slave quilters may have learned many techniques from Euro-American quilting traditions, they brought with them from Africa a rich heritage of textile art. Many of their patterns, especially the strip quilt, exemplified clear continuities with a widespread West African textile tradition in which the strip was the basic cultural and design unit. Gifted black basketmakers all along the rice coast of South Carolina and Georgia produced beautiful coiled fanner baskets for winnowing rice by wrapping palmetto butts or oak splits around bundles of bullrush or sweetgrass in the African manner. Talented black potters, incorporating elements of both African and Native American pottery traditions, made a low-fired unglazed earthenware known in South Carolina as Colono-ware, but strikingly similar to pottery excavated from plantation sites in Barbados and Jamaica.[33]

A speech community, even more than a political community, implies shared culture and a shared world view. Creole languages were the shared property of everyone in the speech community. Whenever enslaved African-Americans communicated with one another, whether in the Caribbean or in the Carolina or Georgia lowcountry, they had to use the symbols held in common by their speech community. The creole language thus became the principal channel of African-American thought and African-American culture. In the creole, enslaved Africans and their descendants created their magnificent spirituals and folk songs. In the creole, they developed the extraordinary folktales of the animal trickster and of the slave trickster. In the creole, they transmitted their culture to posterity and gave voice to their deepest aspirations.

Thus, when they spoke, when they told stories, when they worshiped, when they sang, when they cooked or quilted or built houses or made baskets or pottery, enslaved Africans and their descendants in Carolina, Brazil, and the Caribbean manifested not only African continuities but also African creativity. In a world of exploitation, they created a complex and beautiful culture, a culture that drew upon their various African heritages but adapted them creatively to the new environment. For out of African traditions as well as New World circumstances they created a new language, a new religion, indeed a new culture. The culture African-Americans made in their new home not only helped them to endure the horrors and indignities of slavery, but also enabled them to pass on something of value to generations of descendants. That beautiful culture, forged in the crucible of slavery and tempered in the fires of discrimination, is a legacy beyond price.[34]

As I stood there that summer day in Dakar in 1991, berated by friends and colleagues, I understood the sense of shame that underlies slavery, the sense of shame that underlies the demand for positive images. I may have understood it even better than my skeptical African-American friends. My ancestors were small farmers who labored in economic competition with the great planters, unevenly matched against men who grew rich on the labor of others. I am not aware of a single one of my ancestors who was a slaveholder. But I am aware that slavery was not a peculiar institution in the sense that it was unusual in human history. In fact, slavery was so common in human history that it is highly unlikely that anyone on the planet is not descended from both slaveholders and slaves. And I am also uneasily aware that it was not African traders who peopled the New World with enslaved Europeans.

How dismaying, I thought, that the origins of the exciting cultural transformations wrought by Africans in South Carolina, in the Caribbean, and in Brazil that I had been studying should somehow remain shrouded in shame. Just three days before departing for Dakar, I had returned home to South Carolina from a Fulbright Conference in Australia. While there, I had visited an academic friend at his family's farm in northern New South

Wales. His father, recently retired from the public school system, had written a book about his family. He showed me a copy of the indictment notice for his first ancestor to come to Australia. Her name was Ann Forbes, and she was fourteen years old in 1787 when she was charged with stealing ten yards of printed cotton cloth in London. Handwritten across the top of the indictment notice was the verdict and the sentence: "Guilty, No Chattels. To be hanged." Ann Forbes languished for five months in the cold and filth of the prison hulks that constituted England's death row. As she awaited her date with the hangman, Parliament decided to rid Britain of some of its "criminal population" by sending the first fleet of convicts to Australia. Ann Forbes was among them. Her sentence was commuted to transportation and seven years hard labor in New South Wales.[35]

Australia never amounted to much as a nation until it faced up to its convict past. Australia only became a great nation when Australians looked at cases such as Ann Forbes and realized that the shame of their convict past was less the shame of the convicts, the shame of fourteen-year-old girls so pitifully poor that they stole ten yards of cloth, than it was the shame of the British penal system, which sentenced children to hang.

Similarly, there is shame enough to go around in the epic tragedy of slavery, but it is not the shame of those brave men and women who were ripped from their homes and families in Africa, herded like cattle aboard slave ships, and transported across the Atlantic to a strange new world, taking nothing with them except what they could carry in their heads. For out of what they could carry in their heads, they created something profound and beautiful. As I noted in *Down by the Riverside*, "Out of pride and compassion as well as anguish and injustice, out of African traditions as well as American circumstances, they created a new language, a new religion—indeed a new culture—that not only allowed them to endure the collective tragedy of slavery, but to bequeath a notable and enduring heritage to generations to come."

Someday the achievement of those slave men and women who created that magnificent culture will be recognized and honored as it should be. Someday the word *slave* will be a source of pride rather than a badge of shame. Someday the descendants of slaves and the descendants of slaveholders will all lay the burden of slavery down. But how soon is someday? That will depend on us.

Commentary / Stanley L. Engerman

I

In this paper Charles Joyner has drawn upon numerous primary and secondary sources and his very rich historical insights, to present a detailed picture of the slaves's culture in the New World, most particularly in the southern United States. The picture which is presented is of a rich culture that was accomplished, even under the institution of slavery, by the slaves own choices, and is to be presented as a source of pride to their descendants today—of the accomplishment achieved under extreme adversity. Joyner presents the formation of new cultural patterns and describes these adjustments in several categories, including religion, language, music, folktales, food and cooking, material culture, and the design of huts and villages. These cultural features are seen as mixtures of African, European, and American patterns, the mixture varying, as he suggests, according to demographic and other factors.

This creation of new patterns from old African and old European and American patterns leads Joyner to place proper emphasis on the dynamic process of cultural formation. This approach, as Joyner has suggested at another symposium, helps to finesse the earlier attempts by anthropologists and historians to show the slave's humanity by arguing for the persistence and presence of African survivals in slave culture, as well as to put aside the problem of limited return by former slaves to Africa. Thus Joyner along with other recent scholars, including the anthropologist Richard Price and the historian Lawrence Levine, seems to be arguing that the previous long, hard-fought debate on African survivals is somewhat irrelevant to understanding the nature of the adjustment to enslavement in the Americas. The observed mixture suggests that slaves had the ability to choose and form cultural patterns as a separate and distinct, if not an independent, people. Joyner suggests, also, that this distinctive culture should not just be looked at as a type of resistance or rebellion in an Apthekerian sense, as if that was what was needed to demonstrate the slaves humanity—although he does accept this as "a form of resistance." This type of need to prove resistance is not really necessary since we do know what the slaves did once the opportunity to flee the system arose during the Civil War. It is not always clear whether Joyner is arguing that these cultural patterns were in some sense optimum or even the most appropriate, either under slavery or afterward. The point is that these cultural patterns developed under terrible conditions and that they existed for long periods often into the rather different post-slavery era.

Not all issues of cultural interest are covered. For example, little is said about marriage, childbearing, and work patterns, which also have important implications for both slavery and the post-slavery experience. These could be interesting to examine since, for various reasons, they were perhaps of more direct economic and social concern to slaveowners than were some of the cultural patterns described.

II

It is useful to remember that the proponents of negative views of the culture of black slaves included not only slaveowners and pro-slavery advocates, but also abolitionists, as well as later anti-slavery scholars and activists. Some observers attributed these slave problems to their being black Africans, while others pointed to the influence of their having been slaves. Thus if we rewrite the slave experience as Joyner has suggested, and, on the basis of our reading of the available material do so more accurately, do we not also have to adapt our understanding of how slavery itself operated and how slaveowners controlled slave behavior? What, for example, did it mean to have such a broad diffusion of certain cultural patterns? What did it mean for slaves to be able to choose and determine patterns for themselves? Did the masters care deeply about the specific patterns or, at least in some cases, as long as they were able to maintain power and control, were they willing to accept the patterns that slaves chose? And, also, did the cultural patterns of free blacks and of maroons present differences from the enslaved? At the same time slaves were arriving in the colonies, convicts were also coming from England. Joyner discusses the Australian settlement by convicts, which arose only after the American Revolution forced a change in location, but significant cultural interaction between these groups may have taken place in the Chesapeake and elsewhere.

III

The issue of cultural diffusion which Joyner presents gives rise to questions about whether there were some differences among patterns formed in different regions of the Americas and what could account for these, noting some differences which may have seemed minor and others quite large. In the U.S. there were several different sources of slave supply. At first slaves arrived primarily from British West Indies, then from various parts of Africa. Some arrivals came to Louisiana from the French West Indies after the Haitian Revolution. The flow from Africa occurred for about one and one-half century, a period that saw rather dramatic changes occurring within African societies, as well as changing sources of location for slaves brought to the Americas.

The U.S. had an extensive internal movement of slaves (and whites) after 1800. In terms of geographic location, major crops produced, and size of units, the last 60 years of slavery in the U.S. were quite different from the much longer period of nearly two centuries that preceded it. Also important to examine is the quite different economic and demographic basis of slavery in the U.S. compared to elsewhere in the New World, most particularly for my purposes here the British West Indies. To use evidence from throughout the Americas to suggest one particular set of patterns is to ignore the different circumstances and conditions that formed the basis of cultural adjustments in different places. There are two major differences to note at the start. In the U.S. the main crops in the colonial era were tobacco and rice, then, in the nineteenth century, cotton, while for the British West Indies it was, after a very early start with tobacco, for a long time, sugar. The size of units differed, the health of plantation and farm locations differed, and given that whites, unlike black slaves, could generally locate where they wanted, the racial compositions of the populations differed.

Second, as had been well known for centuries, the U.S. slave population grew at an extremely rapid rate, while elsewhere slave mortality exceeded fertility, and the surviving populations were lower than the numbers imported over time. These demographic differences may themselves have been influenced by differing cultural adaptations, regarding marriage, childbearing, and child-nursing, raising U.S. slave (and white) fertility.

Several important points are worth considering in understanding the process of cultural diffusion. First, at any moment of time the U.S. had less need for slave imports from Africa than did the other New World slave powers, and thus the share of native-born to African-born was always much higher in the U.S. than elsewhere. Indeed, U.S. blacks were more frequently American-born than were U.S. whites. This native born-African born pattern is true for the U.S.—B.W.I. comparison, where the transatlantic slave trade closed in the same year, but the slave trade (and continuing new African influence) continued in Brazil to about 1851 and Cuba to 1867, making for some even more striking differentials in the African-born/Native-born ratio than at later, twentieth-century dates.

The size of producing units differed dramatically between crops, with sugar plantations ranging in the hundreds of slaves, while the general numbers of slaves on tobacco- and cotton-producing units were considerably smaller. And since the number of whites varied relatively little by size of plantation, the slaves in the B.W.I. had contact with many more slaves more frequently than did those in the U.S., and they also had fewer direct contacts with those whites on the plantation. The infamous Thomas Thistlewood of Jamaica, whose exploits, economic and sexual, have attracted considerable attention, was rather atypical for that island. He owned a livestock pen with only 27 slaves when he began, increasing only to 35 when he died.

And the various New World societies had rather different racial compositions. The British West Indies were, after the first decades of settlement, about 90 percent black slave, only 10 percent white. The U.S. was only 10–15 percent slave, and even the South was only about 40 percent black slave. The exceptional regions of the South, unusual due to mortality and climatic differences, such as the Gullah regions of South Carolina, had a more recent and a higher percent slave population. Thus they have attracted more attention from scholars of cultural diffusion and differences. This Gullah example does pose one of the many moral paradoxes that arise when discussing slavery. Where, in the South, the demographic performance was most unfavorable it is easiest to argue for some basic African influences within slave culture. These differences between the U.S. South and the B.W.I. not only influenced what happened under slavery, but also would have left some effects seen when blacks both from the U.S. South and from the B.W.I. moved to northern U.S. cities, starting in the earlier part of the twentieth century. And there were apparently also differences in the achievements of ex-slaves from different parts of the South, both within the South and later when they moved northward.

Thus attention to differences in the population of the slaves in different parts of the Americas should indicate some important aspects of the patterns of adjustment, and raises, again, the need to understand the process and mechanics of cultural adaptation over time and space.

IV

Joyner has drawn upon some of the major works of the past two decades regarding the development of slave life and culture, in the United States and in the West Indies, including those by Eugne D. Genovese, Mechal Sobel, Albert Raboteau, Sidney Mintz, and Richard Price, as well as some of his own writings. These are all part of a major scholarly endeavor in rewriting the history of slavery and of slaves, an approach with some deliberate intent to provide a particular message for today's world. Whether it will be successful in this attempt, or whether some will argue that it presents the slavery experience in a misleading manner, here in regard to power relationships and prospects once freedom was achieved, as has occurred before in the attempt to provide a "usable past," remains to be seen.

The Problem of Race in Cuba and the United States*

ALINE HELG

In 1919, in the small town of Regla near Havana, a black Jamaican man was arrested in a store for giving candy to a white girl, allegedly planning to kidnap her for the purposes of witchcraft. A furious mob took him from jail, tied him to the tail of a horse, and dragged the man through the streets until he died.[1] Several Havana newspapers' headlines exultantly praised the people of Regla for their lynching ability. *El Día*, in an editorial entitled "There Is Already One People Who Knows How to Lynch," implicitly measuring Cuba against the U.S. South, qualified the lynching as a "step forward that we take toward civilization."[2]

The Cuban journalists who lauded the similarities between the lynching in Regla and lynching in the U.S. South correctly saw that in both regions, lynching ultimately aimed at teaching blacks their "true place" in society. Yet the motives for lynching differed: in Cuba, it was supposed to punish crimes of alleged black male witchcraft against white children, in the U.S. South, all kinds of alleged black male offenses, especially rapes of white women. Although Cuba's craze against black "witches" lasted for several decades after 1900, it led to few recorded lynchings, whereas in the U.S. South between 1884 and 1930, more than 2,500 blacks were lynched, about a third of them for alleged rape or sexual norm violation against white women.[3] This is not to say that racist violence and the fearful image of the black rapist were absent from Cuban history, however. That image was most dramatically used in the summer of 1912, when, in response to Afro-Cuban protest against the ban of the Western Hemisphere's first black political party, the Independent Party of Color (Partido Independiente de Color), between 3,000 and 6,000 blacks were massacred by the Cuban army and zealous volunteers in the province of Oriente for supposedly planning to transform Cuba into another Haiti.[4]

Founded on archival sources on Cuba and on the secondary literature on the U.S. South, this article proposes to tackle the tantalizing problem of racism by comparing the mechanism of stereotyping and violent domination in two former slave societies: the U.S. South after Reconstruction and Cuba after independence.[5] In the two regions, stereotyping, or the creation of oversimplified mental images to justify the power relationship between dominant and dominated, was expressed in a racial and gendered form. White males asserted their domination of society partly through the use of the stereotypes of the black rapist and the black male witch.[6] These images of the dominated blacks as fearful "others" helped to establish a social hierarchy and boundaries of inclusion and exclusion as well as to fuel the dominant group's racial violence.[7]

The interplay of racial stereotyping and violence raises a series of questions that this article attempts to answer in a comparative way. Why was the stereotype of the black rapist the most likely to provoke indiscriminate racist violence in both the U.S. South and Cuba? Why did it pervade white southern imagery of blacks from the 1890s to the 1920s but in Cuba was limited to 1910–12? Why did the stereotype of blacks take the main form of the male witch in Cuba? Why did racist stereotyping lead to lynching in the U.S. South, whereas in Cuba antiblack sentiments seldom led to mob violence, but took the form of mass killing by the army? Although all people of African descent were generally stereotyped as inferior, why were black men more likely to be represented as fearful "others" than black women? How did stereotypes of black men reflect and affect racial relations, gender hierarchies, and interracial sex in both regions? And, finally, how did differences in black stereotyping and racist violence reflect differences within white society in the U.S. South and Cuba?

This article shows that despite differences between their racial systems, in both Cuba and the U.S. South fear-inducing stereotypes of the dominated emerged roughly two decades after emancipation. Distinct socioeconomic and demographic contexts informed the modality of racial stereotypes and violence. Yet in the two regions racial stereotyping and violence were initiated during a deep crisis in which the white elite's political control was threatened from below. The Cuban and southern elites consciously promoted scapegoating campaigns and stimulated racial violence to regain control of the white lower classes while simultaneously repressing blacks.

1. THE STEREOTYPES OF THE BLACK RAPIST AND THE BLACK MALE WITCH IN THEIR CONTEXTS

As in the Western world at the turn of the century, the representation of people of African descent as savage and primitive pervaded mainstream thinking in Cuba and the U.S. South. In addition, as both regions had been strongholds of slavery and had a large population of African descent, the Haitian revolution had a long-lasting impact on whites. Contemporary histories of that revolution and its aftermath continued to spread images of black revolutionaries and empowered blacks as bloodthirsty beasts naturally prone to sexual excesses and cannibalism. This broad image of barbarism applied particularly to black males, perceived by white society as more threatening than black females.[8] Against this backdrop, in the U.S. South in the 1880s, the icon of fear of the black rapist of white women emerged to remain in force for four decades. In Cuba the fearful image of the black rapist was limited to the 1910–12 government repression of the Independent Party of Color, but the most long-lasting stereotype used against the Afro-Cuban population was that of the black male witch (in Spanish: *negro brujo*) who killed small white children, preferably girls, to use them in cures and feasts. In other words, at the turn of the century, the principal obsession of white society in the U.S. South was that of the black male having sex with white women. In Cuba, it was the black male cannibalizing white children.

Two well publicized cases will serve to illustrate the power of these stereotypes. In the U.S. South in 1899, Sam Hose, a black laborer, had a verbal dispute over money with his white employer, the planter Alfred Cranford, in Coweta County, Georgia. The next day, the planter resumed the argument with Hose, who was chopping wood. As Cranford threatened to kill his employee with a pistol, the black man, acting in self defense, threw his axe at the planter, killing him, and ran away terrorized. Newspapers immediately reported the sensational story that Hose had treacherously murdered Cranford with his axe when he was peacefully eating supper. Allegedly, Hose then injured the planter's baby and repeatedly raped his wife, contaminating her with syphilis. Further newspaper stories added more shocking details of the incident and transformed the farmworker Hose into a multiple murderer and rapist. A few days later, Hose was captured, and a huge infuriated mob tortured, mutilated, and burned him to death.[9] This incident is only one in several hundreds between 1880 and 1930 in which men of African descent were accused of rapes or attempted rapes of white women. Described as infamous beasts, they allegedly threatened white women in their homes, in the fields, and in downtown districts. Even after 1930, the specter of the black rapist continued to haunt southern white men and women.[10]

In Cuba, in 1904, the white toddler girl Zoila disappeared from her parents' farm near Havana. Immediately, the rumor spread that she had been the victim of black male witches to use her blood and heart in specific cures. Although in a first stage all the suspects were released for lack of evidence, after the discovery of Zoila's body and the mobilization of the white villagers by a Havana journalist, the old Domingo Boucourt, a former slave brought from Africa, and several other poor blacks were arrested and charged with the murder of Zoila. Confidential information and testimonies corroborating the "public rumor" served as central pieces of evidence.[11] Mainstream newspapers rivalled in providing details of the toddler's murder and cannibalistic recipes according to which her entrails were prepared. Cuba's best known anthropologist, Fernando Ortiz, theorized then on the atavistic forces that supposedly compelled Boucourt to be the intellectual author of the crime.[12] Months later, five of the defendants were sentenced to life or long-term imprisonment. Two others, Boucourt and his alleged executer, were sentenced to death and garotted. Boucourt, who had consistently denied the charges, allegedly confessed his crime to the prison warden just before his execution.[13] Rapidly, Zoila's murder became the touchstone in matter of black witchcraft and African-based culture. Mainstream newspapers transformed worshippers of African-based religions into potential witches ready to kidnap white children and extract their blood, heart, and entrails, which they would eat in banquets or cure and sell as amulets and remedies.[14] On the basis of Zoila's case, from the 1900s to the 1930s, rumors of alleged black witches' attempting to kidnap white children spread across the island, often producing waves of arrests that the press avidly reported. White children were taught by their parents to run away at the sight of a black man carrying a bag, because he could well be a witch ready to kidnap them.[15]

Although the myth of the black male witch permeated Cuba's white imagery during the early century, one case of alleged rape of a white women by blacks made a powerful contribution to racist violence in the island: the nationally publicized story according to which at the beginning of the Afro-Cuban protest in Oriente in 1912, members of the Independent Party of Color had collectively raped and semi-cannibalized a white female teacher who subsequently died of her wounds. Although later denied by the schoolteacher herself in an open letter to the press, the story, printed simultaneously with other false reports of rapes of white women and editorials announcing that Afro-Cubans had launched a race war against whites, gave the image that Cuba was about to be the stage of a revolution along Haitian lines. Moreover, the President of the Republic alluded to the story of the raped teacher to justify the army's indiscriminate repression and called the Cuban people to volunteer to fight for "civilization" against the "ferocious savagery" of the party's followers.[16] In 1912, thus, the myths of the black rapist and the black witch were conflated to officially justify army repression and to galvanize many white volunteers into racist violence. After five weeks of "campaign," thousands of Afro-Cuban men, women, and children had been massacred in Oriente, most of them for no other reason than the darker color of their skins. The impact of the alleged race war and of the ensuing racist massacre of 1912 lasted for years. It prevented Afro-Cubans from organizing again into a political party while it simultaneously allowed whites to transform any collective attempt by blacks to assert their rights into a threat to the Cuban nation.[17]

For today's observer, the fact that at the turn of the century white folks believed in the icons of fear of the black rapist and the black male witch is all the more troubling, especially since there is no evidence that rapes of white women and ritualistic child murders by blacks were then particularly frequent crimes in the U.S. South and Cuba, respectively.[18] Similarly, it is surprising that in 1910–12 the Cuban government managed to brandish the myth of the black rapist and the century-old specter of a revolution along Haitian lines when the facts demonstrated that the Independents of Color's principal demand was the right to democratically organize into a political party.

In both regions, actual rapes of white women by blacks had not fueled collective fear during slavery or during the U.S. Civil War and the Cuban wars for independence. No doubt, Anglo-American slave societies showed a concern with this specific crime not exhibited by Spanish America. Spanish slave codes were not explicit about the crime of rape or attempted rape of white women, but the colonial Spanish penal code increased liability when a crime was committed by a person of color against a white.[19] In the British colonies, pre-nineteenth-century slave codes stipulated the death penalty or castration to convicted defendants, two types of punishments continued in the slave South after independence. However, as shown by Diane M. Sommerville, the fact that death and castration were not systematically implemented and that castration could also punish nonsexual crimes indicate that whites had no collective fear of black sexuality.[20] During the Civil War and from emancipation to 1880, blacks accused of raping white women were often punished through vigilante action, and those brought to criminal courts faced the death penalty, but they were not always convicted, and those convicted not always executed.[21] In colonial Cuba, the Spanish authorities used the myth of the black rapist as a scare tactic to prevent white Cubans from supporting independence with mixed results, and the few cases of actual rape of white women by black proindependence combatants led to swift martial justice and hanging.[22]

During slavery in the U.S. South and in Cuba, blacks and whites lived in a world in which often some human beings, such as healers, midwives, conjurers, and witches, were believed to have special powers. These men and women became sometimes targets of persecution (and those of African descent stigmatized for their paganism), but no systematic campaign was launched against them, and executions for witchcraft and sorcery were exceptional.[23] Black witchcraft involving child murder and cannibalism was unknown during Spanish colonialism and during the first U.S. occupation of the island (1898–1902).[24]

In both regions, in fact, whites worried more about the possibility of slave rebellions than about black males' rape and witchcraft. Actual and alleged slave revolts in the South met with exemplary cruelty. Similarly, in Cuba, during the conspiracy of La Escalera in 1844, Spain persecuted, often torturing to death, thousands of slaves and free persons of color and executed dozens for allegedly plotting to end slavery and Spanish domination. Although some defendants were accused of envisioning mating with white women and of using witchcraft to pursue their aims, these specific charges did not result in death sentences.[25]

In sum, only the Cuban use of the scare tactic of the Haitian revolution in 1910–12 followed a century-long tradition of fear of black mass revolt, but in both regions during slavery and the first two decades following emancipation, black witchcraft and black rape existed without generating collective hysteria among whites. Thus, only a changing context can explain the rise of the fear-inducing stereotypes of the black witch and the black rapist in the subsequent period.

In both regions, the decisive episode in white-black relations had been racial slavery, which had left a social structure based on race. The lynching era in the U.S. South and the witch craze era in Cuba both emerged after slave emancipation (1865 in the United States, 1886 in Cuba), a war (the Civil War in the South, the 1895–98 War for Independence in Cuba), relative empowerment of persons of African descent, and economic crisis. In addition, in both regions, the wars had ended with transitional "foreign" military control (the North's control of the U.S. South until the early 1870s, the U.S. military occupation of Cuba in 1898–1902). In the South, the emergence of the stereotype of the black rapist coincided with the return to power of the white planter elite in a context of agricultural depression, industrialization, and relative dependency on northern capital; in Cuba, the emergence of the stereotype of the black witch coincided with the island's first independent government in the hands of the white Cuban elite, but in the context of increasing U.S. economic and political imperialism. In both regions, white elites were deeply influenced by Social Darwinism and the ideology of white supremacy. Simultaneously, they were facing unprecedented political challenge from formerly dominated blacks. And last but not least, both in Cuba and in the South, the rise of the racist stereotypes corresponded to a period of rapid development of mass communications, photography, and the written media.

Beyond these general trends, there were some important dif-

ferences between the social context of the two regions. The abolition of slavery had shaken the structure of society more suddenly
in the U.S. South than in Cuba, where slave emancipation had
been a gradual process. Throughout the nineteenth century,
Cuba had a substantial free population of African descent who,
though struggling against legal and practical discrimination, comprised a significant economic, political, and military presence. In
the U.S. South, the size and participation of the free black population had been more limited until Reconstruction imposed radical changes such as legal equality and civil rights to people regardless of race.[26] Also, although sociocultural differences among
the population of African descent were important in both regions,
especially between rural and urban dwellers and between subre-
gions, in Cuba these differences were complicated by the fact
that slaves had been brought over from Africa as late as in the
1860s. Much as the African-born were a tiny minority at the turn
of the century, the long-lasting flow of Africans helped the continuing attachment of many Afro-Cubans to African-based traditions.

In both contexts, thus, the social fabric had been upset, affect-
ing race and class hierarchies. Yet, whereas in the U.S. South, in
terms of race relations, the elite was looking backward and using
a variety of means such as disenfranchisement and Jim Crow legislation to "redeem" their society and replace slavery with racial
segregation, in Cuba the white elite was looking forward and attempting to assert, despite U.S. intervention, its new political
power on a very diverse population. In both cases, the use of
racist stereotypes was instrumental in the process as rationaliza-
tion for the exercise of power and the ideology of racial supremacy.

2. STEREOTYPING AND VIOLENCE

Lynching in the U.S. South belonged to a well established tradition of vigilante justice and political violence that had already

served to repress alleged crimes and unconformity of whites and blacks in the antebellum South, a practice that increased during Reconstruction.[27] In the 1880s the stereotype of the black rapist by white Southerners helped justify continuing white violence against blacks. The case of the 1899 lynching of the black farm-worker Sam Hose in Coweta County, Georgia, will again serve as an example. Once Hose's probable homicide of his employer in self-defense had been transformed by the press into a horrify-ing murder and rape, the stage was set for a mass lynching in which the white community rejoiced in the punishment of the alleged culprit. Sam Hose

> was burned at the stake in a public road . . . Before the torch was applied to the pyre, the Negro was deprived of his ears, fingers and other portions of his body with surprising fortitude. Before the body was cool, it was cut into pieces, the bones were crushed into small bits and even the tree upon which the wretch met his fate was torn up and disposed of as souvenirs. The Negro's heart was cut into several pieces, as was also his liver. Those unable to obtain ghastly relics directly, paid more fortunate possessors extravagant sums for them. Small pieces of bone went for 25 cents and a bit of liver, crisply cooked, for 10 cents.[28]

Although most lynchings were not performed by large mobs, still 34 percent of all lynchings in Georgia and 40 percent in Virginia, for example, took the form of public spectacles, such as Sam Hose's lynching, to which hundreds or thousands partici-pated in a well planned and organized ritual of white community revenge.[29] In general, rape and murder were considered the most horrible crimes and attracted the largest participation. Also, the higher the status of the offended white and the more hideous the alleged crime, the greater the likelihood of a class inclusive mob. However, even in the cases in which the elite did not join the mob, politicians and journalists were instrumental in creating the atmosphere of outrage conducive to lynching. Men were the most active lynchers, but women and children participated as well; family and friends of alleged victims often played an active role in the punishment of the presumed offender, and it was not un- common to see women recognize their offenders and initiate the ritual. Although the number of lynchings decreased after 1900, they increasingly involved torture and mutilation.[30]

All lynchings shared common elements. As summary mob exe- cutions of alleged law-breakers or violators of local customs with little regard for proof of guilt, they served as powerful lessons to others, and thus did not need to be frequent to be effective. Lynchings of blacks in particular had white community approval and aimed at enforcing social conformity, at both punishing the individual and collectively repressing blacks. According to W. Fitzhugh Brundage, mobs had clear "didactic aims: their ac- tions both conveyed the degradation that they believed their vic- tim deserved and underscored the legitimacy of extralegal execu- tion."[31] Such aims were achieved by the use of unlimited humiliation and violence against black victims, and by the obser- vance of a planned ritual in their identification and execution. But, as seen in the lynching of Sam Hose, mass lynchings were often also joyful celebrations of white values and white suprem- acy that people immortalized by having pictures of themselves taken with the lynched body and by collecting macabre souve- nirs. Furthermore, some participants were not far from eating the body of their black victim. Of course, the actual lynchers were never prosecuted.[32]

Lynching, however, was not the only form of violence used by white communities to control blacks. In rural areas and towns, mobs terrorized, beat and whipped blacks in order to force them to leave their homes and land. In southern cities murderous race riots multiplied, often triggered by a minor incident involving alleged rape or interracial sex that politicians and the local press inflated into an affront to the white community. Previous to the bloody Atlanta riot of 1906, for example, newspaper headlines escalated from "The Reign of Terror [of the Black Rapist]" to

"The Way to Save Our Women" and "Now It Is Time to Act."[33] Riots usually began with white attacks against blacks in an area of racial interaction and continued with white invasion of black neighborhoods, the beating and killing of blacks, the looting and burning of their properties, and forced black exodus. Unlike lynching, which chose meaningful targets and was often accompanied by a parody of justice, mob terror and rioting were random violence against African Americans and their property in order to dispossess them and oust them from the area.[34]

In Cuba, the stereotype of the black rapist to stimulate anti-black violence was limited to 1910–12, when the government escalated its repression of the Independent Party of Color from mockery and harassment to mass imprisonment, trial, and legal ban in 1910.[35] In summer 1912, the party organized in Oriente an armed protest to regain legality. Newspapers immediately transformed the protest into a race war in which blacks aimed at killing whites and raping white women. The Cuban government, breaking with its tradition of compromise to respond to armed protest, sent the army and hundreds of zealous volunteers to bloodily suppress the movement.[36] Between 3,000 and 6,000 Afro-Cuban men, women, and children were indiscriminately butchered, hanged, and gunned down in Oriente. In 1912, anti-black violence was not limited to Oriente but erupted nation-wide. Throughout Cuba, blacks were killed for minor excuses. The town of Regla was the stage of a two-day riot in which at least two Afro-Cubans were killed, several more wounded, and many forced to take refuge in Havana.[37]

The press transformed the massacre of Afro-Cubans in Oriente into Cuba's long expected "race war" between white civilization and black barbarism. Articles and cartoons symbolically represented the Cuban nation as a white woman, whose integrity, threatened by the "witches" of the Independent Party of Color, dressed up with the attributes of vodun and santería, could only be protected by military force.[38] Mainstream newspapers avidly reported alleged battles between the army and "rebels" that left

dozens of dead and wounded among the enemy and the government forces unhurt. In reality, however, as the unprepared and
poorly armed party's protesters chose to hide rather than to confront the massive forces sent against them, the army and bands
of volunteers increasingly turned against Afro-Cuban peasants.[39]
New armament was tested against them, and the bodies of
hanged men appeared in close proximity to towns, which made
one newspaper ask with satisfaction: "Has Mister Lynch arrived?"[40] Some journalists were ironic about the fact that alleged
rebels who surrendered and those taken prisoner were often
killed "for attempting to escape" and their bodies mutilated.[41]
Simultaneously, newspapers' front pages revealed the stark reality of Oriente's "race war" by displaying cartoons satirizing the
pacificism of the party's protesters and the massacre of Afro-
Cubans by the army. One cartoon, for example, showed the tri-
umphant general in charge of the operation against a backdrop of
countless black dead, their corpses laying on the side of the road
and hanging from trees.[42]

More generally, however, the icon of fear of the black male
witch, rather than that of the black rapist, was raised by Cuba's
journalists, politicians, and social scientists for the defense of
white civilization against black barbarism. Even in 1912, rape
was associated with cannibalism and witchcraft: the schoolteacher supposedly raped by members of the Independent Party
of Color was also reported to have been semi-cannibalized by her
assailants, and some leaders of the movement were rumored to
dominate their "fanatical" followers by "African witchcraft."[43]

Cuba's stereotype of the black witch mixed images of medieval
European female witches with Columbian narratives of Caribbean cannibalism, colonial depictions of African male sorcerers
and cannibals, and pseudoscientific racial theories. Its fear-inducing effect was magnified by the transformation of the unique (and
not fully convincing) case of Zoila's murder into the general rule,
the spreading of false rumors and the juxtaposition of unrelated
incidents. In a Cuban cultural context in which witchcraft[44] was

a reality among the lower class and in which an important portion of the Afro-Cuban population followed religious and cultural practices of African origin, the fearful stereotype of the black male witch worked, at least among large sectors of the white population.[45]

One case in 1919 helps understand the mechanism of stereotyping and mobilization toward racial violence in Cuba. In 1919, the body of Cecilia, a light-skinned mulatto girl, was discovered in Matanzas. The murder was attributed to black male witches who had presumably eaten the girl's entrails. In addition, in conformity with the standard established by Zoila's case, Cecilia began to be identified as a white girl.[46] Eight alleged witches were arrested, put in solitary confinement, and tortured, after which one of them reportedly confessed to the crime. Havana newspapers immediately reacted by publishing edifying articles.[47] One editorial in *La Discusión*, for example, began by portraying the victim as "pretty as a flower, blond as a little corncob, with languorous blue eyes," in order to stimulate white readers' tenderness and racial identification. The next section of the article raised the readers' sense of personal outrage by presenting fanciful details as the general rule, and abruptly closed up on the plight of motherhood.

> Usually, male witches put [their victims] in bags as if they were cats, then they kill them, open their stomachs and their breasts with a can of condensed milk, as they did with little Zoila, they drink their blood, extract their entrails . . . to fry them and serve them as a meal to which they invite their male and female relatives . . . and their friends, they add seasoning, they find it very delicious, they laugh, sing, and dance. . . . . [*sic*]: Come on! Let the mothers speak, they are the ones who can express their feelings.

The cry of wounded motherhood had to be avenged by the men in the community, a call the editorial conveyed by stimulat-

ing violence and raising racist images that cast black witches out
of humanity.

> And could anyone have pity of these monsters, these wild
> beasts? . . . What would these beasts say if we seized them,
> opened them, extracted their organs (which they must have as
> black as carrion crows), prepared them with mayonnaise dress-
> ing, and threw them to pigs (who would not even eat them)?
> . . . And against these jackals who don't take away carrions, but
> small children, . . . couldn't we at least do the same?

The problem, the editorial added, was a lenient justice system
that did not have a special legislation to overcome witchcraft;
the solution, it claimed, was Lynch law. Although lynching was
unsustainable in a state of civilization, it was allegedly justifiable
when people were facing a cannibal organization that threatened
to destroy the family structure by eating defenseless children.
The editorial concluded by calling on national pride to justify
collective violence against the black witches.

> [Witchcraft] is an ignominy . . . that darkens the brightness of
> our national ensign . . . We have to erase it, to scrape it out, to
> extirpate it. And if it is done with blood, it doesn't matter: it
> would be a 'cleaning stain,' which is sometimes imposed on
> individuals or peoples by honor or necessity.[48]

And, indeed, the "people of Matanzas" responded to the
witches' outrage: they massed in front of the prison and threatened to take justice into their hands. The police then killed all
the defendants—one allegedly hanged himself in his cell, and
seven others were shot while "trying to escape." The incident in
Matanzas prompted a nationwide witch craze fanned by newspaper articles conveying the idea that most blacks were cannibals
and that only violence would restrain them.[49] It was in this context that the lynching of the Jamaican man described at the opening of this article took place and led to the exultant headline
"There Is Already One People Who Knows How to Lynch."

Nevertheless, the lynching of the Jamaican remained an isolated case—and one probably caused by racism together with xenophobia.[50] Except when acting under the government's injunction, white Cubans seldom turned to mob violence as a response to an alleged black threat.[51] Generally, supposed witches were denounced by "anonymous citizens" to the police. Most were arrested and sometimes molested and later released from custody. Many were submitted to lengthy judicial procedures and sentenced to short prison terms, because justice found them not guilty of major crimes.[52]

This presentation of the mechanism of racial stereotyping and violence in Cuba and the U.S. South allows for some general conclusions. In both regions, the press and politicians in power were crucial actors in the build-up of white outrage. Without the media's presentation of rape and witchcraft as ubiquitous and simultaneous incidents and without their calls to collective revenge, much of the racist violence would probably not have occurred. The same applies for the transformation of the 1912 Afro-Cuban protest into a race war and the ensuing racist massacre. It is because whites were made to feel collectively threatened by their elites that they responded collectively. Elites knew that by brandishing the stereotypes of the black rapist of white women and the black cannibal of white children, they ignited racist violence. In addition, the very techniques used by Cuban and southern media to provoke outrage were similar: the transformation of rumors into facts, the linking of unrelated and often fanciful incidents to create the sense of a planned black conspiracy against whites, the use of literary effects to make the audience personally threatened, and the call on white men to defend their wives and children and, through them, the sovereign.

3. VIOLENCE AS A PUBLIC MANIFESTATION OF THE POWER OF THE SOVEREIGN

Cuban and southern extralegal racist violence at the turn of the century showed continuity with colonial and pre-emancipation relations to state authority. During slavery in both regions the master's whip had incarnated whites' rights to exert their personal authority over their slave property without state interference, and on the whole the state had functioned as an appendix, rather than a counterweight, to the master's power. Beyond this similarity, however, differences prevailed. Unlike white Southerners who have tended to demonstrate resistance to state and law intervention and a propensity for vigilante justice, whites in Cuba were more prone to turn to state institutions for the repression of alleged social threats. In fact, random racial violence in Cuba appears principally in 1912, when whites acted under the umbrella of the military. Although white Cubans pursuing black "witches" arguably resorted to the law because they knew its antiblack biases, white Southerners, who undoubtedly would have found an even greater support from all-white courts, chose private "justice" and mob violence. Moreover, white Cubans generally entrusted the punishment of "witches" to the justice system despite the fact that witchcraft was not defined as a crime by the penal code, whereas white Southerners sanctioned rape and attempted rape by lynching, when both crimes were punishable by death.[53]

Indeed, southern lynching is an anomaly in the history of Western punishment. As demonstrated by Michel Foucault, with the demise of the absolute power of the monarch and the rise of a conception of the condemned as a human being in the early nineteenth century, the sovereign ceased to be absolute and personal and began to apply to the nation. In addition, "From being an art of unbearable sensations, punishment has become an economy of suspended rights."[54] In the case of the U.S. South, however, the sovereign remained absolute and did not become the nation, but the community of the southern white people. Lynching was a manifestation of the absolute power of a "redeemed" white people who resorted to extralegal punishment to assert their resistance to federal law and their continuing power over free African Americans.[55]

Lynching had the political function of reconstituting the momentarily injured sovereignty and of reactivating its power. It reestablished whites' hold on the bodies of blacks, lost with emancipation. It transformed the alleged crime of a black against a white individual into one committed against the whole sovereign white community. The ceremonial of lynching was a festive display that exemplified the irreversible imbalance between the defiant black subject and the all-powerful white sovereign. It was a public spectacle in which, through the mastering and destruction of the body of the alleged black culprit, the "unrestrained presence" of the sovereign white community manifested itself, deciding and executing punishments for a crime committed against its whole body. Whereas regicide was the absolute crime in monarchical societies, in the post-Reconstruction South black murder or rape of whites were perceived as the crimes that "attacked the very principle and physical person" of the sovereign white community. Within this logic, white society had to respond to the atrocity of the alleged crime with greater atrocity in order "to overcome [the latter] by an excess that annulled it," which was achieved through lynching.[56]

In early twentieth-century Cuba, in contrast, punishment was midway between the monarchical public spectacle of torture and the "democratic" "economy of suspended rights" discussed by Foucault. Most alleged crimes by blacks were punished by prison or hard labor sentences passed by regular courts of justice. Legal executions, though still carried out through the Spanish colonial torture of the garotte, were infrequent and held behind the prison's walls. Lynchings were rare and not planned ceremonials. Yet the 1912 massacre of Afro-Cubans was in many ways a lengthy public spectacle of torture and execution held on a national scale. Although most of the actual gunning down, hanging, and mutilating of black folks was done out of the public view by military detachments and volunteer posses, it was graphically publicized by newspapers' articles and cartoons. In some occasions, such as a testing by the artillery of newly acquired machine guns against an alleged encampment of Independents, in which 150 peaceful Afro-Cuban peasants were killed or wounded, the massacre was genuinely staged for guest journalists.[57]

In Cuba, the injured "sovereign" who took revenge on "criminal" blacks in the 1912 massacre and the 1919 murders of alleged witches was not the white community, as in the U.S. South, but the Cuban republic or nation with its "white civilization." The absolute crime was not the murder or rape of a white individual by a black man which stained the entire white people, but black witchcraft and black political protest which violated the Cuban republic as imagined by the elite.[58] In 1912, in particular, the protest of the Independent Party of Color became a crime of lèse-republic. As a result, punishment and torture were applied in the name of the sovereign Cuban nation and its Western civilization. Reconstituting the republic's momentarily injured sovereignty demanded the full support of all republican institutions and took the form of a national war. Like lynching in the U.S. South, however, the 1912 "race war" showed the unalterable power relation between the sovereign and those being reduced to impotence; and the disproportionate punishment applied to the Independents of Color and ordinary Afro-Cubans served to assert with pomp the republic's control over the entire black population.

From the 1890s to the 1920s southern lynching was an institution by the popular will of local white communities to force African Americans to conform with Jim Crow, economic dependency, and second-rate citizenship. Cuba's 1912 massacre was a unique, government-led operation that mobilized some whites but left most of them indifferent. Nevertheless, its scale and cruelty aimed at preventing any further attempt by Afro-Cubans to politically organize separately from whites. In both regions, the sovereign's racial violence was a powerful political operation that served to manifest the irreversible imbalance of power between whites and blacks. It reinforced white cohesion and terrorized blacks into submission.

4. STEREOTYPING AND VIOLENCE AS MEANS OF TEACHING
BLACKS THEIR "TRUE PLACE" IN SOCIETY

Racial stereotypes and racial violence aimed at teaching a lesson
to blacks: that they should remain in "their place": that of the
dominated. However, different conceptions of the sovereign in
the two societies affected whites' notions of what that place
should be. In the U.S. South, blacks were excluded from the
white sovereign community; in Cuba, they were included in the
nation, but as its lower strata. Such different notions reflected
fundamental differences between the two racial systems. Although both regions were characterized by a two-tier system pos-
iting whites as naturally superior, in the United States the barrier
separating blacks and mulattoes from whites was based on the
"one drop rule," in Cuba, on "visible" African ancestry (skin
color, hair texture, and/or facial features).[59] Moreover, in the U.S.
South, slavery was progressively replaced with Jim Crow laws,
black disenfranchisement, and a rigid color line, in independent
Cuba, with legal equality, universal male suffrage, racial discrimination, and white immigration.

Because the two regions had different racial systems, whites
used different images of otherness to fix the boundaries between
them and blacks. The predominance of one or the other stereotype affected who was targeted in the black population. In the
U.S. South, the icon of fear of the black rapist transformed all
blacks into outcasts. It singled out the alleged barbarism and animal sexuality of the entire male population of African descent; it
ultimately aimed at denying all black men their manhood and
their ability to be family providers and voters. As a result, any
black male could be lynched: a child, a mentally handicapped, a
professional, or an itinerant worker. Globally, most victims were
young black men in the cotton-producing rural areas. Uprooted
or migrant blacks with weak links to the local community were
especially vulnerable. Yet the absence of judicial records on
Lynch murders together with the biases of local newspaper re-

ports, which tended to limits the victims' portrayal to the words "bad niggers," make any sociological and demographic analysis of the phenomenon impossible. What magnified the terror of lynching was exactly this: that any black male who did not conform with the Sambo model of servility and contentment could be perceived as a threat to white supremacy and be lynched.[60]

Similarly, during the summer of 1912 in Cuba, the use of the stereotype of the black rapist and the transformation of the Independent Party of Color's protest into a black war against the sovereign Cuban republic and its "white" civilization pushed Afro-Cubans to the fringe of "Cubanity." The entire black population was racialized and became a potential target of racial violence. Of course, there is no official record of the victims of the army and the volunteer militias in Oriente, and one has to rely on scattered witness accounts. Yet these show that the great majority of the dead were not followers of the Independent Party of Color, but black rural folks and migrant workers. A careful reading of contemporary newspapers also shows that racist violence was not limited to Oriente but erupted nationwide and targeted blacks from all walks of life, though on a much smaller scale than in the eastern province.[61]

In Cuba, however, the most commonly used icon of fear of the black male witch targeted only a portion of the black population: those who practiced religions of African origin. As a result, most persons persecuted for alleged witchcraft were lower-class blacks with little or no formal education. Some were old, African-born, and former slaves, others were freedmen born in Cuba, still others were young Afro-Cubans who had always been free. What distinguished them most was that all worshipped religions of African origin, such as *santería*.[62] However, by denigrating cultural expressions of African origin, the stereotype of the black witch reflected on all Afro-Cubans. It projected the image of the cannibal black witch, thus casting a negative shadow on the image of heroes that Afro-Cubans had collectively acquired for their mass participation in the War for Independence. It presented the legal equality guaranteed to them by the constitution as a favor granted by whites and helped to justify Afro-Cubans' lower position in society on educational grounds.

Yet in both societies the stereotypes of the black rapist and the black male witch also targeted the small but rising black middle class, the "uppity blacks" who threatened the mythology of black inferiority and had the potential of changing the balance between dominants and dominated. That these two stereotypes emerged simultaneously with those of the loyal slave during the Civil War and the faithful black fighter of Cuba's wars for independence was no accident.[63]

Shortly before their emergence, individuals of African descent had made important gains that changed the negative image of blacks inherited from slavery. From the 1870s to the 1880s in the South, many had entered the industrial labor force and the federal bureaucracy and advanced in education; some had acquired land and property, opened businesses, established newspapers, and become elected representatives.[64] Between 1895 and 1902 in Cuba, many had been soldiers and officers in the proindependence army; a few had returned from exile with new means and an experience as journalists; others had been appointed to minor offices during the U.S. occupation and a few had become professionals; a handful had been elected at the national or local level.[65] In addition, black political leaders had showed that they had power balance in close votes between Republicans and Democrats in the South and between Liberals and Conservatives in Cuba. In both regions, these achievements had increased the expectations of people of African descent across class.

Against this backdrop, the economic depression of the 1890s in the South and the postwar crisis in Cuba deeply affected blacks as well as poor whites and created the conditions in which a crossracial alliance of the lower classes or an all-black mobilization could challenge white elite political control.[66] Whites perceived black middle-class assertiveness with increasing concern. In both regions, the white elite envisioned the "true place" for the small black middle class only in terms of white paternalism. They could not accept black independent political leadership, which they stigmatized as "social equality" in the South and "black separatism" in Cuba.

At first sight, the myths of the black rapist and the black male witch, by targeting the black lower classes, indirectly recognized "civilized black males" as part of manhood, as family providers and voters, thus as competitors. But the myths did so as long as middle-class blacks acknowledged their supposed inferiority and grew away from the "barbarian" lower class. The stereotypes, thus, had a double function with respect to the black middle class. On the one hand, they aimed at further fragmenting blacks into "civilized" and "savage," in order to prevent their united challenge to white-dominated society. On the other hand, they allowed whites to blame black "barbarism" on a black middle class supposedly unable to "civilize" its lower classes, and by extension to stigmatize the entire "black race" as prone to rape and witchcraft.

In the South, when universal male suffrage was still in force, the Ku Klux Klan and vigilante action repressed black leaders who showed unconformity. In the 1890s, the white elite began to claim that if blacks voted en bloc, they limited the freedom of whites and threatened them with black dictatorship. Black education began to be seen as the root of "the black problem" and to be equated with African Americans not accepting their place in society and demanding political rights and "social equality."[67] As aptly analyzed by Glenda E. Gilmore,

> By positing lust for refined white women as a universal trait in black men, whites explained away black Best Men's [middle-class blacks'] good behavior by arguing that they sought success simply to get close to white women. Likewise, when a poor black man stood accused of rape, the New White Men argued that the rapist had been stimulated by the black Best Man's elevated position. Black progress of any sort meant a move toward social equality, a code word for sexual equality.[68]

In Cuba, throughout the wars of independence, autonomous black leadership and black military success had concerned whites, who had raised more than once the specter of a revolution along Haitian lines to neutralize black challenge.[69] After independence, any attempt by Afro-Cuban leaders to push for a agenda benefiting blacks continued to be stereotyped as "black separatism" and equated with a threat to national unity. Simultaneously, the stereotype of the black male witch served as a powerful reminder of African "barbarism" and black alleged inferiority to both whites and Afro-Cubans demanding full equality on the basis of their advancement and their fundamental role in Cuba's independence. In 1908, whites' nightmare seemed to become true when a group of "civilized" Afro-Cuban men defied white politicians and founded the Independent Party of Color. Most founders were middle-class war veterans frustrated that independence had given Afro-Cubans formal, rather than real equality. The party rapidly gained thousands of black and mulatto lower-class supporters nationwide and threatened the political monopoly of the island's Liberal and Conservative parties.[70] Government response escalated from harassment to trial and legal ban in 1910. In that process, government officials and journalists twisted two claims of the party to brandish the specters of the Haitian revolution and of the black rapist. First, they transformed the Independents of Color's plan to run in elections into an attempt to overthrow the legally elected government and to impose a black dictatorship. Second, they used the party's claim that, if racial equality really existed in Cuba, black men should be allowed to court and marry white women, to accuse the party of inciting black men to rape white women. In addition, they repeatedly presented the party's leaders as "uppity mulattoes."[71] On this basis, the 1912 armed protest organized by the party to regain legality was easily transformed into a "race war" in which blacks aimed at killing whites and raping white women, which justified the ensuing massacre.

More generally, in the South as in Cuba, the stereotypes of the black rapist and the black male witch confronted middle-class blacks with an unsolvable dilemma. If they denied the myths' veracity through factual refutation, they failed to annul their irrational and emotional meaning and they exposed themselves to accusations of instigating black crime. If they subscribed to the myths and proposed to "uplift" and "civilize" poor blacks, they had to simultaneously conform to negative views of blacks that affected them as well.[72]

Like stereotyping, violence as a means of teaching blacks their "true place" was used differently in the two regions. In the U.S. South, verbal and physical antiblack violence was institutionalized to preserve the color line. Lynching helped to maintain southern society and to reestablish economic and political domination over blacks, when the economy continued to depend on cotton and to require a large, cheap, and docile labor force.[73] Whites believed that coercive acts against blacks, such as flogging and lynching, helped to remind the latter of their inferior social position. In addition, they resorted to extralegal violence rather than to formal justice because it allowed them to terrorize specific blacks and entire black communities. In order to survive, African Americans needed to learn the unwritten and ever changing rules of interracial relations set by white individuals and local white communities.[74] In Cuba, in contrast, white antiblack violence was not institutionalized, and blacks who individually challenged the racial order generally incurred retaliation, not death. In fact, the white elite chose to keep them in check mostly by preventing black unity and mobilization through a rhetoric of racial equality, while simultaneously promoting white immigration from Spain, which reduced the proportion of people of color in the island's population and increased the competition for jobs to the detriment of Afro-Cubans.[75] However, when Afro-Cubans protested collectively the racial order, the white elite did not hesitate to use massive and indiscriminate violence against them.

Although most of the black victims of racist violence in Cuba and the South belonged to the lower class, middle-class blacks were not spared. Southern urban riots often targeted black business and middle-class residential areas, leading to the forced exodus of middle-class African Americans. In 1912, the Cuban government took care of eliminating the two principal leaders of the Independent Party of Color. Only after they had been shot, their bodies exposed to the public and buried on a common grave, did the army began to withdraw from Oriente.[76]

No doubt, with two different racial systems, the use of racist stereotyping and violence to keep blacks in their "true place" led to different "solutions" to the "black problem": public segregation and disenfranchisement in the U.S. South, selective integration and white immigration in Cuba. In the 1900s, Jim Crow affected all aspects of life from birth to death in the South. It meant the rigorous separation of the races in such domains as health care, education, justice, employment, entertainment, trade, housing, worshipping as well as in all public and private facilities. Public segregation was guaranteed by racist laws and local practices and upheld by the U.S. Supreme Court.[77] In post-independence Cuba, Afro-Cubans were victims of discrimination throughout their lives, but there was no rigid separation of the races and no mandatory segregation, which allowed for substantial racial mixing in popular neighborhoods, in the work place, and in several social activities. Nevertheless, as in colonial Cuba, many social clubs, places of entertainment, hotels, and private schools, for example, excluded blacks. Most theaters accommodated Afro-Cubans only in the back of the upper circle, ballrooms and swimming pools were often divided into two sections, one for whites and another for persons of color. Blacks were barred *de facto* from certain trades and professional positions, and over-represented in the lesser paid and lower-status jobs. In the government and the public sector, Afro-Cubans were not treated equally with white Cubans.[78]

In matters of civil rights, in the 1900s the U.S. South and Cuba were at the antipodes. Although (or because) since Reconstruction African-American men enthusiastically participated in south-

ern politics, generally behind the Republican Party, by the end
of the century they had been stripped of their voting rights. In
contrast, Cuba stood out in the Western Hemisphere as the only
nation with a substantial population of African descent and universal male suffrage. In the U.S. South, the ideology of white
supremacy then ruled all aspects of life and prohibited the mere
advocacy of social equality, which was equated with "miscegenation" leading to the disappearance of the "white race." Even in
the 1880s and 1890s, when black men could vote, white politicians, including Populists, recruited their suffrages behind the
banner of political rights but opposed equality between the
races.[79] In Cuba, the ideology of white superiority coexisted with
legal equality, which Afro-Cubans gained because of their decisive contribution to the nation's wars for independence. Racial
equality was part of the official discourse, but in reality was primarily used to prevent Afro-Cubans from protesting racial discrimination and from organizing to defend their rights. In 1910,
in particular, the Independent Party of Color was banned on the
grounds that, in representing only the interests of the Afro-
Cubans, it discriminated against whites and thus violated the
equality guaranteed by the constitution.[80]

At the turn of the century, thus, the margin of action allowed
to Afro-Cubans was broader than the one allowed to southern
African Americans. The latter were often limited to retreat into
black communities and resist as discreetly as possible, or migrate
to the U.S. North. Still many courageously stood up to protest
political oppression, labor exploitation, and racist violence.[81] In
addition, the very system of Jim Crow that marginalized African
Americans also allowed them to promote racial consciousness
and to organize separately from whites.[82] Afro-Cubans, in contrast, did not face institutionalized restrictions as long as they
did not collectively question the racial order; however, if they
mobilized on racial lines, they were forced into silence, repressed, and even murdered en masse.

5. STEREOTYPING, VIOLENCE, AND INTERRACIAL SEX

Stereotypes affected the ways black men and their alleged white victims were sexualized. The image of the rapist, which pervaded white Southerners' views of blacks at the turn of the century, oversexualized black men and, by equating their sexuality with animality, stripped them of all attributes of humanity. Simultaneously, the image of the assaulted white woman elevated her to sanctity but also desexualized her and stressed her dependency on the white man supposed to protect her purity.[83] In Cuba, the predominance of the image of the black male witch served rather the opposite purpose: to desexualize black men. Although the abduction and carving of the body of the white child showed some similarities with the rape of white women, the presentation of the black male witch seasoning and cooking human stews in big pots had a rather feminizing connotation, especially given the tradition of Spanish witchcraft which targeted poor women. Even during the "race war" of 1912, once the army had begun random killing, editorials and cartoons played down the virility of the protesters to portray them as carnivalesque cowards. How did these stereotypes, then, reflect the sexual dimension of racial relations in both societies?

In Cuba, the witch craze corresponded to a period of mass migration to the island, comprising mostly young white males from Spain but also, in the 1910s, Afro-Caribbean men in substantial numbers.[84] As a result, men outnumbered women in the island's population, and the proportion of people of color reached its lowest proportion since the beginning of sugar production. Male competition for women intensified. Simultaneously, the competition for jobs increased to the detriment of Afro-Cuban men but, with still few white Cuban women in the labor force and few females among the immigrants, it remained relatively favorable to Afro-Cuban women, especially in industry and personal services.[85] In the U.S. South, the opposite phenomenon took place. No mass immigration occurred, but until 1900 important intraregional migration happened to the agricultural frontier and to cities, which increased the black population in relation to whites in several areas. However, this trend did not benefit blacks in their competition for lucrative jobs, because the new economic sectors increasingly turned to the overwhelmingly black convict lease system and to poor white women for labor. The racial and gender balance of the southern population was not changed, but gender roles were affected as poor black and white families increasingly depended on female labor to survive. Only after the first two decades of lynchings, when the convict lease system faded away and African Americans began to emigrate en masse to the North, did the southern labor shortage become acute enough to make black free labor desirable in sectors other than agriculture and personal services. By the 1910s, both regions saw the relative "whitening" of their population, but in Cuba the labor supply increased, whereas it decreased in the South.[86]

Demography and economics, thus, appear to be powerful factors explaining the rise of racist icons of fear. As some recent historiography has shown, in the U.S. South the position of lower-class white women and their relations to white men were profoundly modified by the new context. White fathers, brothers, and husbands seemed to lose control over their female relatives at the same time as they were often losing the ownership of their land. As the depression of the 1890s made their condition more precarious, the black economic destitute and the progressing black appeared more threatening to them. In this context, the myth of the black rapist of white women allowed whites to repress, segregate, and disenfranchise black men while simultaneously bringing white women under the protection and responsibility of white men.[87]

In Cuba, lower-class native white women continued to overwhelmingly work in their homes. White Cuban men's control over them seemed less in jeopardy. Moreover, in the competition for women, they probably felt less threatened by Afro-Cubans than by white immigrants from Spain. Interestingly enough, however, unlike in Argentina where a similar phenomenon occurred, the Spanish immigrant to Cuba did not become stereotyped as a rapist or a criminal, but as the naive and stupid Galician victim of the lustful and astute mulatto woman.[88] The myth of the black male witch, by desexualizing black men and stressing their supposed barbarism, helped to discredit black men's competition for women and jobs.

In the two regions, the changing context affected black women and their relations with black men. Suffering from the dual effects of racial and sexual discrimination, they were excluded from the definition of womanhood by white society and viewed as sexual objects, which opened the door to unrestricted exploitation. Although a small minority of women of African descent were able to advance, among the lower classes male unemployment or underemployment increased black men's difficulties to conform with the dominant model of patriarchalism and often put the burden of family providing on women's shoulders. Black women also played a major role in black community organizations in both societies. In the U.S. South, as disenfranchisement silenced African American men, middle-class educated black women were often in the forefront of the struggle for equal rights.[89]

A comparative study of Cuba and the U.S. South confirms the recent challenge to studies explaining lynching and the rape myth in the U.S. South by the existence of a southern code of honor, with its corollaries of the glorification of motherhood and feminine virtue as a gauge for measuring a man's worth.[90] Although the southern code of honor is important to understand the dominant mentality in the white South, it was linked to slavery and preexisted the wave of lynching of alleged black rapists. Moreover, despite the fact that in Cuba the Hispanic code of honor, with its emphasis on feminine virginity and purity of blood, was strong as well,[91] the use of the stereotype of the black rapist and lynching were rare there. Other studies of lynching in the South have stressed the role played by white male sexual frustrations in the process.[92] Comparison with Cuba indicates the paramount importance of demography, economics, and politics in the rise of racist stereotypes and violence, but does not exclude the contributing role of white male sexuality. Quite likely, Cuban white males found more ways to fulfill their sexual desires, thus were less frustrated and less prone to violence than white Southerners when a global crisis affected them.

In both regions, forced or consensual sex between white men and slave women had been widely tolerated during slavery. As the children born out of these relations inherited their mother's status, these relations represented no threat to the social hierarchy. Black women were cast out of womanhood, which included only white women, and stereotyped as lustful females lacking the attributes of motherhood.[93] Such images transformed white rapists of black women into victims of black seductresses and freed them from guilt feelings. After emancipation, interracial sex between white men and black women continued, but took different paths. In the U.S. South, African-American women won the legal right to bring rape charges against white men. However, whites' rape and casual exploitative sex with black women continued unopposed by white society, whereas consensual sex became increasingly less tolerated, especially if it concerned white men who showed other signs of unconformity with the social order.[94] In Cuba, sex between white men and black women did not encounter the same level of opposition and continued to be attributed to the lust of women of African descent. Society did not challenge elite white men's colonial practice of having darker lovers, as long as they did not marry them. In general, in a culture free from Protestant puritanism and lacking a strong Catholic Church, male extramarital liaisons were tolerated. Traditionally, many adults, especially in the popular classes and among Afro-Cubans, did not legalize their unions through marriage.[95] In addition, unions with darker women were often depicted as the sorry privilege of poor Spanish immigrants, and the offspring of such unions generally inherited the lower racial category of their mothers.[96] In short, interracial sex between white men and black women was not opposed because it did not threaten the color hierarchy and the social position of white women.

Both regions, however, were characterized by a taboo on interracial sexual relations between black men and white women. As a result, both in Cuba and the U.S. South such unions were rare at all levels of society. In the South before the Civil War and even during Reconstruction, liaisons between poor white women and black men had enjoyed some degree of toleration, partly because they corresponded to the white planter ideology about the depravity of lower-class white women. In Cuba, during slavery, interracial marriage was prohibited, but some exemptions were granted for a handful of poor white women and self-sufficient black men, because the higher economic status of the man was supposed to compensate his lower racial status.[97] In the 1880s in the U.S. South, the sociopolitical changes brought about by emancipation and Reconstruction dramatically modified white views of black men. The potential that men among the former slave population had to destroy the racial caste system led to the taboo of sex between white women and black men with a new urgency. Some states issued laws reaffirming opposition to interracial marriage. Increasingly, all white women, regardless of class, were required to follow the ideal of virtue of the white southern lady in order to protect the purity of the white race. Sex between poor "immoral" women and black men began to be violently combatted.[98]

In the 1890s, as the "one drop rule" determined status, white women, regardless of class, became the "symbol and repository of white racial purity" and white civilization. Any perceived assault against white women by black men became an attack on the sovereign white community and on white male honor that had to be avenged. White women in interracial relations were either punished with their black mate or, increasingly, considered raped, even if they protested their consent to the relation.[99] In many southern states, interracial marriage and cohabitation were prohibited, and in Mississippi in 1920, even the advocacy of interracial marriage was considered a crime.[100]

In Cuba after independence, in contrast, there were no legal restrictions on interracial marriage, but the marriage or free union of white women with black men continued to be a taboo, thus a rare phenomenon. Sometimes such relations were called rapes or attributed to the power of black witchcraft, which restored the morality of white women having sex with black men.[101] Yet within a dual racial system based on "visible" African ancestry, racial mixture was sometimes possible to conceal. Moreover, unlike southern African Americans, Afro-Cubans did not oppose "miscegenation," and many subscribed to the ideal of "whitening."[102] As already mentioned, the Independent Party of Color's claim that racial equality should also apply to sexual relations, thus that black men should be allowed to mate with white women, provoked outrage and was transformed by the white press as a call on black men to rape white women. However, unlike in the U.S. South, where such a statement by a group of black men would have prompted an immediate wave of lynchings, in Cuba it served at first to heighten racial tensions and to mobilize white men.[103] Only in 1912, when the Independents of Color rallied to protest the ban of their party, did it help to fuel antiblack violence. In general, however, with no mandatory segregation and no rigid color line, Afro-Cuban men having consensual sex with poor white women were less likely to face violence, because they were so few that they could not challenge the color hierarchy of society.[104]

6. WHITE UNITY AGAINST BLACKS

In the U.S. South and Cuba, as in most of the world, the representation of the dominated as "other" helped to assert what civilization meant and to unite the dominant group behind what they believed they were not. Violence against the "other" reinforced the dominant group's boundaries and reaffirmed its superiority.

To be fully effective, however, domination requires the existence of a politically and economically strong elite who has no doubt about its own superiority. After Reconstruction the southern white elite was able to progressively retake the political control of the South and to reassert, despite increasing dependency on northern industry and financial capital, its economic domination over the region through continuing control of land and labor.[105] In contrast, in Cuba after independence many in the white native elite were experiencing political power for the first time and under the narrow limits of the Platt Amendment. Whereas some of them gained economic power through politics and others preserved their preindependence wealth, still others were displaced by the growing U.S. control of the island's infrastructure, land, labor, and capital.[106]

In the South, the Civil War at least in the beginning brought whites closer together. The poor, the small farmers, and the planters united in the defense of slavery, independence from the North, and white supremacy. As the extension of the war exacted a disproportionate contribution from the non-planter classes, white unity eroded, bringing the Confederacy on the edge of internal collapse. Yet no crossracial rapprochement between poorer whites and blacks could grow out of this erosion, because the interests and war allegiances of these groups were antagonistic. Moreover, after the end of the war, Reconstruction met with broad white opposition, even from the poor whites who could have benefited from its social policies.[107] In Cuba, in contrast, the War for Independence, by mobilizing mostly the east of the island, by dividing the white population along national (Cuban versus Spanish) and political lines (in favor of Spanish colonialism, or autonomy, or U.S. annexation, or independence), and by bringing proindependence white and black Cubans closer together in the Liberation Army, weakened racial identification. The U.S. occupation continued this trend through policies that favored U.S. and Spanish interests to the detriment of those of the veterans of the Liberation Army.[108] The two regions, thus, had not the same experience of white unity to build upon.

After Reconstruction in the U.S. South and after independence in Cuba, white elites used the black threat to unite lower-class whites behind them and to prevent any class alliance between blacks and poor whites, but they fared differently in their endeavor. In the U.S. South, tensions between planters on the one side, and farmers and poor whites on the other, continued after the war, due to increasing landlessness, indebtedness, and dependency on world market prices. As a result, from the late 1870s to the early 1890s, planter political domination through the Democratic Party was threatened by such movements as the Farmer Alliance and Populism, as well as by some local successes of the Republican Party. However, during these years, the ideology of white supremacy was never questioned. The Farmer Alliance and Populism, for example, accepted black political cooperation as a means of countering the Democrats but rejected racial equality.[109] By the mid-1890s, the southern elite had recovered political control of the region, thanks to terrorism, intimidation, and fraud. But the elite also successfully used the threat of the "black rapist" and of "black domination" to induce guilt among the deserters of the Democratic Party and to offer a new definition of manhood to poor white men loosing control over their land and partially depending on the wage labor of their wives and children: militant racial identification.[110] In addition, white Southerners cleverly associated lynching with black rape of white women to globally justify extralegal violence, because it served to gain the white North's sympathy on the "necessity" of lynching.[111] In the 1900s, black disenfranchisement was accepted throughout the South with the support of the former challengers to the Democrats. Antiblack racism and the ideology of white supremacy then reached their paroxysm. As most whites benefited from the caste system and from black exploitation, after blacks were disenfranchised, there was a crossclass and crossregional white consensus against blacks' equal rights and in favor of lynching. In the press and politics, elite whites consciously used the icon of fear of the black rapist to channel poor white discontent and to bring a sense of caste solidarity to the white lower class. They were willing to see blacks terrorized and lynched because it helped to strengthen control over rural workers and to widen the gap between blacks and lower-class whites. Poor white farmers were equally willing to use antiblack violence when economic adversity threatened their tenuous claim to social superiority and when revolt against the elite was too risky.[112]

In Cuba, in contrast, although the racial order also worked to the advantage of whites in general and although most whites believed in black inferiority, antiblack violence only occasionally united whites across class and national lines: when some Afro-Cubans actually organized to challenge the white-dominated sociopolitical structure. In 1910, notably, in several towns, poor whites volunteered in all-white militias to defend their communities against alleged attacks by members of the Independent Party of Color. More significantly, white unity was realized in 1912 against the black party's armed protest in Oriente. Some whites then did not hesitate to butcher Afro-Cubans because of their race. Operating under the government's umbrella, they felt unaccountable, and indeed they were. Many in the elite openly rejoiced at the massacre. Most saw the killings as a necessary lesson to teach Afro-Cubans the limits of their freedom. A few analyzed the bloody outcome of the "race war" as a sure sign that blacks were doomed to disappear in Cuba, allowing the island to have a bright future as a white nation.[113] Among the white lower class, the indiscriminate killings of blacks prompted enthusiastic support mostly among those who volunteered to fight with the government. But few, if any, protested racial violence, and the white-led labor unions kept a conspicuous silence. Although they knew what was going on, most white Cubans remained indifferent to the fate of their darker fellow citizens.[114]

When blacks did not challenge Cuba's racial order, however, whites were too entangled in their own internal divisions to dem-

onstrate unity against blacks. White Cubans clashed with Spaniards, white veterans of the War for Independence with former
supporters of Spain, white Liberals with white Conservatives—
and some of these clashes produced crossracial alliances between
Cubans. Lower-class white Cubans competed not only among
themselves and with Afro-Cubans for employment and access to
land, but also with Spanish immigrants, which weakened racial
allegiances. The racist stereotype of the black male witch, for
example, worked mostly among elite and working-class whites in
cities and small towns, but failed to raise much alarm among rural
whites, who often had traditional healing practices and were beyond the reach of Western medicine.[115]

The white Cuban elite itself was insecure in its dominance of
society. Apprehensive of Afro-Cuban demands for full participation after the end of the War for Independence in 1898, many
upper-class whites had welcomed U.S. intervention and the Platt
Amendment. In the fourteen years that followed, as a result, the
U.S. military ruled Cuba during almost six years, and U.S. interests controlled most sectors of the Cuban economy. Thus, unlike
the southern elite, after independence the white Cuban elite was
politically and economically weak.[116] In addition, it was not unusual for U.S. officials and travellers to portray all Cubans, including the white elite, as an inferior and Negroid people and to
use the theory of white racial supremacy to justify U.S. control of
Cuba.[117]

Rather than taking the risk of confronting U.S. imperialism,
the Cuban political elite chose to direct their resentment and
frustration against Afro-Cubans as a means of recovering self-confidence in their own whiteness and superiority. The repression
of black male witches, by caricaturing Afro-Cuban otherness as
barbarism, delineated the white Cuban elite as a part of the Western modern world and justified its domination of Cuban society.
Similarly, in 1912, when the Cuban government sent troops and
volunteers to fight a fictional "race war" led by the Independent
Party of Color, this enabled the elite to win a battle in the name

of white supremacy, as some contemporary interpretations claimed.

Also indicative of elite white Cubans' insecurity was their ambiguous attitude toward the United States, which oscillated between rejection and adulation. Whereas some advocated the reaffirmation of Cuba's independent status together with subsidized Spanish immigration, others welcomed U.S. supervision as a safeguard against Afro-Cuban challenge. Still others looked toward the U.S. South for a blueprint for race relations.[118] Even during the peak moments of the witch craze and during the 1912 "race war," although the elite agreed that immediate repression was necessary, they diverged on the long-term solutions to Cuba's "racial problem." Some questioned the fundamental institutions of Cuba's democracy for allegedly not suiting a people as racially diverse as Cubans and proposed their replacement with limited male suffrage, legal segregation, and lynching, among other things. They were defeated, however, by those who supported legal equality on the grounds of Afro-Cuban overrepresentation in the struggle for independence.[119] Afro-Cubans themselves were slowly recovering from the shock of the 1912 massacre and raising their voices against racist violence.[120] Despite the example set by the people of Regla who lynched the Jamaican man in 1919, lynching was to remain a prerogative of the U.S. South.[121] Moreover, although Cuban anthropologist Fernando Ortiz and others tried to add witchcraft to the penal code's list of crimes, they failed because most legislators found the existing law well equipped enough to face the threat.[122]

Just as a majority in the Cuban elite was rejecting lynching as unfit for a civilized nation, by 1920 the southern elite was beginning to see the first signs that their domination was threatened by forces that could not be undermined by racist violence and terror. Blacks were migrating to the North en masse, creating a labor shortage and reducing the competition between them and poor whites. They were also organizing against white supremacy, notably behind the National Association for the Advancement of

Colored People. In addition, opposition to lynching was growing from within the elite. The "silent South" who had vainly opposed specific racial policies since the aftermath of Reconstruction was becoming more vocal and began to organize, notably in the Commission on Interracial Cooperation and the Association of Southern Women for the Prevention of Lynching. Black resistance and emigration, the beginning of southern white dissent, northern activism and economic interests were all forces that explain the waning of lynching in the 1920s.[123] By the end of the 1920s, both in the U.S. South and Cuba, extralegal racist violence was on the decline. The racial systems in which violence was exerted, however, continued unabated for several more decades.[124]

CONCLUSION

At the turn of the century, Cuba's dual racial system was less rigid than the "one drop rule" system prevailing in the U.S. South. Blacks' freedom and rights were broader in Cuba than in the segregated and disenfranchised South. Similarly, the existence of distinct socioeconomic and demographic contexts had a fundamental influence on the shaping of racial stereotypes and on the actual manifestation of violence in the two regions. In particular, lower-class white women's proletarianization was a southern phenomenon without equivalent in Cuba which contributed to the successful use of the gendered race card in the South.

Whereas the stereotype of the black rapist was periodically used in the South to justify lynching and to terrorize African Americans into conformity with Jim Crow and the racial etiquette, in Cuba it was used mostly in 1912 to justify the army massacre and to force Afro-Cubans into integration in the white-controlled political system. In fact, in Cuba the most long-lasting stereotype was that of the black male witch, which served to divide Afro-Cubans between "civilized" and "barbarians" in a context in which universal male suffrage increased white fears of black unified political challenge. In the South lynching was broadly accepted by lower-class whites; in Cuba, whites generally entrusted repression to state institutions. Whereas the southern elite was quite successful in reasserting its control of society after Reconstruction and in uniting whites across class behind the necessity of lynching, the Cuban white elite only managed to do so in 1912, when some Afro-Cubans actually mobilized to challenge the racial order. Nonetheless, despite its claim that Cuba was the embodiment of racial equality, when faced with Afro-Cuban challenge the Cuban white elite, like their peer in the U.S. South, resorted to racial stereotyping and racial terror to force blacks into submission.

This comparative discussion of the two processes allows for some broad conclusions about the mechanism of racist mobilization. In Cuba as in the U.S. South, two decades after emancipation, fear-inducing stereotypes of black males emerged that helped to justify antiblack violence. In both societies, racial stereotyping and violence were initiated and promoted by white elites undergoing a crisis of confidence in order to prevent a lower-class crossracial alliance and/or an all-black mobilization that could transform the socioracial structure of society. It was a top down, not a bottom up, process in which the rapidly expanding media of mass communication played a major role. It was an ideological campaign of intoxication that pursued political goals: the compliance of the white lower class with white elite politics and the annihilation of black autonomous challenge.

In both societies, the white lower classes did little to resist the elite racist call. The two regions were then going through deep economic crises that threatened to assign to poor whites the same lot as to the majority of blacks, thus to destroy their claim to a status superior to that of the former slaves. In particular, the rise of a small middle class of African descent increased whites' fear of a future in which they would have to compete with blacks on an equal basis. In both cases, lower-class whites were encouraged to blame the dominated blacks. This concealed the real sources

of the crisis and gave them the illusion of power, when simultaneously people of African descent were deprived of the means of
effectively countering the attack.

Indeed, the icons of fear of the black rapist and of the black
male witch had irrational and rational components that hindered
counteraction. They represented principles difficult to refute:
that rape and cannibalism were criminal. Built on traditional
fears of black "barbarism," stereotyping artificially and methodi-
cally made these specific crimes ubiquitous and the propensity
of the dominated group, and by doing so, generated an atmosphere of fears. Used together with the image of the docile "good
black" of former times, the new icons powerfully countered the
more frightening possibility of black postslavery success. Supported by actual violence and terror, they helped to draw a line
between whites and blacks and to teach people of African descent
their "true place" in society. Ultimately, however, both regions'
emphasis on annihilating black political voice—through the
physical elimination of an autonomous black party in Cuba,
through black disenfranchisement in the South—showed whites'
and blacks' beliefs in the potential of universal male suffrage to
radically transform former slave societies into racial democracies.

Commentary / Daniel C. Littlefield

Professor Helg develops a very interesting comparison between
the United States and Cuba in their race relations and race stereotyping, and I have very little basic disagreement with her. I
think, however, that the Cuban situation is so interesting partly
because it is influenced by two contrary traditions: one coming
from Spain and the other from the United States. From the nineteenth century when Cuba became an important slave society,
and particularly after the 1830s when slavery was abolished in
the British Empire, leaving Brazil, Cuba, and the United States
as leading slave societies in the New World, Cuba looked to the

United States for support and as something of a model. After the
Spanish-American War and Cuba's linking to the United States
as a protectorate, she had of necessity to look to the United
States. But, it seems to me, that at least some American values
were in conflict with those derived from Iberia, and I would be
interested in a little more discussion of that kind. For example,
was the discrimination against blacks in certain hotels or clubs,
and their segregation in theaters derived from American practices or indigenous Cuban creations? They may have been either
or a combination of both, but I would like to see the issue explored because the historic relationship between the two countries has been so important and because such a consideration
underlines the complexities of Cuban racial attitudes.

Although Professor Helg stresses the differences between the
1919 Regla lynching and U.S. lynching, for me the similarities
still stand out: witchcraft was the rationale in 1919 Cuba; rape
was most often the rationale in the U.S. South; but in both cases
the motive was the same: to terrorize and dominate blacks. Significantly, however, the difference in rationale might partially signal a difference in the meaning and significance of blackness.
Assuming that it was not a simple expression of xenophobia (the
victim having been Jamaican), the Regla lynching sounded a clear
warning not to practice witchcraft or African-derived traditional
religions. It points to the more African-based nature of slave culture on the islands, where African-derived religions were more
openly practiced. But it also suggests, as Professor Helg indicates, that if Africans rejected their traditions, and particularly if
they were genetically-mixed, they might in some sense cease to
be black.

There was indeed a strong emphasis on purity of blood within
the Spanish tradition, but it was a much more elastic concept
than Americans understood. Originally, in Iberia, it had a religious rather than a racial significance: people were theoretically
prevented from doing certain things if they had Jewish or Moor-
ish "blood." In the New World it developed a racial meaning, but

in either case it was not so strongly enforced that other things like wealth, appearance, meritorious military service, or signal contributions to the crown could not override it. There was a disposition to overlook minor defects for the common good. There remained throughout a white ideal, but the ideal was not a genetic one except in theory. Other things intervened. Particularly important was an assimilation to Spanish culture. In sixteenth-century Spain, according to Ruth Pike, Africans were considered to be more trustworthy and were consequently more acceptable, than Moors or Moriscos because of their greater amenability to hispanization, including the adoption of Christianity.[1] Admittedly, they were in fewer numbers than the other two groups. A number of considerations, therefore, might offset the misfortune of a black progenitor. And once the person accepted his new position as white, he might be more ardent than others in opposition against those who had not his degree of acceptance. So blacks—or what would be called blacks in the United States— could be divided against each other. On the other hand, white immigrants into Cuba from Spain, coming out of a tradition where race of color was not the most important consideration, might not be easily constrained to change that opinion even on the island—especially in view of the existing racial mixture they found there.

Of course, excepting the United States, it was part of a widespread New World practice to separate what we now call people of color on the basis of phenotype and pigmentation. Certainly many people who would be called black in the United States would not be so-called in Cuba or in other parts of Latin America or indeed, the World. Walter White, second "black" president of the NAACP, was a blue-eyed blond. On one occasion, when they traveled together overseas and were announced as an interracial couple, Europeans thought his white wife, who was brunette, was the "black" of the group.[2] Similarly, Sidney Barthelemy, mayor of New Orleans in the 1980s, would not be considered black anyplace else. He looks absolutely no different from *his*

white wife. He had to fight to be considered the black candidate
in the New Orleans mayoral race and among the charges he had
to fight was that he had previously passed for white. By contrast,
I had a Cuban friend who was a lot darker than either White or
Barthelemy, and who, by any objective opinion, clearly had black
genes but did not consider himself black. If his gene pool were
analyzed, he may have had at least as much right on that basis to
consider himself white as black. But from an American point of
view he clearly was not white. Indeed, he was only a shade
lighter than my father and looked phenotypically the same.
Which was one of the things that attracted me to him in the first
place. He reminded me of my father. But his identity was different and he did not seem to notice the stunned expression on the
faces of a group of us, white and black Americans together, when
he made a statement separating himself from blacks in no uncertain terms. But the expression on the faces of all of us in the
group, black and white alike, was: "who and what do you think
you are?" We were too polite and perhaps too conscious of a
cultural difference to say anything to him, though some of us did
mutter among ourselves later. But it is a very clear example of
how, as Professor Helg points out, the Cuban elite (and the Spanish elite before them) was able to divide what Americans would
consider blacks, among themselves. Indeed, many people the
color of this Cuban may have engaged in the slaughter of blacks
in 1912.

The more African-based nature of black culture in Cuba, particularly the more African character of religious expression, might
well have caused the Cuban elite some discomfiture. If the Haitian Revolution did anything, it showed the power of African religion, in combination with other factors, to mobilize Africans in
rebellion. Yet it is curious to me how Cubans, especially the elite,
could rationalize their apparent belief in witches with their conviction that they were prime exemplars of modern "civilization."
Because the fear seems to be somewhat deeper than the threat
that some white girl might be sacrificed, or that blacks might

rebel. It seems to be a projection and recalls the hysteria in seventeenth-century Salem, Massachusetts, during the witchcraft trials. Most late nineteenth- and early twentieth-century white Americans, whatever their private beliefs, would not likely have operated openly on the assumption of witchcraft, confining that to an earlier, benighted age. There is a certain irony, therefore, in a Cuban elite arguing for a defense of modern civilization based on a medieval belief in witches. Of course, this is no more ironic than basing a defense of civilization of the even more barbaric practice of lynching. Yet I can imagine some white Americans getting a perverse joy out of learning that black Americans believed in witches which they would point to as evidence, as did white Cubans, that blacks were savages in need of firm control. But the actions of Cubans implicitly warned blacks to change. White Americans at the time essentially wanted little or no change among blacks, just their subordination. So long as blacks were simple and subservient there was a disposition to tolerate and even to romanticize their divergent beliefs—as evidenced in the popularity of the tales of Uncle Remus.

Being aware of a Latin background in which the view of race was comparatively elastic, but taking as an ideal a society where race was an absolute concept, Cubans were of necessity insecure. They were aware that some people accepted as white on the island would not be so considered in the United States and they were afraid, as Professor Helg suggests, that all would be painted with the same brush. Fortunately, there remained in Cuba white people who could not agree that an overweening focus on race was as important as the elite could with to make it. They were aware that this elite was mostly concerned with outside acceptance. By contrast, foreigners coming into American society normally had to bend to an overwhelming consensus in opposition to blacks; and usually to acquiesce in a commitment to an aggressive white supremacy as an aspect of Americanization. The difference between the North and the South is this respect was not unimportant, but it was marginal. Thus Thomas Nelson Page, who helped stimulate national popularity of a genre of literature that presented the most nostalgic vision of the Old South, knew his audience when he told a largely northern readership in 1892 that "The white race, it is reasonably certain, is not going to be ruled by the Negro, either North or South."[3]

In the United States, blacks by their very presence posed a threat; it was a genetic threat symbolized by the cry of rape, which encapsulated a cluster of interrelated concerns. Living within a historic tradition that imposed upon blacks a passionate sexuality, a situation of which white men had been previously able to take almost exclusive advantage, there was now a fear that black men and white women might do likewise. But the onus was placed on black men. Consequently, when Page discussed "the Negro question" with the Italian king in 1906, he said "the trouble was that the Negroes wanted to marry the whites."[4] The issue was nowhere expressed more honestly, starkly, or succinctly. At no time during the discussion did he attempt to prove that assertion and no proof was necessary; it was an assumption rooted firmly in his own mind.

His 300-page disquisition on *The Negro: The Southerner's Problem*, published in 1904 (a copy of which he offered to the king), was a diverse, discursive, and defensive extenuation of the southern argument that blacks were inferior. But he did not hide his central concern. The problem arose after Reconstruction when there was a "teaching that the Negro was the equal of the white, that the white was his enemy, and that he must assert his equality. The growth of this idea was a gradual one in the Negro's mind. This was followed by a number of cases where members of the Negro militia ravished white women; in some instances in the presence of their families."[5] The syllogism was clear: black equality meant miscegenation and that, in the nature of things at the time, had to mean rape. That charge was the easiest way to mobilize white people to action. It was shorthand for black domination, which black equality also came to mean. And there was logic to the reasoning. For if black men were truly—socially, politically, and economically—equal and they were also, as white men argued black women to be, irresistibly sensual, then there was every reason to expect that they would displace white men. And lynching was a ritual enactment of a determination that black men, quite literally, should never be on top.

In Cuba, there was also a desire that the island remain mostly white, and that white people remain dominant, but the sexual fear was not as great. There was indeed a great deal of opposition to interracial marriages, as Verena Martinez-Alier in her book *Marriage, Class and Colour in Nineteenth-Century Cuba* (1974) has shown. Yet the plethora of cases she adduces illustrate clearly that interracial marriage was omnipresent. This is aside from the more casual racial mixing. Moreover, there was a serious liberal argument, even if it did not prevail, that Cuba could achieve whitening through miscegenation. Thus the nineteenth-century planter Francisco de Arango y Perreno wrote in 1816 that "Nature . . . shows us that black yields to white and that it disappears if one continues mixing both races."[6] Antonio Saco took up the argument in the twentieth century: "The great evil of the Island of Cuba consists in the static nature of the black race, who always preserving its colour and primitive origin, keeps itself apart from the whites by insurmountable barriers; but if one got it moving, mixing it with the other race and allowed it to continue this trend, this barrier would gradually be broken down."[7] In Cuba, therefore, the idea of racial mixture had not the same import as in the United States. Blacks had to be presented as an immediate physical threat before whites could be mobilized to violent action, and then only some whites, and only temporarily.

It is not entirely clear to me the precise meaning of Professor Helg's statement that "with no legal segregation and no rigid color line, Afro-Cuban men were less likely to face violence for having consensual sex with poor white women, because they were so few that they could not challenge the color hierarchy of society." I assume she means that few poor white women would have considered a relationship with blacks, rather than that there were few poor white women. But I assume it also to be true that many of these women would have been glad to consider a relationship with many light-skinned men who in the United States, but not in Cuba, would have been considered black. In this case, the issue does indeed become one of color and not race and emphasizes the greater elasticity of the Cuban system. In the United States, by contrast, by the late nineteenth century, any such relationship could have been considered objectionable. Yet even in the United States, in exceptional cases, and depending on local circumstances, it might have been tolerated. The sheriff who arrested Richard and Mildred Loving for transgressing Virginia's antimiscegenation law in 1958 was promptly turned out of office at the next election. They lived in a region where the results of racial mixing had been highly visible for years and where one resident explained, "We have a community of our own. Our mores apply only here. We've done more integrating than any other part of the U.S."[8]

It might be true, as Professor Helg points out, that "in the early twentieth century Cuba stood out in the Western Hemisphere as the only nation with a substantial population of African descent and universal male suffrage." But is also true, as she also points out, that they could not exercise that right except on an individual, unorganized basis. If they organized as blacks they were suppressed. The Cuban system was therefore more insidious, for it obliged blacks to deny who they were if they desired to get ahead, at the same time ensuring that most would not.

Both societies had images of blacks that bore little relationship to reality. Both societies had images of blacks that in some ways looked the same. Moreover, in situations where blacks were punished because of these images the differences may have had little practical significance. But behind the images lay a divergent cultural content and distinctive historical traditions that still influence modern attitudes.

Afro-Caribbean Culture and the South: Music with Movement

ROGER D. ABRAHAMS

The eminent Caribbeanist, Sidney Mintz, warned me when we first met in the mid-1960s that identifying oneself as a scholar of New World creole societies was tantamount to committing professional suicide. As he explains it even today, the Caribbean has been only grudgingly admitted as a subject of study in cultural anthropological research. Both in terms of historical variety and linguistic difference, the Caribbean defies easy analysis of its institutions, to say nothing of Old World influences and New World developments. For Mintz and other investigators of this area, a constant difficulty involves accounting for cultural enclaves constituted from the gathering of historically and geographically uprooted peoples.

Now in bringing together the American South with the Caribbean, the problem becomes that much more profound, but also more interesting. In examining the record of cultural interchange between and within the two regions of greater Afro-America, patterns of belief and practice emerge, patterns which reside not in their construction, but in the ways in which they organize the energies of the *celebrating* group responding to the *call* of the *spirit* (I use these terms in both secular and religious senses), using the performing moment as a potential flashpoint for the emergence of a new sense of community.

From these moments have emerged styles of music and dance that, as they were recognized and imitated by the larger public, led to fads and frenzies that have deeply influenced popular culture even as it has elevated the place of the master performers. That these developments do not follow the political or social lines of power alerts us to the existence of counter hegemonic forces constantly emerging from within dislocated and dispossessed communities.

As a folklorist with both historical and ethnographic inclinations, I can more easily describe the operation of such cultural hotspots than to account for them in any larger theoretical scheme. But this disability I share with others interested in how culture is produced locally and caught up in the development of a public sphere, an international popular culture. My observations are built on the voluminous work of other investigators. Because it is such a large body of reported cultural productions, rather than burdening my argument with references within the text, I have given a list of works at the end that I have drawn upon most often.

The expressive inventions found in one African American enclave seem to arise from the social and aesthetic disposition of New World black communities, which Robert Farris Thompson, John Szwed and I, and Sidney Mintz and Richard Price outlined some years ago—a disposition that has received widescale acceptance in more recent scholarly endeavors. Whenever one form of music and dance emerges in one particular African American community, and is brought to the attention of the world through devices of popular dissemination, it is likely to have a cognate form in many other communities in spite of the differences in the historical and linguistic situations.

The record here is both consistent and revealing. Blacks and whites have been involved in a mutual cultural transfer ever since the plantation world came into being. Sheer propinquity in a sparsely populated part of the world led to the development of stylistically adventurous syntheses of the two Old World traditions, usually under the aesthetic guidance of slaves and exslaves. If one wishes to search for some kind of agency for enslaved African populations, one can find it in abundance in the area of expressive culture, especially while work, play, or celebration is taking place.

One of the problems experienced by scholars studying this area is understanding the ways in which social and cultural cohesion is conceived and voiced within African American communities. For these peoples simply did not develop the pan European Romantic nationalist attitude toward territory and land based traditions. Rather, community identification was achieved through significant movement together through an improvised value space, a togetherness that can be transported anyplace.

Looked at, then, against the backdrop of emerging nation-states, I will outline the cultural innovations of a people who identify, not with any local genius emerging from the land, the language, and the grounded lore of a race, but rather with the danced and sung occasions in which the idea of community and spirit arise in performance, celebration, and worship. Not that these black expressive forms are not associated with specific places: the Cuban Habanera, the Samba of Rio, Reggae and Kingston, the Mississippi blues. But these are also recognizably vernacular inventions that achieved a place in the transnational entertainment industry rather than providing the kind of cultural reflexiveness that leads to the formation of a *patria*.

Indeed, if a sense of homeland appears in African American communities during their formative periods, an idealized Africa engages the soul and the spirit of the individual. Africanness is fully articulated both musically and gesturally in performances. More than this, as Morton Marks and a number of other scholars have demonstrated, the more intense community performances and celebrations become, the more the interlocked voices and movements of its members come to the fore. This interlock is most deeply expressed through the growing metrical complexity of the expressive interaction, as well as the sharing of spirit as it descends on the celebrating group as a whole. At such moments, a return to the places in which the spirit or soul of the ancestors is called for. For most of the New World black communities, this has meant some sense of return to Africa.

This, then, evokes a culture area of a different sort than those previously addressed by anthropologists—for it is one in which the festive and religious music and dance provides a greater organizing force than territory or language. Even the events in which the musics developed travel well, especially if they found their most masterful form through a singing, dancing, even stylized fighting format: the *bois* stick dance of Trinidad, *capoeira* in Brazil, the jazz jam session, the tap-dance streetcorner *cutting*, the disco contest made into such a powerful instrument of stylistic confrontation in the movie "Saturday Night Fever." As the recent diaspora of Carnival to Brooklyn, Toronto, and London shows, even the complex events through which these local styles developed have represented cultural pride occasions, for the participants a way of going back home while making a place for themselves in new metropolitan milieux.

These musics, and the peoples identifying themselves through them, knit together the entire region, even as they advertise local cultural invention to worldwide popular audiences. It is a region which not only includes the Caribbean and the U. S. South, but many coastal outposts in South America on both the north, east, and west coasts, and many areas of the latifundium of Central America, including Mexico, Belize, and Costa Rica. Transcaribbean cultural variety here is as significant as questions of history, social formations, and economic networks. This imitation occurs over great distances, often through the mediation of radio, television, phonograph recordings, and movies. Before the confrontative developments of skiffle or punk musics in England, Central or Eastern Europeans used first jazz and then rock and roll as emblematic of dissent. More recently, and more subtly perhaps, "hipster" movements in England, Germany, Sweden, Japan, and other places have embraced the blues, bluegrass groups, and most recently, salsa.

Many profound differences characterize Afro-American and European-American expressive forms and styles. Under the sway of an emerging world economic system centered on surplus crop agriculture, the two Old World peoples came together in the Caribbean Basin, in areas in which the most profitable extractive industries emerged. Driven by European capital and markets, but produced primarily through the labor of slaves of African descent, sugar, tobacco, rice, indigo, and cotton all fostered New World fortunes. While political and economic power and surveillance techniques clearly privileged Europeans and their practices, a plethora of scholarship in the last thirty-five years argues that influences, indeed cultural mimicry, often called for those in power to copy their slaves. More than this, the research on the history and development of expressive styles has brought about a reappraisal of the interactional processes not only of play and display forms, but of work and worship as well.

Scholarship does not suggest any necessary lack of respect for non-blacks involved in these transactions. Far from it. Rather the problem is that play, itself, enters into the lives of African Americans in decidedly different fashions. Throughout the Caribbean Basin, and well into North and South America, music is seldom encountered without a significant set of stylized movements by the performing group as a whole, whether in play, work, or worship. Different systems of standing, walking, and running are hypertrophized in the alternative habits of the heart, the body, the ways of thinking and moving. Or to put it somewhat differently, body, soul, and community all have had to be reassessed and even reconceptualized in the light of the growing understanding of African and Afro-American practices.

A case in point: for well over two-and-a-half centuries, black and white children have found themselves playing together, under the supervision of black dance instructors. This happened under conditions of enslavement as they have persisted in settings in country and city-play areas since emancipation. We hear of it reported by those lonely European planters seeking entertainment from the workers, often in the yards outside the Big House, the Upstairs House.

Whenever I think about this subject of intercultural imitation, I am reminded of my conversations with my friend Bess Lomax

Hawes, who conspired to write a book with her friend and ring-play teacher, Bessie Jones, from the Georgia Sea Islands. When Hawes first tried to enter into the playworld which Jones was calling out for her to respond to she stumbled through the lesson. A teacher herself, and thus a willing learner, as she moved into the ring of play, Hawes became aware that she was just not getting it. "Suddenly the cultural gulf between us yawned very wide indeed," she records in their book. She continued: "To me, as to all white Americans, I suspect, a person who is 'with' me [will] do just what I am doing."

Perhaps it is this dimension of "withness" that most characterizes the stylistic differences between Euro- and Afro-Americans. With the former, entering into a conventional interaction empathy (withness, friendliness, being there for each other) is established by making one's eyes available in face-to- face encounters. The body movement which emerges from this friendly environment is built on the principle of immediate imitative responsiveness—that is, taking on the posture and gestures of the others in the interaction. When this norm finds itself expressed in dance, the focus will be on partnering, that is, establishing a sense of trust in the ability and willingness of each other in a dyadic relationship to maintain the physical and psychological balance inherent in the pairing. One can see this principle spelled out fully in the couple dances from the waltz to the foxtrot to the jitterbug, and on.

To this we must contrast a different set of interactional emphases in African American interactions. These rather place greater value on a group cohesion developed through a shoulder-to-shoulder arrangement. The eyes of the group commonly come to focus upon a single spot, one or two performers who take the center of the floor or stage. The bodies of the dancers respond together to a pulse system that encourages each to both play apart and maintain a sense of group cohesion, an effect achieved through an overlap of voices and an interlock of responsive movements. All of these effects underscore the presence of the whole moving group, against which a single performer displays himself or herself.

Again, Hawes discusses just this difference in her usual common sense terms: "To Mrs. Jones and the Sea Islanders, to be 'with' somebody means to respond to them, to complement and support their silences, to fill in their statements (musical, physical, and verbal) with little showers of comment, to answer their remarks, to clap a *different* pattern." As instruction to the dancers emerges from the master teacher, other voices enter over and under, weaving encouragement to each other, and demanding that all play a part in the overall energetic responsiveness of the social body.

Not that one does not find couple dancing in African American communities. Especially in metropolitan centers, as the black dances begin to be imitated by white elites, a new and more genteel rendering of a new-fashioned dance commonly arises in which the sex-paired couple, rather than the individual performer, takes center stage. These take on the pattern of couple-dancing, teasing and romantic dances of sexual advance and retreat like the *Beguine*, the *Mambo*, the *Lindy* or *Disco Dancing*. Just as commonly, they represent a call for each performer in some manner to repeat some motion taken from life: *hip hop*, the *chicken wing, turkey trot*, the *breakdown, breakout, break dancing*. Or the master-performer leads all of the others, taking the head of the line.

Further complicating the subject historically, an active exchange of musical and dance styles occurs between regions. This is precisely the interaction that has taken place between various Caribbean enclaves and the American South ever since the late eighteenth century, and probably before. Indeed, this commerce of expressive forms and fads extends far beyond the Transcaribbean to those areas of Central and South America in which European, African, and indigenous peoples came together.

Under the awful shadow of enslavement, the dynamic features of cultural creolization were little studied until recently. Com-

mon sense says that those in political and social control carry
with them the institutions of surveillance and control that prevail
in stylistic as well as political and social points of contact. That
such an argument betrays a deeper common sense occurs to investigators of the cultures of this part of the world only when
the dynamics of expressive exchange are addressed directly. The
vectors of invented and recycled cultural styles provide an entirely different tale, one involving a good deal of imitation across
social boundaries. Even under the most repressive conditions,
expressive exchange events developed between dominant and
subordinated groups under particular conditions. Moreover,
within specific bounded groups of African Americans, much of
the shared aesthetic features of subsaharan performance, celebration, and worship were maintained and reformulated to attend
to local conditions and the emergence of master performers and
innovators. This has been widely reported in the face of "the
myth of the Negro past" as Melville Herskovits phrased it, a myth
that presumed radical cultural discontinuities between Africa and
the Americas because of the massive enslavement and transportation of Africans to the New World.

The researches of the last generation have dispelled this myth
to a great degree, most convincingly through richly textured
studies of particular sites of creole cultural production. Little
substantial thought has been given to what produces the cultural
vectors in which those in power come to actively imitate African
American forms and styles.

Singing the Master (1992) accumulated evidence that not only
were African-style entertainment forms not suppressed by some
plantation owners, but an active imitation of slave forms of com-
munity-making entertainment were already conventionalized
throughout the plantation South (and beyond) in the antebellum
South. From this emerged the blackface minstrel show, an explicit white rendering of scenes of slave life which in its earliest
formations drew directly upon slave songs and slave styles of celebration. This was acknowledged, even as it was being devel-

oped, to be the first truly American form of popular theatrical display. Developed in the South through the observation and imitation by whites of black movement and dance style, the minstrel show developed in the North in the period 1828–1858, during a period of extreme social discontent and racial ambivalence.

The story of the minstrel show as it was redeployed by African Americans themselves has received scant notice indeed. While numerous theatrical and musical histories have documented the popularity of blacks in blackface even before the Civil War scholars have little noticed how the songs and dances and stage-craft of such shows affected local communities throughout the black Atlantic.

In the West Indies, for instance, festival celebrations at Christmas and Carnival were strongly marked by conventions derived from blackface minstrelsy. Roaming groups of high stepping dancers dressed in one or another of the standard minstrel costumes. Nighttime roaming groups coaled their faces and wore the exaggerated swallow-tail coats and white gloves most associated with Zip Coon, the dandy. Called "Johnny Walkers," or "Saguas" on Nevis, St. Kitts, groups of performers went from yard to yard (much as the John Canoers did in Jamaica, the Bahamas, even coastal Carolina) "begging" money while performing behind a scrim of joviality.

More than this, the tea meetings and concerts found from the Virgin Islands to Trinibago often included skits and songs and drills derived from the minstrel-theater traditions. I think the same would be found in the African cosmopolitan development of concert-parties reported from Capetown through the Gambia, though little of these parties has made its way into ethnographic reports of popular entertainments.

The tea meeting illustrates just how complicated the story of cross-cultural exchange is. The name is derived from the Methodist tea parties, or meetings, which were to be substituted for the *plays* or *soiree party and dance* developed under enslavement. Primarily made up of speeches on religious or political topics, the event was transformed by the mid-nineteenth century into a combination of variety show and oratorical contest. Organized by *chairmen* or *masters of ceremony* (playing much the same role as Mr Interlocutor), these riotous occasions not only pitted speaker against speaker, but the orators or comic performers against the shouter-abusers in the audience. In the ideal, the chairmen and their students would so dazzle the audience with their virtuosity that they would be quieted. In practice, the bedazzlement did not occur that often in the evening's entertainment.

Before the beginning of the usual tea meeting, the *bum drum* or *bone drum* (fife and drum) ensemble, strongly associated with parades, would begin the march from some distant point to the hall in which the event was to take place. Along the way, the audience would fall in place, singing and dancing behind the musicians.

This ensemble will be familiar to those from many regions of the South where, for so many years, festive events were initiated and enlivened by the parading of black fife and drum groups. This marching band tradition illustrates a similar complex exchange of musical and movement styles reflecting the mixture of peoples that have historically come together here. As in the West Indian *bum drum*, a set of musical instruments found throughout the Old World are deployed in an Africanized, or Afro-Americanized, set of situations. Throughout the Caribbean, as well as in the American South, musical bands led by a melodic instrument, such as a single flute or fiddle, move around a community along with a trap and a bass drum and a further ratcheting rhythm instrument, like the shak-shak, the clave (or some other scratched and notched wooden block), even a stray piece of metal which is clanged in tonal and textural contrast to the other instruments. This is both a parade and a dance ensemble, found throughout the Caribbean and American Southeast and Gulf Coast areas, sometimes suggesting a military march, sometimes an European dance form like the quadrille or reel.

A similar story of cultural interaction might be told of the inter-play between Afro- and Euro-American impulses in the African American appropriation of European set dances. In many planta-tion and metropolitan communities, slaves were delegated the duties of both music making and dance calling at various Euro-American entertainments. Taking much of their calling vocabu-lary from French dancing masters, local adaptations of jigs, reels, and quadrilles formed the basis of the dance repertoire in both black and white communities from late in the eighteenth to late in the nineteenth centuries, and well into the twentieth in some Caribbean village enclaves. When I carried out my first fieldwork on the smaller islands in the British Leewards and Windwards, quadrilles and reels were still danced by the older people wanting to demonstrate old-time ways in concerts and on moonlight night spontaneous entertainments. On Nevis, old set dances had also been maintained within the *Masquerade* dance, another roving performance group performing on holidays from yard to yard. The leader of the Masqueraders was a dance caller cum scare figure, who playfully whipped performers and audience alike if they failed to get into the spirit of the occasion.

Becoming a dancing master or musician was one way in which slaves and freemen could find a means through which to achieve mobility on the plantation, where they were hired out for such occasions, and in towns and cities where freed blacks could achieve social status through such occupations. African American adaptations of European set dances were a logical outcome of black callers and musicians playing for white elites whether in country or town. From this racial mix, in fact, grew the American *square dance.*

This event, so deeply associated with white country dancers, actually owes a good deal of its style and spirit to the nuanced performance techniques of African American musicians and call-ers. This group of dances, still often called by its slave names, the breakdown or hoedown, is commonly accompanied by an instru-ment—a banjo or a fiddle, or both playing in unison—that establishes both the metrical regularity and the melodic line of the tunes associated with specific dances. Commonly, counter-rhythms were established even when a single fiddle was played, as the fiddlers' second man would beat a straw on that portion beyond the bridge of the instrument. American fiddling, commonly thought to derive from Celtic sources, has been demonstrated to be grounded in a syncopated string of rhythms that are ineluctably Afro-American in aesthetic principles.

Another set of song-dances commonly associated with white dancers might be reexamined in these same terms: the *play-party*, or *josey* (from the game elaborating the minstrel song, "Jump Along, Josie.") These song-dances were found on the frontier wherever the community did not have a fiddler, or where the settlers did not countenance the use of any stringed instruments because of their association with the devil. With one or two exceptions, the dances were performed in the round with a central figure or couple being isolated and sung at by the rest of the group, much as Bessie Jones described the ring-plays of the Georgia Sea Islands. Often the accompanying songs directed the focal dancers to move in certain ways. The black ring-play origins of this kind of dance is patent.

As John Szwed and I suggested in the introduction to *After Africa* (1980), this same story may describe essentially how high school cheering developed as well—that is, in the playful opposition between song and dance leaders and those attracted to the competitive sporting event. In the United States, this meant gridiron football. This pedigree receives startling confirmation in the recent development of *cheering, double-dutch jumping,* and *stepping* practices in the wide range of voluntary organizations that thrive in Afro-American communities throughout the United States. Like the school cheers, these forms involve pre-choreographed movements intended to dazzle and viscerally involve onlookers, usually during a contest formated event.

This intuition has been startlingly advanced by the historian of black movement styles, Jacqui Malone, in her important book.

Significantly, the Malone work does not focus on the most exotic forms of African American song and dance but on group presentational formats within the bourgeois segment of African American communities: college marching bands, fraternity and sorority stepping shows, and the choreographical backgrounding for Motown singers developed by the great tap dancer Cholly Atkins.

Many scholars have documented the origins and development of one or another dance craze emerging from metropolitan flashpoints. The recent vogue for the *Macarena* reminds us of how many other dance manias captured the public imagination over the last hundred years and more. Can anyone doubt that this craze—like the Conga, Samba, Rhumba, Mambo, Limbo, Merengue before it (to name a only a few)—will run out of vigor just as quickly as it came into fashion as a public entertainment?

These song-dances become fashionable in a flash and then tend to burn themselves out, often to reappear in slightly altered form and with a new name. Each of these has produced fans who seem to know the performers and their songs by heart, and a fan literature that knows no bounds. (For instance, see the masterworks by Gordon Rohlehr and by Donald Hill on the history of calypso in Trinidad, both of them replete with texts that presume a depth-of recognition that strains the imagination. Just as both blues and jazz have engendered a great number of hipster fan publications and recordings, rap and hip hop culture now has led to a number of books, popular publications, fanzines and webpages devoted to the subject.) Many of these song-dances have topical references and carry heavy social messages in the places in which they arise. Forms like calypso, the samba, and rap replay the traditions of praise and scandal singers of subsaharan worlds, but they emerge out of festive contests in which cleverness is as valued as the catchiness of the song and dance.

While the song-and-dance crazes may undergo name changes all of the time, the terms for the interactive movements and vocal interactions have remained constant. Such terms as *breaking, jamming, calling* (and *calling out* and *calling in*), *cutting* and *strut-*

ting, getting down and *jumping up, shuffling, patting, rapping* and *tapping* and *patting* drift in and out of the vocabulary of stylistic elaboration, many of them on loan, translations of West African terms of art. Even *marching* and *shouting, getting happy,* even *spirit* and *soul* and *the word* are given a different set of meanings, especially as they are employed in sanctified settings. These terms of description are joined with those of encouragement— *get down, amen, do it, right on*—to constitute an enlivened music-and-gesture system that remains the bedrock of African American notions of community and creativity.

In fact, the vocal dimension of African American movement events has only been noted in a systematic way in the last thirty-five years. Here, Robert Farris Thompson's life-work alerting the world to the richness of the Transatlantic visual, gestural, and vocal traditions has lined out the ways in which the entire sensorium is drawn upon in African American spirit formations. The work by John Szwed, with Morton Marks early on, and Sally Banes more recently, on African American dance-musics is nicely complemented by Jacqui Malone's book mentioned above.

Szwed and Banes, drawing primarily on material found in commercial recordings, discuss the periods of black/white rapprochement, in which black performers have taken it upon themselves to teach a larger popular audience how to move. They have identified hundreds of recordings performed by African Americans, which extend the role of the dance-master into more funky forms of bodily expression.

One final example that comes from the work world rather than that of play: throughout the maritime world of the late eighteenth century and the nineteenth, work on board ship was coordinated by the use of sea shanties. These clearly built upon the model of subsaharan African worksong, with interlocking of the many voices, and an overlapping of vocal lines developing in dialogue between song-leader and the rest of those engaged in the task at hand. While the same shanties were recorded from tall-masted ships of many European registers, a widespread understanding existed that the best shantymen were West Indian. Yet when I collected shanties in various West Indian settings, the singers often related them to places in North America, remarking on this fact in their discussions of the songs. Furthermore, the many accounts of travellers in the antebellum South indicate a limited repertoire of these songs, many being used in one slave setting or another, from boat-loading to hoeing and reaping, to cotton picking and cornshucking.

Usually, these would be reported as having been improvised on the spot by the shantyman. Would expropriation account for this phenomenon? Obviously, I think not. Rather, a song-style arose that was adaptable to a number of work-tasks both on and off-ship; these songs were recorded widely as slave compositions, even when sung by sailors from all over the world. This tale could be repeated for a variety of other styles of musical production from ringplays to blues—subsaharan styled songs being developed by New World black populations and sung by anyone with sufficient musical acumen to learn the nuances.

The constant movement of African American workers, players, and worshipers accounts in some part for the spread of now one, now another New World adaptation of African styles of coordinating movement. Built on the bedrock of the richly textured interaction of leader and response, plantation and post-plantation, rural, small town, and metropolitan black music and dance were all strongly marked by the complementary deployment of European instrumentation and an African contrapuntal style of attack.

These forms of performance and entertainment, which gather much of their power from their rootedness in Greater Afro-America, become a part of the larger development of popular musics. They arise from communities made up essentially of peoples dislocated, first from Africa, and then from their adopted homes in the New World. But in a global economy, such uprooting is the norm. Focusing on the constantly uprooted but persevering and loyal old slave figures, like Old Black Joe or Uncle Tom or Faulkner's Dilsey, allows us to see how much a sentimen-

tal nostalgia affects the white representations of black figures.
They become representative of all dislocations along with the
sense of loss of homeplace characteristic not only of the enslaved
but of settlers in general.

To regard these developments simply as white cultural expro-
priations is both too easy and too given to arguments of historical
victimage. The failure of such a theory to account for continuing
creativity within communities throughout Afro-America indicates
that such explanations do not adequately account for their meanings among those who play, dance, and engage with these dances
and musics. To regard them as simply a response of enslavement
or social exclusion is to miss most of the enchanting power of
these expressive practices.

The events of celebration and entertainment and the dance
and musical styles that emerge from them are seized upon as new
styles for public consumption. Commonly, these developments
arise within black voluntary organizations—churches, fraternal
groups—and other marching societies, or the more casual gather-
ings at street corners, pan yards, or at rum shops and saloons.
When they emerge in a more public formulation, as part of a
festivity or in concert, they become subject to new ways of being
presented and represented in media of record. With the impact
of new audiences and technologies made possible through broad-
cast and other media of record, they are introduced into regional,
national, and international popular cultures. At this point, the
flow of styles is more dynamic even than the often dislocating
movement of peoples that has typified African American life for
the last 250 years.

The problem of any serious acceptance of these creole accom-
plishments is the ephemeral character of the song-and-dance
frenzies that have been launched from the Caribbean Basin and
the American South. Perhaps underscoring the stylistic consis-
tencies contained within these diverse popular forms and styles
will provide a greater respect for these cultural achievements.
For these forms and styles, once released from their community

roots, find very different milieux in which they prosper. They find a different niche in the musical economy of public events. With the rise of interest in popular or vernacular forms of expression as they influence the global economy, perhaps ephemerality will no longer live under the stigma of the irrational and the ephemeral.

Thanks to Charles Reagan Wilson and Douglass Sullivan-González for organizing the Porter L. Fortune, Jr. History Symposium on "The South in the Caribbean," thus providing the occasion for essaying this overview. Thanks, too, for the counsel of John Szwed in the process of the writing, and for my wife Janet who edited my prose and sharpened my argument. My apologies to the number of people who over the years have contributed to my understanding of the cultures of Greater Afro-America, but who for want of space, could not all be mentioned. This has been a great, cooperative adventure that is just now receiving the attention of scholars outside the field.

WORKS CONSULTED:

Abrahams, Roger D. "Afro-American Worksongs on Land and Sea." In *Folklore on Land and on Sea: Studies of Folklore of Work and Leisure, in Honor of Horace P. Beck,* eds. Roger D. Abrahams, Wayland D. Hand and Kenneth S. Goldstein. Hatboro, Pa.: Legacy Books, pp. 1–9.

Abrahams, Roger D. *Deep the Water, Shallow the Shore.* Austin: University of Texas Press, 1974.

Abrahams, Roger D. *The Man-of-Words in the West Indies.* Baltimore: Johns Hopkins University Press, 1983.

Abrahams, Roger D. "The West Indian Tea Meeting: An Essay in Creolization." In *Old Roots in New Lands,* ed. Anne M. Pescatello. Westport, Conn.: Greenwood Press, 1977, pp. 173–208.

Abrahams, Roger D. *Singing the Master: the Emergence of African-American Culture on the Plantation.* New York: Pantheon, 1992.

Banes, Sally and John F. Szwed. "From 'Messin' Around' to 'Funky Western Civilization: The Rise and Fall of Dance Instruction Songs." *New Formations,* 27 (winter 1995–96) pp. 59–79.

Bilby, Kenneth. "The Kromanti Dance of the Winwrd Maroons of Jamaica." *Nieuwe West Indische Gids,* 55 (1981), pp. 55–101.

Botkin, Benjamin A. *The American Play-Party Song.* New York: Ungar, 1963.

Cantwell, Robert. *Bluegrass Breakdown: the Making of the Old Southern Sound.* Urbana: University of Illinois Press. 1984.

Chernoff, John Miller. *African Rhythm and African Sensibility.* Chicago: University of Chicago Press, 1981.

Clark, VeVe. "Performing the Memory of Difference in Afro Caribbean Dance in Katherine Dunham's Choreography, 1938–187." In *History and Memory in African-American Culture,* eds. Genevieve Fabre and Robert O'Mealy, New York: Oxford University Press, 1994, pp. 188–204.

David, Jonathan. "The Sermon and the Shout: A History of the Singing and Praying Bands of Maryland and Delaware." *Southern Folklore,* 51 (1994), pp. 241–63.

Hazzard-Gordon, Katrina. *Jookin': the Rise of Social Dance Formations in African-American Culture.* Philadelphia: Temple University Press, 1990.

Hill, Donald R. *Calypso Calaloo: Early Carnival Music in Trinidad.* Gainesville: University of Florida Press, 1993.

Jones, Bessie, and Bess Lomax Hawes. *Steppin' It Down: Games, Plays, Songs and Stories from the Afro-American Heritage.* New York: Harper and Row, 1972, p. 24.

Joyner, Charles. *Down By the Riverside: A South Carolina Slave Community.* Urbana: University of Illinois Press, 1984.

Kinser, Samuel, *Carnival, American Style: Mardi Gras at New Orleans and Mobile.* Chicago: University of Chicago Press, 1990.

Lomax, Alan. *Folksong Style and Culture.* Washington, D.C.: AAAS, 1968.

Lott, Eric. *Love and Theft: Blackface Minstrelsy and the American Working Class.* New York: Oxford University Press, 1993.

Malone, Jacqui. *Steppin' on the Blues.* Urbana: University of Illinois Press, 1996.

Manuel, Peter Lamarche, Kenneth Bilby, and Michael Langey. *Caribbean Currents from Rhumba to Reggae.* Philadelphia: Temple University Press, 1995.

Marks, Morton. "Ritual Structures in Afro-American Music." In *Religious Movements in the United States,* ed. Mark Leone and Irving Zaretsky. Princeton: Princeton University Press, 1974.

Mintz, Sidney. "Enduring Substances, Trying Theories: The Carribean Region as *Oikoumene." Journal of the Royal Anthropological Institute,* (N.S.) 2, (1974) pp. 289–311.

Mintz, Sidney and Richard Price, *The Birth of African American Culture.* Boston: Beacon Press, 1992.

Piersen, William. *Black Yankees.* Amherst: University of Massachusetts Press, 1988.

Price, Richard, and Sally Price. *Two Evenings in Saramaka.* Chicago: University of Chicago Press, 1991.

Raboteau, Albert. *Slave Religion.* New York: Oxford University Press, 1978.

Rohlehr, Gordon. *Calypso and Society in Pre-Independence Trinidad.* Port of Spain: Gordon Rohlehr, 1990.

Stearns, Marshall and Jean Stearns. *Jazz Dance: the Story of American Vernacular Dance.* New York: MacMillan, 1968.

Stuckey, Sterling. *Slave Culture: Nationalist Theory and the Foundations of Black America.* New York: Oxford University Press, 1988.

Szwed, John F. and Roger D. Abrahams, eds. *After Africa.* New Haven: Yale University Press, 1980.

Szwed, John F. and Morton Marks. "The Afro-American Transformation of European Set Dances and Dance Suites," *Dance Research Journal,* 20, #1 (1988).

Thompson, Robert Farris. "An Aesthetic of the Cool: West African Dance." *African Forum,* 2 (1966), pp. 88–95.

Thompson, Robert Farris. *African Art in Motion: Icon and Art.* Los Angeles: University of California Press, 1974.

Thompson, Robert Farris. *The Flash of the Spirit.* New York: Random House, 1983.

Toll, Robert C. *Blacking Up: the Minstrel Show in Nineteenth Century America.* New York: Oxford University Press, 1974.

Waterman, Richard. "African Influence on the Music of the Americas." In *Acculturation in America,* ed. Sol Tax, Chicago: University of Chicago Press, 1952.

White, Shane. *Somewhat More Independent: The End of Slavery in New York City, 1770–1810.* Athens: University of Georgia Press, 1991.

Wood, Peter. *Black Majority.* New York: Knopf, 1974.

Commentary / Kenneth Bilby

Running as a motif through Roger Abraham's paper, as through much of his work over the last thirty-five years, is that perennial, seemingly intractable question: what, precisely, has remained of the complex ancestral heritage carried in the heads and hearts of the Africans brought to American shores in past centuries? And what difference has this made in the larger scheme of things?

From a North American perspective, the Caribbean region has always occupied a special place in the investigation of this problem. For it was apparent from early on that African-derived cultural practices were much more pervasive and obvious in the Caribbean than farther to the north—a disparity often attributed to the very different ratios of blacks to whites in the two regions. Indeed, it was Melville Herskovits' early trip to Suriname, by way of Haiti, that changed his views on what was then called the "Negro question," and led him to launch the field of Afro-American anthropology in the United States. Stunned by his encounter with the Saramaka Maroons, who seemed to have succeeded in regenerating remarkably African-like villages, social structures, and religions in the isolation of the interior rain forest, he was forced to reject the deculturation hypothesis and begin from different assumptions.[1] Since then, the Caribbean has continued to serve as a sort of comparative baseline for North American scholars grappling with the African-American past and present.

This reliance on the Caribbean as a sort of testing ground—a cultural preserve harboring traditions that would appear to be related to, but have remained more clearly African than, those in the southern United States—is especially evident in studies of music and dance. Many are the students of African-American music, dance, and related forms of expressive culture who have carried out fieldwork both in the United States and the Caribbean—Zora Neale Hurston, Katherine Dunham, Alan Lomax, Harold Courlander, Richard Waterman, Frederic Ramsey, Marshall Stearns, Arthur Alberts, Samuel Charters, Roger Abrahams, William Ferris, John Storm Roberts, Morton Marks, Robert Farris Thompson, Donald Hill, Barbara Hampton, and Jacqueline DjeDje, to name a few.[2] Not just fieldworkers, but historians and others working primarily with written sources have also made ample use of Caribbean materials to throw light on African-American music and dance in the antebellum South.[3]

That this dual regional focus should occur so often together with an interest in music and other varieties of performative behavior is not surprising. For music has proven to be particularly amenable to the task of establishing African cultural continuities in the Americas. Whereas economic systems and social structures, for instance, tend to present vexing and sometimes insurmountable problems to the researcher interested in processes of cultural transmission, the raw materials that constitute music, like the vocabularies that make up languages, often remain relatively easily identifiable, using empirical methods, with cognate forms distributed across large stretches of time and space.[4] Nowhere in Afro-America has this been clearer than in the Caribbean, where certain genres of religious music, and the drumming styles on which they are based, can be traced unambiguously to specific African ethnolinguistic groups. One thinks, for instance, of the *batá* drumming of the Cuban *lucumí* religion, or some of the songs of the Shango (Orisha) religion of Trinidad, both quite clearly derived from Yoruba traditions; or the *kumanti* drumming played by Maroons in the interior of Suriname, which betrays quite obvious Akan origins.[5] But just as importantly, the Caribbean is also home to dozens of other neo-African drum-based musical genres that *cannot* be traced to specific African peoples, yet whose ultimate African background is no more in doubt than is that of Cuban *lucumí* or Surinamese *kumanti*.[6] One might ask, however, how much the existence of such unquestionably African-derived musics in the Caribbean really reveals about musical life among African Americans in the United States, where drums of African design, for whatever reasons, appear to be absent from most historical accounts, as well as from present-day vernacular musical traditions.

Ethnographers have long recognized that most Afro-American musical events, even in the Caribbean region, bespeak complex and convoluted cultural histories, through which various African, European, and colonial strands have all become closely interwoven.[7] But it has taken them some time to realize that it is precisely those traditions that are most mixed and culturally ambiguous that may actually raise the most interesting questions for

cultural historians. Roger Abraham's contribution to this symposium, like much of his work, is a testament to the advances in
understanding that may result when this realization is put into
practice.

An important implication of Professor Abraham's work is that
any serious attempt to fathom traditions that have arisen from
diverse sources—as have almost all forms of music, dance, and
community celebration in the Caribbean—necessitates a shift of
focus away from surface features and their apparent origins, and
an engagement with *both* past and present contexts of social interaction. Cross-cultural exchange and social interaction, rather
than apparent geographical derivation and paths of cultural transmission, must be placed at the heart of analysis. West Indian tea
meetings are in some sense derived from practices introduced
by British Methodist missionaries during the nineteenth century;
though this fact is certainly not without significance, it is less
important than the question of how those who originally came
together in these contexts were able to create a common ground
through their interactions, and what this might say about present-
day versions of the tradition. Similarly, that corn-shucking celebrations on slave plantations in the American South can be traced
to the manorial harvest feasts of the English countryside is of
less interest than the patterned interactions between whites and
blacks that evolved in these contexts, what these meant to participants, and what they might say about present-day forms of expressive culture that were once tied to such contexts.[8]

The approach exemplified here, which applies insights gained
from close ethnography to the analysis of historical texts, and
views these through a performance-centered lens, has made an
important contribution to our understanding of the process of
creolization, particularly the creolization of music, dance, and expressive culture more generally. In its focus on process over
form, on deep cultural themes, styles, and principles over surface
manifestations, it parallels and complements the work of a number of others who have attempted to come to grips with the com-

plexities of Afro-American cultural history, most notably the anthropologists Sidney Mintz, Richard Price, and Sally Price, as
well as a number of historians of slavery.[9]

An interesting contrast emerges here. Whereas Roger Abrahams began his explorations of African-American expressive culture on the streets of Philadelphia, a diaspora location thought to
be culturally as far from Africa as possible, the Prices, like Melville Herskovits before them, came to their understandings
through the experience of living in the Surinamese forest with
Saramaka Maroons, long regarded as the culturally most African
people in the entire western hemisphere. That Roger Abrahams
and the Prices ended up, theoretically speaking, so close to the
same place, is, I think, significant. One might add that Abrahams
was led to the various Caribbean islands where he later conducted fieldwork by a desire to shed further light on his Philadelphia material; the Prices, on the other hand, were able to use
their previous field experience to the north in Martinique as a
foil against which to view their Saramaka data. Starting out at
opposite ends of the Afro-American geographic and cultural continuum, then moving from each direction toward the middle,
they developed overlapping perspectives that would seem to be
particularly well-suited to the challenge of bridging the full ex-
panse of the African diaspora.

Because this perspective gives greater weight to the cultural
logics—the deep structures or "grammars"—that underlie and
inform surface forms than to these forms themselves, it is easily
misconstrued; indeed, it has on occasion even been interpreted
as a denial of the very real, concrete traces left by specific African
cultures in the Americas—particularly when applied to cases
such as the Surinamese Maroons, where expectations of cultural
preservation are especially high. More careful consideration,
however, leads to the conclusion that by depriviledging the most
obvious manifestations of African cultural continuity—the surface "traits" to which the Herskovitsian legacy is too often un-
justly reduced—the way is opened to a more meaningful appreci-

ation of both the depth and breadth of the African contribution. Indeed, only by this means is it possible to begin to grasp just how powerfully the African past continues to resonate not only in the southern United States, but throughout the urban North.

My own primary field experiences have been in Maroon communities founded by escaped slaves, which have long been considered the ultimate exemplars of African cultural survival in the Americas—first, among the Windward Maroons of eastern Jamaica, then among the Aluku or Boni, a people who live along the border of Suriname and French Guiana, and who are closely related, historically and culturally, to the better-known Saramaka and Ndjuka Maroons.[10] Dramatic examples of cultural continuities that can be traced directly to specific parts of Africa are not hard to come by among either of these peoples, particularly in the domains of religion, music, dance, and language. The work of relating these to their original social and cultural matrices on the other side of the ocean continues to move ahead.[11] Yet, as the Prices have argued, to ignore the fundamentally creolized nature of these Maroon societies and cultures is to overlook not only their originality, but much of what is essentially African about them.[12]

In investigating such questions, one need not limit one's comparative scope to data gathered on the African continent itself. Indeed, the insights gained by Abrahams in his studies of expressive cultural events in Philadelphia, the West Indies, and the plantation South have enriched my own understanding of cognate events in the Guianese rain forest. Aluku Maroon musical performances, for example, are replete with the kinds of verbal contests, interactive social commentary, and group-supported individual displays of creativity that Abrahams has found in each of his field sites, and which, indeed, he and John Szwed have documented historically throughout the anglophonic Black World. In fact, there exists in Aluku, as well as among the neighboring Ndjuka Maroons, an important musical genre called *awawa*, yet to be documented in the literature, which is entirely

devoted to the competitive singing of formulaic as well as improvised insults, providing a socially-sanctioned vehicle for public
moral commentary.[13] This Guianese Maroon tradition represents
but one more point—though one that remains more obviously
African than most—on a creole continuum of cognate forms represented among Jamaican Maroons, for instance, by a song genre
known as *kyazam*, in Trinidad by *picong*, and in both the southern
United States and the urban North by traditions of verbal play
such as "the dozens" (as well as the various related forms of expression known as "signifying").[14] Even within Aluku culture itself, a whole range of related practices and behaviors exists, such
as drummed and spoken praise names that can be used both to
exalt and to ridicule the people and animals they describe; or, to
take another example, licensed joking relationships centering on
good-natured exchanges of personal insults.[15] That tea meetings
in the West Indies, verbal contests such as the dozens in the
United States, or indeed, corn-shucking songs performed on
southern plantations in past centuries can be used to enhance
understanding of traditions practiced by Maroons living in the
Guianese forest says much about the potential for continuity
within change that has characterized the creolization process
throughout the Americas. While the point I am making here is
hardly a new one, it deserves continual stressing, for the possibilities it opens to researchers interested in expressive cultural phe-
nomena such as music are far from being exhausted.

Further comparative work should be carried out, for example,
on the Afro-American fife and drum marching bands discussed by
Abrahams, variants of which are found from the southern United
States all the way down to the southern Caribbean, and on the
set dances and masquerade processions with which they are
sometimes associated.[16] The limited information available hints
at many complex, parallel histories of cross-cultural exchange
that have yet to be fully explored, but which promise to
strengthen understanding of the larger picture. One thinks, for
instance, of the "jumbie dances" of Montserrat and Tobago, dur-

ing which Africanized versions of jigs, reels, polkas, and quadrilles are sometimes used to invoke ancestral spirits to come
and take possession of dancers' bodies; or the *balakadri* (*bals de
quadrille*) of the sugar growing regions of Guadeloupe, where
performances of the quadrille and mazurka are driven by the
forceful, African-influenced rhythms of a frame drum (*tanbou
d'bas*) and a notched percussion instrument called *siyak*.[17] During recent fieldwork in a non-Maroon section of western Jamaica,
I located a surviving older variant of the *jonkonnu* dance that is
accompanied not by the fife and drum band typical of present-
day Jamaican *jonkonnu*, but a musical ensemble centering on a
square frame drum called *gumbe*. In the present-day village
where this tradition survives, *jonkonnu* dancing not only includes
the house headdress mentioned in eighteenth- and nineteenth-
century accounts, often taken by contemporary observers to be a
representation of the plantation Great House; but it forms an in-
tegral part of a living community religion in which possession by
ancestors, many of whom are buried in local family plots, plays a
central role.[18] What do music and dance events such as these tell
us about social interaction and cultural exchange between blacks
and whites during the period of slavery? One suspects that a
closer look at the historical sources in such cases would clearly
reveal, as it did for Roger Abrahams while he was investigating
southern American corn-shucking celebrations, that those in positions of near-absolute power, and the institutions of surveillance
and control on which they relied, were often less capable of setting and maintaining the course of cultural change and exchange
than they or their ideological successors imagined. If this was
true of large public observances such as the corn-shucking celebration, which brought together all segments of the plantation
universe, it was doubly so of those "insider" events staged by the
slaves for themselves.

This question of cultural vectors in situations of unequal power
is, as Abrahams suggests, one that has been given too little
thought. One can only marvel at the extent to which whites have

actively imitated, and sometimes built upon, African-American
forms and styles throughout American history, whether while in-
teracting directly with blacks, or in contexts somewhat farther
removed. But the Caribbean, with its rather different balance
of cultural and socio-racial components, has produced complex
cultural vectors of its own, and these too deserve attention. In
the Maroon community of Accompong in western Jamaica, long
held up as a bastion of New World African culture, Katherine
Dunham found during the 1930s that Jamaican-style quadrille
dancing was all the rage; and in the eastern Jamaican Maroon
community of Moore Town, up until a few decades ago, the tea
meeting was a favorite entertainment, rivaling the African-ori-
ented Kromanti Play in popularity.[19] It is almost certain that Jamaican Maroons did not adopt the tea meeting—and probably
not the quadrille either—through direct contact with whites, but
rather, as a result of interactions with non-Maroon black Jamai-
cans. Why would these particular historical examples of cultural
exchange have occurred, and what might their deeper meaning
have been? Or to take a much more recent example, urban popular music in Suriname over the last few years has come to be
dominated almost entirely by the contributions of young Ndjuka
and Saramaka Maroon city dwellers, who have remade a number
of the most popular urban genres with stylistic innovations that
draw heavily on their own ancestral musical traditions. Creole
musicians from the coastal region have been quick to adopt this
new musical vocabulary, and have continued to follow along with
each new Maroon trend.[20] What are the forces lying behind such
cultural exchanges?

As Abrahams reminds us, the flow of styles in the Atlantic
world is even more dynamic than the movement of people. It is
not always easy to distinguish cultural parallels that arose inde-
pendently from those that stem from migration and diffusion.
Clearly both kinds have played a role in the cultural and musical
development of what may be called Greater Afro-America. That
variants of the instrument we call the banjo were shared across

the great arc traced by the African slave trade, from the American South to Suriname and farther south, cannot be explained solely by migration between these points.[21] That festivals bearing the name *jonkonnu*, to take another important example, were once found not only in Jamaica and other parts of the anglophone Caribbean, but in eastern North Carolina, probably *can* be so explained.[22] Yet, in the end, this distinction may prove to be less important than the underlying fact of cultural connectedness itself. Such, in any case, was my feeling when a few years ago I learned of the existence in Asheville, North Carolina—that mythical center of "white mountain music"—of a street festival called *goombay*, staged annually by the small local African-American community. As I soon discovered, this event is only a little over a decade old in Asheville, having been introduced there by a Caribbean immigrant in the early 1980s. Originally inspired specifically by the *goombay* (or *gombey*) tradition of Bermuda (a masquerade dance related to Jamaican *jonkonnu* and Bahamian *junkanoo*), the Asheville *goombay* festival has grown into a high-profile celebration of cultural connections between Africa, the Caribbean, and black America.[23] Little did the African-American organizers who launched this reinvented Afro-Caribbean festival know, but a close relative of the *goombay* masquerade dance of Bermuda—a tradition called *"john kuner"*—once existed in their own backyard, at the other end of their state (in Wilmington and the surrounding area, to be precise), where it had survived at least into the early 1900s.[24]

The example I have just cited represents a case of the Caribbean in the South, rather than the South in the Caribbean. But one could probably spend an entire day enumerating examples of cultural and musical flow in the other direction. What, for instance, would the biguine of Martinique and Guadeloupe be without the influence of jazz?[25] Or the ska and reggae of Jamaica without rhythm and blues?[26] The larger point I am suggesting is that when the sounds emanating out of New Orleans began to catch on in the French Antilles in the 1920s, or "blues dances," as they were called in Kingston, became the big thing in Jamaica during the 1950s, jazz and the blues, in a sense, were already there.

The communicative, community-generating power of African-American and African styles of performance have of course allowed musical genres that were once exclusively black to spill over all manner of boundaries and spread across the world. Yet, it has been in the transatlantic black world, of which the American South and the Caribbean form such an important part, that such genres have repeatedly found especially fertile ground. Only by seeing into the past with the gaze of a seasoned ethnographer, as Roger Abrahams and others working in a similar vein have begun to do, are we likely to reach a better understanding than we now have of why this is so.

The Political Economy
of the Caribbean

RALPH LEE WOODWARD, JR.

I debated whether to focus on some narrow aspect as a case example of the history of the political economy of the Caribbean or to attempt a more general overview of the topic. Since I am not presently engaged directly in a Caribbean research project and my involvement in Caribbean history over the past forty years has been one more of teaching than research, I decided on the latter.

Although the lands bordering the Caribbean Sea developed under the tutelage of several different European empires, and more recently under North American dominance, when viewed as an economic unit, there is a certain unity to its development and in its patterns of historical evolution. The Caribbean, in fact, came to be the classic region of plantation society and development, the area to which Europeans came first to plant colonial enterprises, and from which they left last. Thus did the colonial Caribbean became the great laboratory of imperialism in the Americas. We might expect, therefore, to find there both the best and the worst of colonial institutions and practices. More often than not, the imperial interests of the dominant powers in the region have had more to do with its economic and political development than have the inhabitants of the region itself. The history of the Caribbean Basin, in fact, has long been a history of the struggle between imperial interests and those of the local inhabitants.

The Spanish came first, at a time when feudalism was still the dominant socioeconomic system. Early Spanish efforts in the Caribbean were not profitable. Motivated by the primitive mercantilism of the Spanish renaissance, Spain began the process of extending European trade to the New World, but the mentality of feudalism seriously limited the initiative and capabilities of the traders and settlers who came. They moved on quickly to the mainland, and their success in finding gold and silver in Mexico, Peru, and elsewhere blinded the Spaniards to the potential wealth of the Caribbean's fertility, just as DeSoto's march across the southeastern United States suggested that it was a land of little value, harsh weather, and hostile Indians. European diseases and Spanish conquest largely destroyed the native population. Even as they turned their backs on the Caribbean, the Spanish thus left many vacant islands in the lesser Antilles for exploitation by Spain's rivals. Once they and the buccaneers who followed had worn down the Spanish sufficiently they established colonies of their own. French corsairs, English sea dogs, and Dutch sea beggars—as they have been popularly labeled—assaulted Spanish commerce and shore settlements throughout the sixteenth and seventeenth centuries. These assaults inhibited and demoralized Spanish agricultural efforts in both the islands and coastal regions[1].

It is hard to overemphasize the importance of the Dutch in converting these early colonies of Spain's rivals, which often began as commercial trading posts or buccaneering stations, into prosperous plantation colonies. From Virginia to Brazil, the Dutch encouraged and aided the establishment of plantations, not only in their own possessions, but also in the colonies of the British, French, and even of the Iberians. Dutch trade and capital enabled the region to emerge as a producer of tropical and subtropical crops for European consumption. The Caribbean, and parts of Brazil and North America, became major components of a North Atlantic economic system that would generate surplus capital to fuel the Industrial Revolution. Cacao, tobacco, and sugar were important crops first encouraged and traded by the Dutch. Dutch investments in these commodities coincided with Holland's struggle for independence from the Spanish Habsburg empire. Dutch tobacco trading from Virginia southward to the Guianas contributed significantly to Holland's ability to wage that war successfully. Sugar brought even greater profits. Spain successfully beat off the French and English assaults on her American monopoly in the sixteenth century, but after the English defeat of the Spanish Armada in 1588, the Dutch gained the upper hand in the Caribbean, and in the seventeenth century the Dutch West India Company reaped enormous profits from both trade and plunder. The Dutch finally broke Spanish maritime superiority in the Caribbean and permitted greater economic growth not only for themselves, but for the other rivals of Spain as well.[2]

The success of tobacco, however, encouraged imitators, and before long flooded tobacco on Europe's markets, pushing prices down and creating unemployment and economic crisis among tobacco planters and their workers in the colonies. There resulted in the 1630s and 1640s a land and labor revolution that left a permanent impression on the Caribbean. Tobacco profits, trade, and plunder had permitted capital investment in the cultivation of sugar, for which the demand was rising rapidly in Europe. The conversion of much tropical land from tobacco or cattle to sugar resulted in fewer but larger plantations and the displacement of the planters and workers who could not afford the capital investment required for sugar production or processing. Sugar producers turned to African slavery as their principal source of labor. While slavery had not been unheard of in tobacco production, most farms were family-sized operations, with the assistance of indentured laborers who came out from the old country for specified periods of service. They were generally less adaptable as field hands on sugar plantations than African slaves. Many of these displaced people, especially in the English and French islands, turned to buccaneering, and continued the assault on Spanish commerce. New-world based in either their own ports or in those of the French, English, or Dutch from New England to Curaçao, the buccaneers thoroughly crippled what remained of Spanish maritime strength in the region and permitted her

European rivals to dominate not only sugar production, but the economic fortunes of the North Atlantic civilization. Although Spain had been first in the Indies, Caribbean plantation society developed from the seventeenth century forward largely in the colonies of her rivals. The Spanish holdings—Cuba, Santo Domingo, Jamaica, Trinidad, and Puerto Rico—remained largely subsistence oriented, in a more feudal than capitalist mode.

Sugar became King, and the British and French West Indies surpassed the Brazilian production earlier developed by the Dutch as Europe's primary source of sweetness. Profits from sugar funded the development of larger and stronger colonial empires, while they also provided capital for the Industrial Revolution. Richard Sheridan, in his monumental *Sugar and Slavery*,[3] provided convincing evidence that the plantation colonies served as a base for the expansion and diversification of the Atlantic trading empire.[4] It was an industry that quickly became self-financing and yielded surplus capital for investment in Britain. Sheridan argued persuasively in support of Eric Williams' earlier contention that the wealth generated by the plantation colonies helped to stimulate the Industrial Revolution. The British empire also profited enormously from the trade, often illicit, with the neighboring Spanish colonies and from British subjects operating in Dutch, Danish or other colonies of the region.[5] This expansion of production and trade in tropical and subtropical commodities begun in the seventeenth century reached its apogee during the years from the outbreak of the Seven Years' War to the beginning of the American Revolution (1756–1775). It was not, of course, exclusively Caribbean production. Yet, with tea and spices from the East and tobacco, rice, and indigo from the southern colonies of North America, West Indian sugar, rum, coffee, tobacco, cotton, and dyewoods flowing into Britain raised standards of living and paid for the imports of British manufactures, employed ships and seamen, and financed the slave trade and the expansion of plantations and trading stations. "If the colonies of settlement are distinguished from the colonies of exploitation which extended from Tobago on the south to Maryland on the north," concluded Sheridan, "it is clear that the latter were the most important part of the British Empire. They produced the most valuable commodities, consumed more British manufactures and employed more shipping than the New England and Middle Atlantic colonies of North America."[6]

Sugar was intimately related to the growth in the slave trade in the Americas. While the Spanish began the importation of Africans into the Caribbean early in the sixteenth century, in the colonies of her rivals in the seventeenth- and eighteenth-century Caribbean slavery flourished most, becoming the defining quality of plantation society throughout the American tropics and beyond. The trading of slaves was as much an industry in New England as in the Caribbean, and the profits the traders made provided capital for economic development well beyond the region. It was especially important to the rise of the North American maritime industry, and the defense of the slave trade became an economic interest of both private and government sectors in North America, Britain, France, and the Netherlands. The 1974 suggestion of R. P. Thomas and R. N. Bean that "the only group of clear gainers from the British transatlantic slave trade . . . were the European consumers of sugar and tobacco and other plantation crops" who "were given the chance to purchase dental decay and lung cancer at somewhat lower prices than would have been the case without the slave trade"[7] underestimates the close relationship between the Caribbean slave trade and production and the rise of northeastern capitalism in the United States.[8] More recently, William Darity, Jr. has reenforced the argument that West Indian plantations and the slave trade were intimately bound to the rise of British industry and maritime power. He challenges those who have neglected the role of the West Indies and argues that the ratio of profits from the slave trade and plantation production in the Americas to the national income and to total investment in England was quite large, and that the share of imports and exports in the gross domestic product of England during the period in question was also large. He concluded that the British mercantilists thoroughly understood the economic forces of their time, and because Britain was the most thorough and single-minded mercantilist power "in pursuit of the grand mercantilist scheme of commercial conquest, naval power, colonialism, slavery, and metropolitan industrialization," she became "the world's industrial leader by the start of the nineteenth century."[9]

Agricultural estates in the greater Caribbean thus developed along lines that Latin American historians have conveniently categorized as *hacienda* or *plantation*, each symbolizing one of the great socioeconomic systems that have dominated the Western world since the Middle Ages. The hacienda in its classic form was an American version of the feudal manor; the plantation the product of capitalist agro-export refinement. In its idealized form, the hacienda, most prevalent in the Spanish colonies but not absent altogether in English and French America as well, was dedicated to subsistence agriculture, with little or no production for consumption beyond the immediate area. It was single-family owned, and the family lived on the estate. Ideally, it was self sufficient, a complete economic unit, economically independent of the larger world. The owners of such estates favored a decentralized economic and political system, were locally oriented, and had little real commitment to the central state. The hacienda was traditional in most ways, including the relationship between the master and his labor force. Workers were usually serfs, often Indians, in these labor intensive agricultural estates. In the Spanish colonies, the creole masters sought to retain formal feudal institution, such as *encomienda* and *repartimiento*, that kept Indian or mestizo workers under their power. Progress was of secondary importance on these traditional estates, which tended to repeat the economic experience of the past, rather than experiment with new forms. The goal was to preserve existing life-styles and defend against threatened changes. Often short on capital or in debt, the owners were in no position to purchase slaves or invest in productive machinery, so that even where creoles might have had an interest in converting their estates to plantations, they lacked the means to do so.

In contrast, the plantations that emerged in the Caribbean and later in Central America and in the U.S. South were capitalist in fundamental organization. They were export oriented. Family ownership was common, but the trend was toward company ownership, with absentee ownership common in both cases. They were highly dependent on international commerce, often limiting their own production to a single cash crop. They were directly related to the international economy and recognized the authority of centralized states, while lobbying actively to influence their policies in favor of the plantations. Capital intensive, they turned to African slavery for labor, but also sought labor saving machinery and maximum efficiency of production, marketing, and transportation. Regardless of actual ownership, their orientation was European (or North American later on), and they concerned themselves directly with economic and technological progress and competition.

Few estates fit these model characteristics exclusively. Many certainly contained elements of both, especially on the North American mainland. Many were in some stage of transition from hacienda to plantation. These models serve merely to illustrate characteristics of agricultural estates and the differences in outlook and practices from feudal to capitalist mentality.

The mercantilist policies of the European colonial powers continued into the eighteenth century, accompanied by a series of intercolonial wars. Beginning with the English conquest of Jamaica in 1655, British success in these wars brought her more islands, first at the expense of Spain and later of Holland and France. By the mid-eighteenth century the British had achieved a dominant position, but were limited by the size of their markets in the closed mercantilist systems in which markets were reserved for their own producers. Notwithstanding British territorial gains, however, the French sugar producers, with the help of government policies that subsidized and encouraged with tax benefits the Caribbean producers, had achieved greater economy in production and were thus in a better competitive position, especially for the markets of continental Europe. French reexports to the rest of Europe accounted for more than sixty percent of the French production. This helps to explain the phenomenal rise of Saint Domingue (Haiti) as the leading sugar producer in the region in the eighteenth century. After 1763, France had been reduced to only Haiti, Martinique, Guadeloupe, and tiny St. Martin in the Caribbean, and had been pushed off the North American continent entirely. Britain, on the other hand, which had earlier reduced the Dutch to a minor position, had a multitude of sugar islands, led by Jamaica, but also including the Bahamas, Barbados, Dominica, Grenada, St. Lucia, St. Vincent, as well as Anegada, Antigua, Barbuda, the Caymans, Montserrat, St. Kitts, Tobago, and Nevis. To these it would add the large island of Trinidad in 1800. Both the British and the French encouraged expansion of sugar cultivation in these islands, resulting in rapid increases in slave population and exports of sugar. Haiti, especially, experienced rapid growth in its slave population and sugar production. By the 1780s it produced more sugar than all the British islands combined. Overproduction was forcing the prices down for producers everywhere, but the greater volume and markets of the French appeared to put the French producers in a better position. Diminishing returns to the British producers led to their decline by the last third of the eighteenth century.[10] The international rivalries, the rebelliousness of slaves, and overproduction all caused strains on the plantation systems of the eighteenth century. Ultimately, both the French and the British West Indian plantation systems collapsed, opening the way for the rise of Cuban production in the nineteenth century, tied especially to new markets in the United States.

The French Revolution and its Haitian counterpart brought a sudden end to the apparent French success in Saint Domingue. Sociologist Arthur Stinchcombe suggests that the Haitian revolution "was perhaps the first modern case in which a revolution set up a line in the world system between revolutionary third world countries and conservative capitalist world system rulers. The French Revolution briefly became such a symbol of a great divide in the world system in the 1790s."[11] First in Haiti, and subsequently in the British islands, the abolition of slavery undoubtedly hastened the decline of the plantation economy in those colonies, but broader economic forces had already set the trend in that direction. The Napoleonic Wars and Latin American Wars for Independence reduced the Spanish-American empire to Cuba and Puerto Rico, but her Bourbon reforms had begun the process finally of stimulating greater agro-export production in those areas.

Cuban agriculture since the Conquest had been largely subsistence in nature, although by the eighteenth century it exported respectable amounts of tobacco, coffee and sugar. The British captured Havana during the Seven Years' War, however, and quickly opened it to trade with British merchants, an experience that stimulated great interest in freer trade among Cuban creoles. When Spain recovered the island by the Treaty of Paris in 1763 it launched bold new programs both to defend the island against future loss and to stimulate its export economy. Cuban production of tobacco, coffee, cattle, sugar, and other crops surged upward during the last third of the eighteenth century under this encouragement, accompanied by rapid import of African slaves. Advantageously positioned to penetrate the expanding North American market, by the early decades of the nineteenth century Cuba had enjoyed a remarkable rise in exports of all of these commodities and, in what Cuban economic historians have referred to as the "golden age of Cuban economic history," had achieved rising prosperity for the merchant and planter classes. Although comparable to the sort of development that earlier occurred in the British and French islands, owing to the larger established population and more stable social institutions, the rapid rise in slave labor produced less of an immediate shock than had occurred in Haiti or the British islands. Spanish Cuba thus took advantage of the difficulties that would soon plague the British and French West Indies. By the middle of the nineteenth century, Cuba would be the leading producer of sugar, embarked on a path that would tie it in a close dependent relationship to North America. Meanwhile, the independence of Haiti and subsequently the abolition of slavery in the British islands would disrupt sugar production there significantly. They went into a long economic decline from which in certain respects they have never recovered.

The southern United States would also become a more prominent plantation region in the early nineteenth century, supplanting Brazilian cotton production by its more rapid adoption of the technology of Eli Whitney's cotton gin and a better transportation infrastructure. The cotton South would take on some of the characteristics of the slave dependent Caribbean. Only the less intense development of plantation economy saved the mainland colonies from the extremes of dependency as it developed in the islands, but there are still striking similarities of dependency. Unlike the islands, however, the mainland colonies maintained a higher level of local food production and a lower degree of absentee ownership. Thus, southern plantation owners more likely maintained a greater interest in the region's general social and political development than was true among those of the Caribbean.

There were, of course, differences among the plantation regions, creating more complex patterns of economic development than this brief overview might suggest. Sugar was the most significant Caribbean commodity, but it was not the only plantation crop that came to be vital to the region. Tobacco and coffee, and more recently other crops, often were produced best on smaller holdings where a resident owner participated directly in assuring a quality product. In the long run, crops better produced on smaller holdings more likely retained local ownership, for they were less successfully acquired and managed by large, foreign corporations. By contrast, sugar, as well as cotton, and later bananas, were crops well suited to large plantations, slaves, and absentee ownership. Those plantations best typify the classic capitalist plantation in the colonial Caribbean. A modern, twentieth-century counterpart of this pattern would include the banana plantations of the United Fruit Company and other large corporations. Although slavery eventually ended everywhere, the process of emancipation stretched out over nearly a century and accounted for variations in the social and economic development of different regions. Where plantations remained, conditions resembling slavery often continued, with racism and planter control of the local political system, as Arthur Stinchcombe has recently put it, "recreating structures similar to slavery and slave society with formal freedom." The different quality of plantation society, with different crops, differences in the controlled markets for the commodities, as well as the timing of slave emancipation, led to significant differences in the economic and social development of the Caribbean islands and make generalization difficult. There had, of course, been some differences among the islands even before the rise of sugar, but sugar and slavery created very different situations from non-sugar islands. According to Stinchcombe, "the decay of sugar plantations made them different again, less racist and less slave-like in labor relations, although the residue of slave society was always there."[12] Stinchcombe emphasizes the "great variations among the islands in the forces producing slave societies," forces which produced a variety of political situations, even to the present. These variations, he points out, brought

> political autonomy differently on different islands, transmitted democracy at different times and with different intensities, produced rebellion or resistance among planters to imperial power, led to management of the maritime part of the system with different kinds of market politics and administrative apparatuses, and produced environments in which slave sugar production was introduced easily or with great difficulty. And they

varied over time, which produced higher degrees of entrench-
ment of slave societies on the early-developed islands, produced societies that had, and had not, experienced the French
Revolution, and produced an environment for plantation
growth in which planters would buy slaves, contract Asian
labor, or hire free proletarians moving among islands, depending on the historical situation.[13]

The difference in export crops has had much to do with the
variations in local economic and social evolution. Tobacco and
coffee, particularly, thrived best when produced on small, family-
sized farms, where the owner lived on the farm and took a close
interest in the quality of the product. Living in the region, such
owners have characteristically taken a greater interest in regional
development, whether that be in the Carolinas, Cuba, or Costa
Rica, than in sugar, banana, or cotton plantation regions. In those
crops, close supervision by the owner is less essential to quality
production, and the owners have often lived in other places, even
outside the region in Europe or North America, with little interest in the welfare of the local region beyond the production of
the export crop. This difference is important to understanding
the relative differences among development in plantation regions.

Emancipation brought major problems to the plantation economies, in both the Caribbean and North America, even if it was
not the cause of their decline in the first place. After emancipation, the strength of local governments, representing planter interests, in relation to national (or imperial) governments became
an important factor in the ability of the local plantation society to
continue to maintain slave-like social and economic patterns. The
economic impact of emancipation itself is a major theme in the
historical literature on the region. The relatively sudden shift in
British policy from mercantilism to free trade came to espouse
free labor as well. It reflected the rise of classical liberal economic theory, but it also conveniently responded to the problem

of overproduction within the mercantilist-controlled markets. This had caused the British Caribbean plantation system already to enter into decline by the close of the eighteenth century. David Eltis has confirmed that

> Britain was the most successful nation in the modern world in establishing slave-labor colonies overseas. It was also the first to industrialize as well as the first of the major powers to renounce coerced labor in principle and practice. These two developments, industrialization and abolition, evolved more or less simultaneously in the late eighteenth century. But this was only after a century during which the exploitation of Africans in the New World had become the foundation stone of the British Atlantic economy. Indeed the British about face on the issue of coerced labor could be almost described as instantaneous in historic terms. By the early nineteenth century they had become so convinced of its immorality and economic inefficiency that they were running an expensive one-nation campaign to suppress the international slave trade. They went on to free three quarters of a million of their own slaves. Throughout this process their economy underwent major structural change and, of course, continued to expand strongly.[14]

Eltis reminded us that

> soil exhaustion, competition from the French West Indies and the interruption of the trade in staples—stemming from the independence of most of the British North American colonies—all severely reduced the importance of the English-speaking Caribbean to the British economy. At the same time the British manufacturing sector had grown to the point where it required more markets than the slave colonies could provide and, in addition, was no longer dependent on profits from the slave system for its capital needs. The British attack on coerced labor could thus be seen as the first stage of an assault on the trade barriers that reserved the British sugar market for British plantations and restricted trade with the rest of the world.[15]

With the collapse of the British West Indies sugar industry the old planter class disintegrated. The more enterprising or aggressive of them left for new opportunities, in Africa or Australia perhaps. Those who could afford it returned to retire in Britain. Those who stayed formed a reactionary core that did not know how to make the adjustment to the changed economic and social situation.

The British rejection of slavery, of course, did not bring an immediate end to the institution, although it may well have contributed to the emergence of Cuba, the southern United States, and Brazil, as the major plantation economies of the nineteenth century. The United States would play an ever expanding part in the political economy of the region from the 1790s forward, even though its share of the market was relatively small before 1865. Haiti, even before its independence in 1804, had appealed to United States trading interest considerably and been a source of both coffee and sugar. The southern fear of Haitian influence among slaves in the United States, however, prevented a more active role there by the United States. Even at that, a considerable exodus of French Haitians with their slaves headed first to Cuba—where they were not really very welcome for the same reason and did not interact well with the Spanish-speaking creoles—and then to Louisiana. There they swelled the small population by more than 10,000 by 1810, almost doubling immediately the population of New Orleans.[16]

Cuba became the dominant sugar producer from the 1830s through the 1960s. Cuba as a case history of sugar production offers the best example of the evolution of plantation society in the nineteenth and twentieth centuries, as it passed through a series of essentially revolutionary economic changes. The Bourbon reformers had stimulated Cuban agro-export productivity through expansion of slavery, subsidies, tax incentives, and the legalizing of new markets, including that of English North America completely by 1818. When Spain acquired Louisiana it was placed under the political jurisdiction of Havana and trade between the Caribbean and the Mississippi Valley was encouraged from that time. Additional exceptions to Spain's mercantilist exclusion of her colonies from trade outside the empire followed. Given a preferred position in the Spanish trading system, Cuba prospered and diversified, especially from 1818 to 1834, as Cuba failed to follow the rest of Latin America in throwing off Iberian rule. A combination of the benefits of the liberal Spanish economic policies and fear of a repeat of the Haitian slave insurrection account for the loyalty of Cuban creoles at this time. Exports of tobacco, sugar, coffee, and hides all rose dramatically during this period. There followed, however, a trade war among nations resisting the British impetus toward free trade, and retaliations between the United States and Spain led to a second revolution in the Cuban economy when the U. S. applied severe tariffs on Cuban coffee in response to Spanish duties on U. S. wheat flour. Together with the growing North American demand for sugar, this led to a fairly rapid shift from coffee and cattle production in Cuba to sugar production. Although tobacco retained importance, by the 1850s Cuba had become a plantation economy heavily dependent on slave-produced sugar exports, principally to the United States. By 1868 Cuba produced a third of the world's sugar.

This land and labor revolution, however, had displaced large numbers of small farmers, ranch workers, and wage laborers, who increasingly constituted a disgruntled mass, drifting into Havana and other cities and available to support a challenge to Spanish sovereignty in 1868. The ensuing Ten Years' War failed to win Cuban independence, but it did result in the gradual and compensated emancipation of the slaves by 1886 and thoroughly disrupted Cuban sugar production, exposing it to serious competition from European sugar beets, as well as to competition from cane producers in Hawaii and elsewhere. Resurrecting the Cuban sugar industry brought yet another economic revolution to the island, this time in the application of modern technology. Heavy investment from abroad brought the installation of massive mechanical and transportation improvements to the industry. Narrow gauge railroads, steam-operated sugar mills, and other labor-saving machinery made the industry competitive. Once again Cuban production soared, but was accompanied by new social and political dislocation. The modernization of the 1880s saved the Cuban sugar industry, but required the entry of significant amounts of U. S. capital into the production of Cuban sugar. Widespread unemployment, among both former slaves and others, continued.[17]

The resumption of the war for independence in 1895 and subsequent intervention of the United States in 1898 ended Spanish rule, as it delivered the sugar industry more fully into North American hands. Following the war, United States interests assumed ownership of many plantations and mills, while Cuba formally received a favored position within the U. S. market. By 1914, U. S. interests controlled directly thirty-five percent of Cuba's sugar production.[18]

Following World War I, yet another revolution in the industry occurred. Sugar prices first soared to record heights after wartime controls ended. Foreign speculators bought into the industry, with little knowledge or understanding of the market forces at work. Prices then plummeted as it became evident that production outran demand and in the ensuing crash many lost their shirts. This led to an opportunity for major American sugar consumers—Coca-Cola, Hires Root Beer, Hershey Chocolate, and others—to buy sugar plantations and mills to maximize their profits. This reorganization in the industry led to vertical control of sugar production by these large North American consumers. U. S. dominance in the industry continued until 1959, when yet another revolution, this more sweeping than any of the others, led to the collectivization of sugar production. The resulting exclusion of Cuban sugar from the U. S. market abruptly ended Cuban dependence on the United States.[19] While the Cuban experiment made remarkable improvements in the standard of living for rural Cuban sugar workers, it failed to make sugar a successful motor product for a generally prosperous society.[20]

This cycle of dependence on markets and capital investment is a familiar one throughout the region. While Cuban sugar perhaps offers the most stunning example of the possible consequences, less dramatic examples abound in the production of bananas and other plantation crops elsewhere. The social costs of foreign control of plantations have generally led to national reactions against the foreigners. Ironically, it has often been the substantial improvement in health, wages, education, and commerce that have accompanied the plantation societies that have enabled middle and working class interests to rise up against foreign capital.

The profits from monoculture inhibited the development of more diversified economies. Where sugar or other crops were most successful that was all the more true. Justifying monoculture on the theory of comparative advantage, tropical agriculture became characterized by all that went with it, including slavery, dependence on foreign investment and markets, absentee ownership, and impoverished rural working classes.[21]

Plantation agriculture, then, dominates much of Caribbean history from the sixteenth through the twentieth centuries. This long history, however, can be divided into two categorical periods: first, when mercantilist economic policy was dominant, extending into the nineteenth century; and second, when the influence of liberal capitalist economic policy became prevalent, from the late eighteenth century forward. The obvious differences between these two categories are the protection of markets for the production of the plantation versus a free trade environment of open competition. Neither system has ever been exclusive. Even before the eighteenth century the widespread smuggling and contraband trading in the region constituted a kind of "free trade" that undermined the mercantilist official policies. And protectionist policies have persisted among many of the Caribbean colonial powers even to the present. The other obvious difference between the two categories is in the labor systems of slavery versus wage labor. The injustices and inefficiencies of slavery became widely proclaimed by the beginning of the nineteenth century, although slavery continued in Brazil and the Spanish islands until the 1880s. Under liberalism, however, theoretical systems of free labor have often been abusively exploited through collusion between planter interests and governments. Liberal progress for the agro-export interests has often meant poverty for workers.[22] A socialist response in the case of Cuba has ameliorated the poverty of rural workers, but the overall success of that experiment is still very uncertain.

Agricultural exploitation of the tropical and subtropical regions of Middle America hastened the transition from feudalism to capitalism. Profitable plantations of cacao, tobacco, sugar, coffee, and other tropical and sub-tropical commodities expanded the transatlantic trade and contributed significantly to the capital accumulation necessary to the Industrial Revolution. They would also help to provide revenues for the growth of naval and military power, which the imperial powers required to maintain and protect their mercantilist policies in the Caribbean. Plantation agriculture thus became an essential part of the world-system that evolved in the North Atlantic. Eventually, slave labor, which had been so important to the early development in the labor-scarce Caribbean, became both socially and economically less desirable. Technology and exploitation with government collaboration became characteristic of more modern plantation economies. They were also characterized by dependence on foreign markets and investment. Inevitably, soil exhaustion, labor problems, and political opposition to foreign control would diminish the value of many Caribbean plantations. A cycle of the rise and decline of plantations in different regions therefore characterizes the history of the region, not only of the Caribbean islands, but in much of plantation America from Brazil to Maryland. The strong tendency of plantation owners (corporate or individual) to ignore the needs of local inhabitants and the interests of a more diversified regional economy is another characteristic endemic to the region.

Although plantation agriculture produced impressive profits for the owners and contributed to capital investment in a wide variety of economic development beyond the region, there remains a strong heritage of its failures in the region itself. The legacy of the plantation remains a heavy burden on most of the Caribbean even to the present day.

Commentary / David Eltis

This very broad ranging paper—five centuries in twenty pages of text—touches on a number of critically important issues that have preoccupied Caribbeanists for some time. It constitutes an interpretation of the rise and fall of the imperial plantation economy in the Caribbean, or, if we are to take the viewpoint of the peoples who provided labour for the system between enslavement in Africa and eventual freedom, the decline and rise of the people of the Caribbean. In the course of describing the rise and fall of the plantation system, the paper addresses three broad issues: the impact of Europe on the Caribbean; the impact of the Caribbean on Europe; the modern legacies of the former.

On the first of these, I can add some nuance. On the second, I would like to offer an alternative hypothesis, and on the third, and most interesting for non-historians, I can offer very little. The most important nuance I would like to add to the first theme is perhaps that Professor Woodward needs to introduce some non-economic aspects to his treatment of the switch from indentured European to African slavery. If it was cheaper to bring people from Europe to the Americas than from Africa to the Americas, how do we account for the total absence of European slaves on the one hand and African indentured servants on the social and cultural factors surely have to be used to explain why the Irish were not enslaved.

Racism as well as economics counted. Second, Professor Woodward rightly stresses the very high income that the Caribbean plantation economy generated, and it is worth adding perhaps that measured in per capita terms this was high by any standards in the seventeenth and eighteenth centuries. Third, despite this high income, the mercantilist policies that the colonial powers tried to enforce and the protection for producers that these implied meant that part of the high income came at the expense of European consumers of plantation produce. The British consumer increasingly subsidized the West Indian planter as the century progressed. Fourth, while sugar was king, its evolution was not quite as uniform as described here. In the eighteenth century, the production of sugar by-products (rum and molasses) as well as refined sugar increased until by 1770 it amounted to half the value of raw sugar output. Clearly there was a trend toward more processing. In addition to this, however, non-sugar plantation products, chiefly coffee, comprised one-fifth of all Caribbean exports. Thus, at what is usually taken as the height of the plantation system, raw sugar comprised less than half of all Caribbean output. Interestingly, in the course of the abolition era, this trend reversed as production of non-sugar crops migrated to other parts of the Americas, such as Brazil and the U.S. South. By 1850, sugar products accounted for nearly 80 percent of the total, and raw sugar was back up to nearly 60 percent. Freer trade meant more specialization. Fifthly, the Caribbean economy did not decline in any sense after 1770. The growth rate of total output in the whole Caribbean was about one percent a year between 1770 and 1850 compared to four times that in seventy years before 1770. The one percent was, of course, an average which drew on regions where there was an absolute decline in production—such as St. Domingue/Haiti and Jamaica—and very strong growth—such as Cuba and British Guiana. The major immediate forces behind this pattern between 1770 and 1850 were the St. Domingue revolution and the abolition of the slave trade and slavery. Areas such as the French and British Caribbean that had been forced by the metropole to end slavery and the slave trade fell behind the most. From an 1850 pan-American perspective, of the three major plantation regions, Brazil, the southern states of the U.S. and the Caribbean, it was the latter that had grown the most slowly since 1770. The Caribbean also had been the most affected by rebellion and abolition. From the broad perspective, therefore, the plantation economy did not decline before 1850, and any decline of sections of that economy was almost entirely due to rebellion and abolition, not overproduction, soil exhaustion or any innate inefficiencies of slavery. Indeed if the one area where revolution had a major impact—St. Domingue—is removed from consideration in the 1770–1850 era, then total Caribbean output (without St. Domingue) grew at 2 percent a year between 1770 and 1850. In other words the Caribbean economy was doubling in size every 35 years—hardly a decline.[1]

On the contribution of the Caribbean to the economies of the mother countries, Professor Woodward takes the English case as a paradigm for Europe as a whole. Adopting the Williams position in *Capitalism and Slavery*, he argues that the slave economies were important in providing capital and markets for the development of the Industrial Revolution. However, England was not Europe, and as Professor Woodward judiciously points out, the French and Cuban Caribbean overtook their English counterpart, the first in the eighteenth century, and the second in the nineteenth century. How is it then that with plantation economies so much stronger than the English, neither the French nor the Spanish beat the English to the industrial draw?

Even in the English case, total Caribbean output, explosive growth notwithstanding, was always a small fraction of domestic English output. Sugar was a relatively minor consumption item. Sugar refining was an important industry in and around London, as in the Atlantic ports of France, Amsterdam, and Hamburg. But as an input for English industry it by no means approached the importance of such (slave produced) staples as cotton, much less metallic ores, or fossil fuels produced by free labor. Per capita income and profits may well have been above what could have been earned in Europe, but relative to all the other industries that went to feed, clothe, and shelter Europeans (say as percentage of total consumer spending in Europe or England) it was minor. If we estimate the total output of the Caribbean export economies at 3.5 million pounds in 1700 and 14.5 million in 1770, neither could have been as much as one percent of the size of the European economy in either year. If we confine the comparison to the British economy and the British Caribbean then the proportions were larger but still less than six percent. The sugar component of this was, of course, smaller again—less than three percent of British consumption. It is also hard to see how items that formed such a small part of the consumer budget could have had a large impact on patterns and levels of work and investment in the macro-economy.

If such proportions as one or six percent seem significant then it should be remembered that the same procedures used here to calculate the value of sugar production would, if applied to other industries, yield much higher percentages of English total income. Many industries both within and without the agricultural sector had higher outputs and, prima facie, more plausible strategic connections to the process of industrialisation. Wheat production and flour milling, brewing, construction, merchant shipping, woollen textiles, coal mining, and a dozen other industries must have had much larger total products than sugar. Even if growing sugar were five times as profitable as growing wheat or mining coal, it would be hard to see it as a vital contributor to the pool of savings that funded the Industrial Revolution, or to the total demand for goods and services in the British economy. The slave trade and the West Indian trade made up a small fraction of the total British shipping and a smaller fraction again of the transportation sector. The export of manufactured goods to the Caribbean comprised a tiny fraction of the total manufacturing output of Britain—a proportion which does not become significant if we include Africa and the U.S. South. Why would tropical products be more significant as a trigger for expanded output (or expanded work effort) throughout the economy than the goods absorbed by any other single industry (or even group of industries)—also likely to impart multiplier effects—either at home or overseas?

An alternative to Professor Woodward's interpretation of the nature of the Caribbean-British economic links—not much discussed in the literature—is that the impulse for capital intensive development and increased trans-oceanic trade in the Caribbean came from technological improvements within the domestic English economy. The most important of such improvements were not innovations associated with the factory system, but rather changes in social values, vital rates, and market oriented behaviour, which had already raised European living standards beyond those of the rest of the world by 1600. One of the narrower consequences of these changes, all of which preceded the sugar revolution, was reduced production costs. Thus Europeans exported their economic system through cheaper goods and capital outflows. The establishment of overseas colonies that these made possible often meant slavery for non-Europeans. Rather than slavery in the Americas causing growth in Europe, perhaps both long-run economic growth in Europe and slavery in the Americas had the same roots in underlying economic and social trends already well established in north-western Europe by 1650.

Baseball in Southern Culture, American Culture, and the Caribbean

MILTON JAMAIL

When I was asked to write on this topic, I began to reflect on both growing up in the South and my later travels in the Caribbean and Mexico, and how baseball became the link that brought me closer to the people of those regions. I began to do research in Central America and Mexico in the mid-1960s, but never really felt comfortable asking sensitive questions about politics. And I could never quite explain to people why I was more than just another tourist in their country.

In 1974, along with a couple of friends, I embarked on a week-long hike in the mountains that connect the Mexican states of Guerrero and Oaxaca. We went to the end of a road and then walked from village to village until we reached one connected to a highway. In each village we had a guide to take us to the next settlement, in part to make sure we did not get lost, and in part to make sure we did not get in anyone's way.

One day as we rested, our guide came to me and asked, "Cual es tu misión?", basically, "What are you doing here?" I replied that I was interested in getting to know the Mexican countryside better and to meet and speak with people. He nodded and then asked:

"Are you an anthropologist?" I replied I was not.
"Are you a missionary?" No.
"Do you work for the Mexican government?" No.
"Are you a guerrillero?" No.
"Are you up here looking to buy marijuana?" No.

151

Finally, somewhat exasperated, he asked again, "Pues, cual es tu misión?"

Not until I began to do research on baseball in 1987 did I finally have a response—I am here to write about baseball. Interestingly enough, my response is met with surprise and near disdain by many intellectuals in Latin America, especially Mexico. But my interest in a sport that is immensely popular at the grassroots level has taken me into the homes and lives of people throughout the Caribbean and Mexico that I never thought possible. And that trust, built on a mutual love of baseball, has allowed me an insight into politics that I never had before.

While I was trained in political science, and I continue to teach at the university level, I have spent the past ten years writing about baseball. I am much more comfortable in a major league club house than in a departmental meeting.

How does a political scientist end up writing about baseball? What I do is basically a slight variation of a dream I had growing up in Houston, Texas in the 1950s. I had an enormous love of baseball. I learned how to read on baseball cards. I learned math by figuring batting averages. I used to go see the Houston Buffaloes, a minor league team. I remember that Ruben Amaro, a shortstop from Mexico, hit a home run to win a huge series against their main rival, the Atlanta Crackers, in 1956. I did not realize until I interviewed Ruben Amaro a few years ago that, because he is black, he was not allowed to celebrate the victory with his teammates at the whites only restaurant.

When I went to graduate school in the late 1960s, I concentrated on my studies, traveled extensively in Latin America, and did not follow baseball for nearly twenty years. But I did learn a great deal about Latin America, I learned how to write, and I learned how to speak Spanish. And in 1987, I was asked to write an article about Latinos in baseball. So I asked for a press pass, went to Houston, and talked to a few players. This led to a research project looking at both the experiences of Latino players in the U.S., and the experiences of U.S. major league teams searching for talent overseas.

All of a sudden it clicked. I was combining my long-standing love of baseball with the skills I had acquired in school, and I was writing about a subject that few sportswriters grasped. In the past eight years I have written over 100 articles on Latinos and baseball—mostly for *USA TODAY BASEBALL WEEKLY*. And although my book project was temporarily put on hold, I now have enough material for several volumes.

I make no pretense that this paper represents any theoretical breakthrough. It is simply an attempt to look at the relationship between the South and the Caribbean through baseball.

What I want to focus on is the difficult time Latin players, most of whom were black, had in dealing with a segregated South when they began to arrive in the United States in the 1950s and 1960s. These Caribbean youngsters had to come to the United States to receive recognition as the best players in the world, but they were simply not prepared to deal with a segregated society. I have selected four players whom I have interviewed over the past ten years: Vic Power, Felipe Alou, Juan Marichal and Ruben Amaro. Their words will describe their experiences. I have also drawn from the experiences of other Latino and African American players.

I am not going to devote much time to talking about the other side of the coin: southern black players who had to go to the Caribbean to fulfill their baseball dreams and to be recognized as top-flight players. But here we have people such as Willie Wells, "El Diablo" from Austin, Texas, who some consider the best shortstop to play in the Negro Leagues, and who also was a star in Mexico in the 1940s; Ray Dandridge from Richmond, Virginia, who in addition to being an outstanding Negro League star, was a legend in Mexico; and Willard Brown, from Shreveport, Louisiana, who is a hero in Puerto Rico, where he won three consecutive batting titles in winter ball in the late 1940s and where he is known as "Ese Hombre (That Man)."

THE ORIGINS OF BASEBALL

Baseball had its origins in the United States in the mid-nineteenth century but did not stay contained within the national
boundaries for long. In 1866, Cuban students returning home
from their studies in the United States took baseball into the
Caribbean But to Cubans baseball is not foreign; it is an essential
part of Cuban culture. "Growing up Cuban meant growing up in
baseball. In most instances there was no consciousness of the
American origin of the game," writes Roberto González Echevarría.[1]

In the 1890s, Cubans would take the game to Venezuela, the
Dominican Republic, Puerto Rico, and to the Mexican coastal
areas of Veracruz and the Yucatan. Historian Gilbert Joseph has
written on the origins of the game in the Yucatan peninsula of
Mexico in the 1890s. The sons of the elite returned home to Merida with baseball skills acquired at United States boarding
schools. This mix of Cuban refugees, elite support, and a diffusion of the sport among the region's working class would set a
strong foundation for the sport to flourish.[2]

Over time, what began as an upper-class elite sport became a
passion of the working class and the source of dreams. By the
turn of the century, baseball was firmly entrenched in all of these
countries and quickly became the dominant sport (except in Mexico, where it was a regional phenomenon). Several book-length
studies on Caribbean baseball touch upon the history of the diffusion of the game throughout the region. With this expansion of
baseball throughout the Caribbean, an increasing interest appeared in recruiting players to come to the U.S. baseball markets—where teams search for talent and have long gone outside of the U.S. As early as 1892, Miguel Peon Cásares, a pitcher
for the *El Sporting Club*, in Merida, Yucatan, caught the eye
of big league scouts. As Gilbert Joseph has noted, *"El Sporting*
was composed of players twenty and over, who had learned
the game at U.S. boarding schools and colleges." But Peon Cá-

sares' family, wealthy planters, did not envision a career in baseball for their son. The sport was fine as a pastime, but only "vaga-
bonds and people with no future would think of playing it for a
living."[3]

Because baseball in the U.S. was segregated in this century
until 1947, and the majority of players from Latin America were
black, the search for talent in the Caribbean was limited. With
the color barrier shattered in 1947, the principal market for players for U.S. teams was Cuba. Then with the rupture of U.S.-
Cuban relations in 1961 and the decision by the Cuban government to maintain only amateur baseball on the island, the market
shifted to the Dominican Republic, where it remains. Venezuela
is increasing in importance, and U.S. teams are excited about the
possibility of once again being able to recruit players in Cuba.

LATIN BASEBALL PLAYERS IN THE UNITED STATES

The first Latin to play professional baseball in the U.S was Cuban
Esteban Bellan, who was with the Troy, New York team in the
1870s. After Jackie Robinson integrated baseball in 1947, the
door also opened for Latinos. The first of these was Orestes
"Minnie" Miñoso, followed by Vic Power, Chico Carrasquel,
Luis Aparicio, Roberto Clemente, and Juan Marichal. Aparicio,
Clemente, and Marichal are three of the five Latino members
elected to the Baseball Hall of Fame.

Today, some 15% of all major league ball players are foreign-
born, while 25% of players in the minor leagues are foreign-born.
The vast majority of these are from the Caribbean and Mexico.

JACKIE ROBINSON

Before the Brooklyn Dodgers brought Jackie Robinson to the
major leagues in 1947, fewer than fifty players born in Latin
America had played in the big leagues. Since that date, more than
650 have played major league baseball. Regardless of which

major league team a Latino or African American player belonged to, during the 1950s, he would have had to go through spring training in a segregated Florida. Because the Dodgers wanted to avoid problems surrounding Robinson's presence in Florida in 1947, they took their entire squad for spring training in Havana. Robinson thought going to Cuba was a good idea. "It could be reasonably expected that the racist atmosphere I had to face in Florida and other parts of the United States would not exist in another country of non-whites," Robinson recalled in his autobiography.[4]

Ironically, though, Robinson and three other black players were placed in separate and inferior housing in Havana. As Robinson discovered, it was not the Cubans who ordered the segregated housing, but the Dodgers themselves. They feared that some of their players—led by the southern contingent of Hugh Casey (Georgia), Bobby Bragan (Alabama), and Dixie Walker (Georgia), would object to living with the black players. Not only did they object to living together with their black teammates, but these and several other players presented a petition to Dodger owner Branch Rickey stating they would not play on the same team with Robinson. The revolt ended when Rickey told them that anyone not willing to have a black teammate could quit.[5]

Not all major league teams were eager to follow in the footsteps of the Dodgers, but when they did, Latin players were occasionally the first black players for a franchise. Cuban Orestes "Minnie" Miñoso became, for example, the first black Chicago White Sox in 1951, and Dominican Ozzie Virgil was the first black Detroit Tiger in 1958. But Puerto Rican Vic Power was not the first black New York Yankee.

VIC POWER

Victor Pellot Power played in the major leagues for eleven years between 1954 and 1965. "He was an artist at first base. He revolutionized the word fielding," says Puerto Rican journalist Luis

Rodríguez Mayoral. Beginning in 1958, Power won the first seven Gold Gloves awarded in the American League, the honor given to the best player at his position in the league. Power was "an almost sure bet to be the team's first black player," writes David Halberstam. Power had solid years in the New York Yankees minor league system, and it just seemed a matter of time until he was called up.[6]

But he pushed the limits of a segregated society and thus became unacceptable to the Yankees. "He insisted, while in the minor leagues, on driving a Cadillac convertible, not only with the top down, which was bad enough, but accompanied by a white woman in the front seat," writes Halberstam. The Yankees told him they were not going to bring him to the major leagues unless he changed his ways. Power was firm: the Yankees could tell him how they wanted him to play baseball, but, he said, "they cannot tell me which women I can go out with."[7]

When Power was not called to the majors in 1953, Yankee co-owner Dan Topping said, "My information is that Power is a good hitter, but a poor fielder." And in order to rationalize not bringing him up to the big leagues, the management had to discredit Power by giving the New York press negative stories. As David Halberstam describes it, "Typically they planted a story with Dan Daniel, who was, as ever accommodating. 'Power is major-league material right up to his Adam's apple,' Daniel wrote. North of that location he is not extraordinary. He is said to be not too quick on the trigger mentally.' That was it for Power, who was returned to Kansas City in 1953, and soon traded out of the organization. He was not a Yankee type." When asked why the Yankees would not bring him up, Power would tell reporters, "They were waiting to see if I could turn white, but I couldn't do it. You see, I had to make fun and joke so I could *survive* in the game."[8]

Power vividly remembers an incident in a restaurant in Little Rock, Arkansas shortly after arriving on the mainland from Puerto Rico in the early 1950s After he sat down the waitress approached and said, "We don't serve black people." "That's

O.K.," responded Power, "I don't eat black people, I just want
rice and beans." Vic Power loves telling that story. He told me in
1988 as we watched a ball game together in the Dominican Republic. I later found it in a 1963 magazine article about him and
in at least three other sources. "My mother couldn't believe it
when I wrote her that a restaurant wouldn't serve a hungry person who had money," said Power.[9]

Power recalls having to live with a black family in Florida because he could not stay in a hotel near the ballpark with the other
players. Then having to walk the two miles to the ballpark because blacks were not allowed to take taxis. "Eventually," recalls
Power, "they let blacks stay in the same hotels as whites, but they
still told us not to use the pool, look at white women, or eat in
the hotel restaurant." No one could explain to Power why blacks
were not allowed to go downtown after 6:00 p.m., or why he
could not drink from the cold water fountain in the dugout. "I
wish someone would have explained to me about the racial problem because it was confusing," said Power.[10]

Power finished his playing career in 1965, and went to work as
a scout in the Caribbean, recruiting young baseball players for
U.S. organizations, until the early 1990s. He now lives in San
Juan, Puerto Rico.

CURT FLOOD

Latino players often established close relationships with African
American players. They would be grouped together, forced to
stay at the black hotels in spring training, and take out sandwiches rather than eat with their teammates in restaurants. One
of those American players was Curt Flood. Flood is one of the
pioneers in bringing about free agency for major league players,
and thus, the rapid increase in salaries. He was one of the game's
better players for the St. Louis Cardinals in the late 1960s when
he was traded to the Philadelphia Phillies. He refused to go, took
his case to the U.S. Supreme Court, where he lost, and only

played a handful of games after that. But his fight broke open the fight for free agency.[11]

Flood was also the first black player to play in Virginia in the late 1950s. He tells of playing a doubleheader. After the first game, the players would undress and throw their uniforms in a pile. The uniforms would immediately be washed and dried, so that players could suit up for the second game. Flood followed the example of his fellow players, took off his uniform and threw it with the others. The clubhouse attendant rushed over, yelled at Flood, and took a stick and removed Flood's uniform, saying, "This has to go to the black cleaners down the street." When the uniform was late in coming back, and the start of the second game was delayed, Flood recalls his teammates looking at him as if he were to blame. Flood laughed when he recounted the story, but he was humiliated at the time. Flood tried to explain segregation to Leo Cárdenas, a Cuban teammate in Savannah, Georgia, in 1957. "Leo would say, 'Let's eat over here', or 'Curt, let's go to this bar,' and I would have to explain why we could not. I understood the nonsense, but how could I explain it to someone who had never experienced it?"[12]

In 1958, when Flood made it to the big leagues to stay, with the St. Louis Cardinals, his roommate was a young dark-skinned Mexican player, Ruben Amaro.

RUBEN AMARO

Ask Ruben Amaro Sr. for the highlight of his long career and he does not hesitate a second: "It was June 28, 1958, and I was told to report to the St. Louis Cardinals." He talks about the event in detail, as though he were discussing yesterday's game. He remembers what he ate, and he recalls that first walk out of the clubhouse onto the playing field in the old Busch Stadium. Wearing a uniform with the pants two sizes too big, he passed by the locker of veteran Stan Musial. After Musial greeted the rookie, he called to the clubhouse attendant, and said. "Give this man a

pair of pants that fit him." "Getting to the big leagues was of
great satisfaction for me, and for my father, Santos," says Amaro.
"I remember my dad playing, and I thought he should have been
a major league player. Unfortunately, because of the times, he
couldn't play in the U.S."[13]

Santos Amaro, "El Canguro"—the Kangaroo (a nickname he
acquired in the 1930s when he used the long legs on his 6–4
frame to try to catch a team bus that had left him behind at a
restaurant), is extremely proud of his forty-year career as a player
and manager in Mexico, Cuba, Venezuela, and the Dominican
Republic. He is considered one of the best hitters in the history
of the Mexican League, where he had a career average of .314.
Santos Amaro was never allowed to play in the big leagues in the
United States because he is black. But in 1935, he went on an
eighty-game, fourteen-state tour of the United States with a team
from the Texas border city of Nuevo Laredo. The La Junta de
Nuevo Laredo team played throughout Texas and the Midwest,
with the highlight being a three-game series against the Bis-
marck, North Dakota team. Satchel Paige started two of the
games for the home club. "We played everyday," recalls Amaro.
"But in Texas, they wouldn't let Bragaña [another dark skinned
Cuban] and I play much."[14]

Ruben, Santos' son, grew up surrounded by the very best of
baseball in Veracruz. His first memories of the game are of watch-
ing local hero Roberto Avila, who went on to win the American
League batting title while playing second base for Cleveland in
1954, Negro League stars Willie Wells, Ray Dandridge and Josh
Gibson, and Cuban stars such as Martín Dihigo, Ramón Bragaña,
Lázaro Salazar, and his father. Professional scouts took note of
Ruben at the Pan American Games in Mexico in 1954. That same
year, he signed with the St. Louis Cardinals. "When I signed, I
promised my dad I was going to make it," says Ruben. He was
sent to Mexicali of the Class C Arizona-Mexico League, where
he played for two seasons. In 1956 he made the jump to the

Houston Buffaloes of the AA Texas League. "When I moved to Texas it was tough, because I could not live with the other players on the club, even though I was the hero," remembers Amaro. "I was the All-Star shortstop, and I won the Dixie Series with a home run in the sixth game against Atlanta." But being black in Texas in the 1950s meant Ruben could not go out to dinner with his teammates and celebrate.[15]

Returning to Veracruz that winter, Ruben spoke of his misgivings about playing baseball in a segregated environment to his father. "I don't know whether I'm going back to the United States," he told his dad. The elder Amaro looked at his son, and with a wisdom based on his own experiences, and a vision of Ruben's future, told him: "I thought you promised me you were going to go to the top. I guess you are not going to make it. I believed when you told me that you were going to make a commitment to play baseball, that your goal was to play in the big leagues. Maybe you can give it some thought, I don't think you are going to stay in Houston too many years." Santos Amaro had a broad smile on his face when he told me this story in 1989, sitting in his living room in Veracruz.[16]

Ruben reconsidered his decision to retire, and Santos Amaro proved right, as Ruben did not stay long in Houston. In 1958 he was promoted to Rochester and by the end of the 1958 season, he had made it to the majors with the Cardinals. After spending most of his career with the Philadelphia Phillies, he retired in 1970 to became a minor league coach in the organization, and becoming in 1974 coordinator of their Latin scouting program. In the 1996 season Ruben managed the Class A team of the Chicago Cubs in Williamsport, Pennsylvania. His son, Ruben Jr., who graduated from Stanford University, considers himself Mexican American. He made it to the big leagues and played with Cleveland in the 1995 World Series, and later with the Philadelphia Phillies.

JUAN MARICHAL

Juan Marichal, "The Dominican Dandy," began playing baseball when he was six and at age ten decided he would become a pitcher. Still in his youth, he developed a high leg kick, which was to become his trademark. In 1957 Marichal signed with the New York Giants, left his home in the Dominican Republic, and, like all other players in the organization, was sent to their spring training camp in Sanford, Florida. He, along with other black players, lived in segregated housing and was denied service in restaurants. "When I left my country and encountered discrimination in the United States, I couldn't understand it," Juan Marichal told me in 1988, recalling his first days in Florida thirty years earlier. "When you come to a country so advanced, and you encounter this, you don't believe it."[17]

"Racism was something that I didn't let bother me, but it did bother a lot of other players," says Marichal. "Not me. I have always said, if you don't want me in your house, why should I go there?" "When we would go through places that were not going to serve us in the restaurants, there were some of the white players who would bring us sandwiches out to the bus. And I stayed calmly waiting on the bus. But some guys tried to enter the restaurant and see if they would get served, and I told them, 'Don't go, they are not going to serve you.' But they went and often came back crying. This happened to José Tartabull."[18] Tartabull was from Cuba and played in the major leagues for nine years. His son Danny has played for the Chicago White Sox.

Marichal survived these early battles with racism and went on to become one of the best pitchers in the history of baseball. He made his major league debut in 1960, and during the next ten years with the Giants won more than twenty games in a season on six occasions. In 1983 he became the first Dominican inducted into the Baseball Hall of Fame in Cooperstown, New York. Following his playing career, Marichal worked as scout for the Oakland Athletics until 1995.

FELIPE ROJAS ALOU

Although Ozzie Virgil was the first player born in the Dominican Republic to make it to the big leagues when he played with the New York Giants in 1956, the first Dominican who grew up in the Dominican Republic to get to the major leagues was Felipe Rojas Alou. "When I was signed by the Giants in 1956, I was sent to a Class-D team in Lake Charles, Louisiana, in the Evangeline League. It was the first time I was in the United States, and I guess I should have learned more about conditions in the South, especially if you have dark skin. There is discrimination of some sort all over the world. There is a little bit—not much, but some—in my own country. But I was not prepared for what happened in Louisiana," wrote Alou in 1963.[19]

In Lake Charles, Alou lived with another ball player, Ralph Crosby, an African American from New York City. They were the only two black players on the team. "I did not know a single word of English. I followed Crosby all over," wrote Alou. "We had played five games, when one day they told me I had to leave, and they put me on a Greyhound bus, and shipped me to Cocoa, Florida." Team owners had met and decided that they did not want blacks playing in the league. "Later," Alou writes, "I heard it was the governor, Earl Long, who sent word down to Lake Charles. 'Get them out of here,' he said."[20]

Alou was an early and outspoken critic of discrimination against Latinos in the United States. In 1963 he wrote an article in *Sport* magazine, "Latin-American Ballplayers Need a Bill of Rights," detailing the prejudice Latin players faced in the United States. "That article should tell you something about me and why I'm here now," Alou responded when I asked him in 1995 to comment on what he had written over thirty years earlier. "I have always been able to say what I think is right, and stand by it. I'm not afraid to lose my head for what is right."[21]

Alou played for seventeen seasons in the major leagues with six different ball clubs. On September 10, 1963 he, along with his brothers Mateo and Jesus, comprised the outfield for the San Francisco Giants, marking the only time three brothers played together on the same team in the major leagues. After his playing career ended in 1974, Alou managed for twelve years in the minor league system of the Montreal Expos. In 1992, the Expos named Alou manager, becoming the first Dominican to guide a major league team. In 1994 Alou led the Expos to first place and was chosen as the manager for the National League team at the 1995 All-Star Game, becoming the first Latino to manage the mid-year event.

Alou and the other Caribbean players not only had to deal with institutionalized segregation and racism, but also with being foreigners, and they had to cope with all of this in another language. When Alou first signed a contract before he came to the United States, he purchased a mail order course to learn English. But when he got here he often found it difficult to understand the accent in some of the towns where he was sent to play. "Living in the drawl-heavy South did not help," wrote Alou. "Nowhere on the records or in the textbooks that had been sent to me from Hollywood was there anything similar to, 'Y'all come'n back tumarrah, heah?' "[22]

CONCLUSION: BEYOND THE SOUTH

The one aspect that runs through all of my interviews and research is the sense of dismay that players from the Caribbean had when confronting a segregated society in the 1950s South. They were confused and wished that someone could have explained to them what they might have expected before they came. They simply were not prepared to deal with segregation—an institution which hit them head on. How would you begin to explain an institutionalized practice that was so foreign to these players who had come from cultures where economic status, not skin color, was the most important factor? As Curt Flood said, he understood it, but how could he explain it to someone who had not experienced it.

The stories I have told are about survivors. There is no doubt, though, that the segregated South adversely effected the performance of the Latino players in the 1950s and 1960s and possibly accounted for the failure of many to play up to their potential. It must have been difficult to concentrate on baseball, when confronting an institution designed to destroy your humanity, self-esteem, and self-confidence. No statistics in the *Baseball Encyclopedia* record Latino players who went home broken by racism.

Today those same cities where the early Latino players suffered injustices during the era of segregation have made dramatic changes. The Atlanta Braves, Florida Marlins, and Houston Astros now are among the leaders among major league teams in recruiting Latino players. The Cuban national amateur baseball team, which has an overwhelming majority of black athletes, usually plays three or four games each year at the U.S. Olympic baseball facility in Millington, Tennessee, a suburb of Memphis, where they are received with great courtesy and warmth and hospitality. And in Houston—the city where Ruben Amaro could not go out to eat—the Astros send their young baseball players from the Caribbean to play in Jackson, Mississippi. And the players have no problems.

However, as the institution of segregation gave way, Latin black players realized they still faced other hurdles, and these problems were not limited to the South. They still had to deal with racial discrimination, now in more subtle forms, and they were perceived as foreigners playing a game that Americans thought they should dominate.

"We are strangers. I need a passport to come here," wrote Felipe Alou in 1963.[23] Today, the United States Department of Labor tightly restricts the number of foreign-born baseball players allowed to compete in the United States. Each of the thirty organizations is allotted an average of twenty-five visas for their minor league systems.

While the visa process is complex, the "visa problem" is basically very simple: U.S. teams are developing more talent in Latin America and Australia, Asia and Europe, than the U.S. government or organized baseball is willing to let compete in the United States. The real problem is the lack of "visa slots" allotted to Major League Baseball. And the result is that some foreign-born players are passed over, others cut early, and still others never get an opportunity to play in the U.S.. The quota imposed by the U.S. government is the greatest single factor limiting the participation of foreign-born players in organized baseball in the United States, the vast majority of whom are from the Caribbean. Part of the problem is the reluctance of the U.S. government to approve more visas for the baseball industry for fear of a backlash from U.S. citizens about foreigners taking U.S. jobs. But restricting the number of foreign-born players allowed to compete in the U.S. is akin to keeping blacks out of baseball. Under segregation, baseball set up regulations restricting the entry of top quality players. In doing so, baseball limited—and limits—its own potential. Visas serve the same purpose as segregation.

So while Caribbean blacks no longer have to deal with segregated water fountains, or housing, and they can eat at McDonald's, they still have to deal with the other barriers to participation in baseball in this country, barriers not limited to the South. They are often considered foreigners at their own game.

Notes

Notes to THE SOUTH AND THE CARIBBEAN: A REGIONAL
PERSPECTIVE
by Bonham C. Richardson

I am most grateful to three colleagues at Virginia Tech—Jim Campbell, Joe
Scarpaci, and Randy Shifflett—who read an early draft of this paper, made valuable suggestions, and commented very helpfully from their different perspectives.

1. D.W. Meinig, *The Shaping of America*, Vol. 2, *Continental America, 1800–
1867* (New Haven, 1993); p. 538; Terry G. Jordan, "The Creole Coast: Roman-
Caribbean Ethnicity and the Shaping of the American South," paper read at the
Annual Meeting of the Association of American Geographers, San Francisco, 1994.

2. Sidney W. Mintz and Richard Price, *The Birth of African-American Cul-
ture: An Anthropological Perspective* (Boston, 1992); Eugene D. Genovese, *From
Rebellion to Revolution: Afro-American Slave Revolts in the Making of the Modern
World* (Baton Rouge, 1979); Rebecca J. Scott, "Defining the Boundaries of Free-
dom in the World of Cane: Cuba, Brazil, and Louisiana after Emancipation,"
American Historical Review, 99 (1994), pp. 70–102.

3. Rupert B. Vance, *Human Geography of the South: A Study in Regional
Resources* (Chapel Hill, 1935), p. 351; Special report on "The American South,"
The Economist, December 10, 1994; Carl N. Degler, *Place Over Time: The Conti-
nuity of Southern Distinctiveness* (Baton Rouge, 1977), p. 10.

4. Bonham C. Richardson, "Detrimental Determinists: Applied Environ-
mentalism as Bureaucratic Self-Interest in the Fin-de-Siècle British Caribbean,"
Annals, Association of American Geographers, Vol. 86 (1996), pp. 213–34; Vance,
Human Geography of the South, p. 367.

5. David McCullough, *The Path Between the Seas: The Creation of the Panama Canal, 1870–1914* (New York, 1977), p. 323.

6. Gordon K. Lewis, *Main Currents in Caribbean Thought: The Historical
Evolution of Caribbean Society in Its Ideological Aspects, 1492–1900* (Baltimore,
1983), p. 3.

7. Christopher Columbus, *The Four Voyages of Christopher Columbus*, ed.
Cecil Jane (New York, 1988), p. 2.

8. Carl O. Sauer, *The Early Spanish Main* (Berkeley, 1966), pp. 206–207.

9. Alfred W. Crosby, *The Columbian Exchange: Biological and Cultural Consequences of 1492* (Westport, Ct., 1972); Kenneth F. Kiple, *The Caribbean Slave:
A Biological History* (Cambridge, 1984).

10. Sidney W. Mintz, "Can Haiti Change?" *Foreign Affairs*, Vol. 74 (January/
February 1995), pp. 73–86; Richardson, "Detrimental Determinists," pp. 213–34.

11. Malcolm Gladwell, "Black Like Them," *The New Yorker* (April 29 and
May 6, 1996), p. 75.

12. Malcolm Gladwell, "Louis Farrakhan's Journey," *Washington Post National Weekly Edition* (January 22–28, 1996), pp. 6–8.

13. Rob Ruck, *The Tropic of Baseball: Baseball in the Dominican Republic*
(New York, 1991), p. 160.

14. Carl Bridenbaugh and Roberta Bridenbaugh, *No Peace Beyond the Line: The English in the Caribbean, 1624–1690* (New York, 1972), pp. 249–256.

15. Richardson, *Caribbean Migrants*, pp. 56–57; Walter Rodney, *A History of the Guyanese Working People, 1881–1905* (Baltimore, 1981), p. 3.

16. Sidney W. Mintz, *Caribbean Transformations* (Baltimore, 1984), pp. 146–156.

17. Richardson, *Caribbean Migrants*.

18. Carol Stack, *Call to Home: African Americans Reclaim the Rural South* (New York, 1996).

19. George L. Beckford, "The Social Economy of Bauxite in the Jamaican Man-Space," *Social and Economic Studies*, Vol. 36 (1987), p. 1; Chalmers Archer, *Growing Up Black in Rural Mississippi: Memories of a Family, Heritage of a Place* (New York, 1992), p. 104.

20. Kusha Haraksingh, "Culture, Religion, and Resistance among Indians in the Caribbean," in *Indian Labour Immigration*, ed. U. Bissoondoyal and S.B.C. Servansing (Mauritius, 1986); Orlando Patterson, "Migration in Caribbean Societies: Socioeconomic and Symbolic Resource," in *Human Migration: Patterns and Policies*, ed. W.H. McNeil and R.S. Adams (Bloomington, 1978), p. 139.

21. Jervis Anderson, *This Was Harlem: A Cultural Portrait, 1900–1950* (New York, 1982).

22. David Quammen, *The Song of the Dodo: Island Biogeography in an Age of Extinctions* (New York, 1996), p. 128.

23. Derek Walcott, *The Antilles: Fragments of Epic Memory* (New York, 1992), pp. 34–35.

Notes to COMPARATIVE SLAVERY: AFRICAN CULTURE IN THE SOUTH AND THE CARIBBEAN
by Charles Joyner

The research on which this paper is based was conducted during the course of two fellowships at Harvard University, one as a fellow in Comparative Slave Societies on a stipend from the National Endowment for the Humanities, the other as an Associate of the W.E.B. DuBois Institute for Afro-American Studies.

An earlier and much shorter version of this paper was presented at the annual meeting of the Association of Caribbean Studies in Manaus, Brazil, in 1995 under the title, "African Cultures in the Caribbean, Brazil, and Carolina: the Need for Discourse." Most of the "discourse" included in that paper is omitted from this version.

1. The significance of the slave trade to the rise of industrial capitalism has proved to be an enduringly controversial question. Reaction to Eric Williams' *Capitalism and Slavery* was rarely neutral. The prevailing mainstream position of the 1990s would appear to be that Williams considerably overstated the case, but slavery and the slave trade did in fact play an important role in the economic development of Western capitalism. The precise dimensions of the controversy remain unsettled at the end of the twentieth century and bids fair to continue into the next one. See Eric Williams, *Capitalism and Slavery* (Chapel Hill, 1944), 10, 19–21, 51–52. Williams acknowledged the inspiration of C.L.R. James, *Black Jacobins: Toussaint L'Ouverture and the San Domingo Revolution* (New York, 1938) 48. See also Richard B. Sheridan, *Sugar and Slavery: An Economic History of the*

British West Indies, 1623–1775 (Baltimore, 1974); Stanley L. Engerman, "Slave Trade and British Capital Formation in the Eighteenth Century: A Comment on the Williams Thesis," *Journal of Business History*, 46 (1972), 430–43; Eugene D. Genovese, *In Red and Black: Marxian Explorations in Southern and Afro-American History*, 2d ed. (Knoxville, 1984), 27; Elizabeth Fox-Genovese and Eugene D. Genovese, *The Fruits of Merchant Capital* (New York, 1983), 392–93; Jay Alan Coughtry, *The Notorious Triangle: Rhode Island and the Slave Trade, 1700–1807* (Philadelphia, 1981); James Walvin, *Slavery and the Slave Trade* (Jackson, Miss., 1983); David W. Galenson, *Traders, Planters and Slaves: Market Behavior in Early English America* (Cambridge, 1986); and Joseph C. Miller, *Way of Death: Merchant Capitalism and the Angolan Slave Trade, 1730–1830* (Madison, Wis., 1989). For a sweeping bibliographic essay covering an extraordinary range of 19th- and 20th-century materials on the subject, see Ronald W. Bailey, "Africa, the Slave Trade, and Industrial Capitalism in Europe and the United States: A Historiographic Review," *American History: A Bibliographic Review*, 2 (1986), 1–91. Among briefer surveys of the literature are Jan Hagendorn, "Review Essay: The Economics of the African Slave Trade," *Journal of American History* 70 (1984), 854–61; and Hilary Beckles, "Down but Not Out: Eric Williams 'Capitalism and Slavery' after Nearly Forty Years of Criticism," *Bulletin of Eastern Caribbean Affairs*, 8 (1982), 29–36. An indispensable study that deftly blends history and economics with anthropology is Sidney Mintz, *Sweetness and Power: The Place of Sugar in Modern History* (New York, 1985).

2. Culture, as Lawrence W. Levine reminds us, is "the product of unremitting interaction between the past and present." See his *Highbrow/Lowbrow: The Emergence of Cultural Hierarchy in America* (Cambridge, Mass., 1988), 33. Sidney Mintz observes that culture constitutes "a repository of historically derived beliefs, values, etc., upon which societies may draw, particularly for symbolic purposes." See his *Caribbean Transformations* (New York, 1974, 1989), 325. Raymond Williams calls culture "one of the two or three most complicated words in the English language" and urges study of the "modes of change" of cultural meanings and values. Raymond Williams, *Keywords: A Vocabulary of Culture and Society* (London, 1984), 87, 90; Raymond Williams, *The Long Revolution* (Harmondsworth, Middlesex, 1965), 58–70. See also Raymond Williams, *Culture and Society* (Harmondsworth, Middlesex, 1963) 127; and Raymond Williams, "Base and Superstructure in Marxist Cultural Theory," in *Problems in Materialism and Culture* (London, 1980).

3. Eric Williams, *Capitalism and Slavery* (Chapel Hill, 1944), 2; Despite M.G. Smith's insistence that an African heritage can be established in the Caribbean only by tracing particular cultural practices directly back to particular groups in Africa, Mintz notes that "it would be extremely difficult to attribute a significant part of the culture of any contemporary Caribbean people to specific African cultures." See his "The African Heritage in the Caribbean," in *Caribbean Studies: A Symposium*, ed. Vera Rubin (Seattle, Wash., 1960), 34–36; Sidney W. Mintz, "The Caribbean as a Socio-cultural Area," *Journal of World History*, 9 (1966), 921–22; Michael Mullin, *Africa in America: Slave Acculturation and Resistance in the American South and the British Caribbean, 1736–1831*, Blacks in the New World, ed. August Meier and John H. Bracey (Urbana, Ill., 1992), 26; Michael Craton, *Sinews of Empire: A Short History of British Slavery* (London, 1974), 211–12; Richard S. Dunn, *Sugar and Slaves: The Rise of the Planter Class in the English West Indies, 1624–1713* (Chapel Hill, 1972), 236.

4. Roger Bastide, *African Civilisations in the New World*, [*Les Amériques noires*] trans. Peter Green (New York, 1971), 92–93. Cf. Craton, *Sinews of Empire*, 212–13; Bryan Edwards, *The History, Civil and Commercial, of the British Colonies in the West Indies* (Dublin, 1793), 2, 155.

5. On Great Traditions and Little Traditions see Robert Redfield, *Peasant Society and Culture* (Chicago, 1956, 1965), 41–42. With no disposition to romanticize racial harmony in the West Indies, it is obvious that I do not share M.G. Smith's characterization of them as a "plural society," subject to endless tensions and alienation, unlikely ever to produce an indigenous culture. See his *The Plural Society in the British West Indies* (Berkeley, Cal., 1965); Bastide, *African Civilisations in the New World*, 189–90.

6. Sidney W. Mintz, "Tasting Food, Tasting Freedom," in *Sonderdruck aus: Slavery in the Americas*, ed. Wolfgang Binder (Wurzburg, 1993), 257–75, quotations on 271 and 269. I have explored slave culture as a form of resistance in *Down by the Riverside: A South Carolina Slave Community* (Urbana, Il., 1984); in *Remember Me: Slave Life in Coastal Georgia* (Atlanta, 1989); in "History as Ritual: Rites of Power and Resistance on the Slave Plantation." *Australasian Journal of American Studies*, 5 (1986), 1–9; and especially in "Texts, Texture, and Context: Toward an Ethnographic History of Slave Resistance," paper presented at conference on "Unfree Labour" at University of Sydney in August, 1993, in *Varieties of Southern History*, ed. John Salmond and Bruce Clayton (Westport, Conn., 1996).

7. I have tried to explain this epic cultural transformation by using the concept of creolization. I was influenced by the "anthropological approach" proposed in 1976 by the Caribbeanists Sidney Mintz and Richard Price, who suggested that the culture of the slaves was less a matter of "borrowing" or "retaining" than it was of "creating." Through Mintz and Price I was led back to an earlier work by the Jamaican poet and historian Edward Kamau Brathwaite. I was much influenced by Brathwaite's concept of creolization as "a cultural action—material, psychological and spiritual—based upon the stimulus/response of individuals within the society to their environment and—as white/black, culturally discrete groups—to each other." See my *Down by the Riverside*. See also Sidney W. Mintz and Richard Price, *An Anthropological Approach to the Afro-American Past: A Caribbean Perspective* (Philadelphia, 1976). A second edition, with a new preface and some updating of terminology, but largely unchanged, is published as *The Birth of African-American Culture: An Anthropological Perspective* (Boston, 1992). See also Edward Kamau Brathwaite, *The Development of Creole Society in Jamaica, 1770–1820* (Oxford, 1971), 296–307 (quotation on 296).

8. Joyner, *Down by the Riverside*, esp. 196–224; Joyner, *Remember Me*; Charles Joyner, " 'If You Ain't Got Education': Slave Language and Slave Thought in Ante-bellum Charleston," *Intellectual Life in Antebellum Charleston*, ed. Michael O'Brien and David Moltke-Hansen (Knoxville, 1986), 255–78. Implicit creolist formulations may be detected in Peter H. Wood, *Black Majority: Negroes in Colonial South Carolina from 1670 through the Stono Rebellion* (New York, 1974); Margaret Washington (Creel), *"A Peculiar People": Slave Religion and Community Culture among the Gullahs* (New York, 1988); and Littlefield, *Rice and Slaves*.

9. On the definition of creolization, see Dell Hymes, introduction to pt. 3 of Dell Hymes, ed., *Pidginization and Creolization of Languages* (Cambridge, 1971), 84. That volume also contains useful essays on the complexity of the relationships involved in the creolization process: see esp. Sidney W. Mintz, "The Sociohistorical Background of Pidginization and Creolization," 153–68; Mervyn C. Alleyne,

"Acculturation and the Cultural Matrix of Creolization," 169–86; and David De-Camp, "Introduction: The Study of Pidgin and Creole Languages," 13–39. See also Robert A. Hall, *Pidgin and Creole Languages* (Ithaca, 1965), 15; Loreto Todd, *Pidgins and Creoles* (London, 1974), 5–6, 54, 67; Douglas Taylor, *Languages of the West Indies*, Johns Hopkins Studies in Atlantic History and Culture (Baltimore, 1978); and Ian Hancock, "Componentiality and the Origins of Gullah," in *Sea and Land: Cultural and Biological Adaptations in the Southern Coastal Plain*, ed. James L. Peacock and James C. Sabella, Southern Anthropological Society Proceedings, No. 21 (Athens, Ga., 1988), 13–25.

10. Ian F. Hancock, "A Survey of Pidgins and Creoles of the World," in Hymes, ed., *Pidginization and Creolization*, 512–15; Neville A.T. Hall, *Slave Society in the Danish West Indies: St. Thomas, St. John, and St. Croix* (Mona, Jamaica, 1992), 113, 192; Mintz, *Caribbean Transformations*, 16; Douglas Taylor, "New Languages for Old in the West Indies," *Comparative Studies in Society and History*, 3 (1961), 277–88; Mintz, "Caribbean as a Socio-cultural Area," 935–36. On the special case of the development of an African-English creole in Dutch Surinam, see Charles R. Boxer, *The Dutch Seaborne Empire, 1600–1800* (New York, 1965), 241.

For an eighteenth-century description of "creolsk," creole language of the Danish West Indies, see C.G.A. Oldendorp, *Geschichte der Mission der evangelischen Bruder auf den caraibischen Inseln S. Thomas, S. Croix und S. Jan* (Barby, 1777) trans., Arnold R. Highfield and Vladimir Barac, in George F. Tyson and Arnold R. Highfield, eds., *The Kamina Folk: Slavery and Slave Life in the Danish West Indies* (St. Thomas, VI, 1994), 89–92.

11. My own contribution to the study of this broad process of culture change, other than applying creolization to South Carolina, is perhaps to have used the model of *linguistic* creolization in a systematic way toward explaining the emergence of the totality of African-American culture. Instead of looking for static "retentions" or "survivals" of African culture, I have sought out records of the slaves' active creation of a new culture. The premise of the linguistic model is that the crucial element in the formation of African-American culture was the slaves' acquisition of a common language. E. P. Thompson notes that both "resistance to change and assent to change arise from the whole culture." See his "Time, Work-Discipline, and Industrial Capitalism," *Past and Present*, 38 (1967), 80. Cf. Herbert G. Gutman, *Work, Culture, and Society in Industrializing America* (New York, 1977), 1–78. A somewhat similar approach was pioneered by Richard Price and Sally Price, *Afro-American Arts of the Suriname Rain Forest* (Berkeley, 1980); Richard Price and Sally Price, "*Kammbá*: the Ethnohistory of an Afro-American Art," *Anthropologica*, 32 (1972), 3–27; and Richard Price and Sally Price, "Saramaka Onomastics: An Afro-American Naming System," *Ethnology*, 11 (1972), 341–67.

12. Charles Joyner, "A Single Southern Culture: Cultural Interaction in the Old South," in *Black and White: Cultural Interaction in the Antebellum South*, ed. Ted Ownby (Jackson, Miss., 1993), 1–22.

13. Johan Lorentz Carstens, *En Almindelig Beskrivelse om Alle de Danske, Americanske eller West-Jndiske Ely-Lande* (an eighteenth-century mss. published in Copenhagen in 1981), trans. Arnold R. Highfield, in Tyson and Highfield, eds. *Kamina Folk*, 5–7; Mary Turner, *Slaves and Missionaries: The Disintegration of Jamaican Slave Society, 1787–1834* (Urbana, 1982); Charles Joyner, " 'Believer I Know,': The Emergence of African-American Christianity," *African-American*

Christianity: Essays in History, ed. Paul Johnson (Berkeley, 1994), 18–46; Charles Joyner, "The Creolization of Slave Folklife: All Saints Parish, South Carolina, as a Test Case," *Historical Reflections/ Reflexions Historiques* [Canada], 6 (1979), 435–53; and his "Creolization," in *Encyclopedia of Southern Culture*, ed. Charles Reagan Wilson and William R. Ferris (Chapel Hill, 1989), 147–49. See also Bastide, *African Civilisations in the New World*, 88–90, 128–29; 180–90; Craton, *Sinews of Empire*, 207–13; Dunn, *Sugar and Slaves*, 250; Mintz and Price, *Birth of African-American Culture, passim*, esp. 2, 8, 15, 33, 39, 48, 52–53.

14. Franklin W. Knight, *Slave Society in Cuba during the Nineteenth Century* (Madison; 1970), 106; Herbert S. Klein, *Slavery in the Americas: A Comparative Study of Virginia and Cuba* (Chicago, 1967), 87–105; Jerome S. Handler, *The Unappropriated People: Freemen in the Slave Society of Barbados* (Baltimore, 1974), 92, 155–56, 161–65; Edward L. Cox, *Free Coloreds in the Slave Societies of St. Kitts and Grenada, 1763–1833* (Knoxville, 1984), 112–13; Oldendorp, *Geschichte der Mission der evangelischen Bruder*, 95–98; Hall, *Slave Society in the Danish West Indies*, 111–14; Craton, *Sinews of Empire*, 217; Dunn, *Sugar and Slaves*, 249; Richard Price, *Alabi's World* (Baltimore, 1990), 99; George Eaton Simpson, "The Belief System of Haitian Vodun," *American Anthropologist*, 47 (1945), 35 According to Roger Bastide, enslaved Africans newly arrived in Catholic America were required "only to learn a few prayers or ritual postures to be granted baptism." See his *African Civilisations in the New World*, 153.

15. [Lt. Brady], *Observations Upon the State of Negro Slavery in the Island of Santa Cruz, the Principal of the Danish West India Colonies; with Miscellaneous Remarks Upon Subjects Relating to the West India Question, and a Notice of Santa Cruz* (London, 1829), in Tyson and Highfield, eds. *Kamina Folk*, 172–74; Cox, *Free Coloreds in the Slave Societies of St. Kitts and Grenada*, 116–21; Hall, *Slave Society in the Danish West Indies*, 58, 81, 113; Philip D. Curtin, *Two Jamaicas: The Role of Ideas in a Tropical Colony*, 1830–65 (Cambridge, Mass., 1955), 35–37; Craton, *Sinews of Empire*, 219–20; Handler, *Unappropriated People*, 168; Gwendolyn Midlo Hall, *Social Control in Slave Plantation Societies: A Comparison of St. Domingue and Cuba* (Baltimore, 1971); Emilia Viotti da Costa, *Crowns of Glory, Tears of Blood: The Demerara Slave Rebellion of 1823* (New York, 1994), esp. ch. 1; Roger Anstey, "Slavery and the Protestant Ethic," in Michael Craton, ed., *Roots and Branches: Current Directions in Slave Studies* (Toronto, 1979), 173–77.

16. Charles Ball, *Slavery in the United States: A Narrative of the Life and Adventures of Charles Ball, A Black Man, Who Lived Forty Years in Maryland, South Carolina and Georgia, as a Slave* (New York, 1837), 164–65. On the presence of Muslims in the Caribbean, see da Costa, *Crowns of Glory, Tears of Blood*, 195; Bastide, *African Civilisations in the New World*, 105, and Craton, *Sinews of Empire*, 211. On the Islamic presence in the South Carolina and Georgia lowcountry, see Charles Joyner, " 'Believer I Know': The Emergence of African-American Christianity," 19–20; Savannah Writers Project, *Drums and Shadows: Survival Studies Among the Georgia Coastal Negroes* (Athens, 1940, rpt. 1986), 161, 166; and Alan D. Austin, *African Muslims in Antebellum America* (New York, 1984). Sterling Stuckey argues that "the great bulk of the slaves were scarcely touched by Christianity." See his *Slave Culture: Nationalist Theory and the Foundations of Black America* (New York, 1987), 37–38.

17. Or were Christian saints transubstantiated into African deities? Roger Bastide contends that such dances were "in fact addressed to African divinities." He considers this form of African-American Christianity to be "simply a mask put

over the black gods for the white man's benefit." See Bastide, *African Civilisations in the New World*, 156; Monica Schuler, *"Alas, Alas, Kongo": A Social History of Indentured African Immigration into Jamaica, 1841–1865* (Baltimore, 1980), 86. Sterling Stuckey argues that the distinctive attributes of African-American Christianity were outward and visible manifestations of inward and invisible African cognitive orientations. Most important, according to Stuckey, "by operating under cover of Christianity, vital aspects of Africanity, which were considered eccentric in movement, sound, or symbolism, could more easily be practiced openly." See his *Slave Culture*, 35–36, 57, 54. See also Mintz, *Caribbean Transformations*, 18; da Costa, *Crowns of Glory, Tears of Blood*, 146, 162, and Bastide, *African Civilisations in the New World*, 153, 164.

18. Mintz and Price, *Birth of African-American Culture*, 45; Bastide, *African Civilisations in the New World*, 103.

19. Albert Raboteau, "African-Americans, Exodus, and the American Israel," in *African-American Christianity*, 1–17; Joyner, *Down by the Riverside*, 141–171; Joyner, *Remember Me*, 35–44; Bastide, *African Civilisations in the New World*, 163.

20. John Lang's Diary, 1816, quoted in Brathwaite, *Development of Creole Society in Jamaica*, 219; Martha Warren Beckwith, *Black Roadways: A Study of Jamaican Folk Life* (Chapel Hill, N.C., 1929), chs. 2, 6; Brathwaite, *Development of Creole Society in Jamaica*, 219–25; and Bastide, *African Civilisations in the New World*, 180. John A. Lomax, Field Notes 1935–1937, John A. Lomax Papers, Archive of Folk Culture, Library of Congress; Bremer, *Homes in the New World*, I, 290; "Tom-toms Sound for Edisto Rites," in Murray Papers, South Carolina Historical Society; Smith, "A Plantation Boyhood," 75–76; Charlotte Forten, "Life on the Sea Islands," *Atlantic Monthly*, 13 (1864), 593–94, and *The Journal of Charlotte L. Forten*, ed. Ray L. Billington (New York, 1953), 153, 184, 190, 205; Zora Neale Hurston, "Shouting," in Nancy Cunard, ed., *Negro: An Anthology* (London, 1934), 49–50; Willie Lee Rose, *Rehearsal for Reconstruction: the Port Royal Experiment* (Indianapolis, 1964), 91; Mechal Sobel, *Trabelin' On: The Slave Journey to an Afro-Baptist Faith* (Westport, Conn., 1979); Erskine Clarke, *Wrestlin' Jacob: A Portrait of Religion in the Old South* (Atlanta, 1979); Lawrence W. Levine, *Black Culture and Black Consciousness: Afro-American Folk thought from Slavery to Freedom* (New York, 1978); 1–55; Raboteau, "African-Americans, Exodus, and the American Israel," 1–17. The importance of a continuing Yoruba and Ashanti influence and declining Bantu religious influence in African-American Christianity (despite Bantu demographic dominance) is discussed in Bastide, *African Civilisations in the New World*, 104–15.

The importance of "shouting" in African-American Christianity is underlined by an exchange between a Gullah preacher and a white folklorist in 1936. After a field trip to All Saints Parish in the South Carolina lowcountry for the Library of Congress, John Lomax wrote in his field notes, "Once I asked the Reverend Aaron Pinnacle of Heavens Gate Church, South Carolina, why he deliberately attempted in his sermons to influence his congregation to 'shout.'" The black minister responded to the white visitor, "If I did not preach shoutin' sermons, my congregation would pay me nothing." Lomax mused, "Even in religious matters, the economic factor is dominant. We can't get away from it." See John A. Lomax, Field Notes, 1935–1937, John A. Lomax Papers, Library of Congress.

21. Brathwaite, *Development of Creole Society in Jamaica*, 220; Bastide, *African Civilisations in the New World*, 91–92, 180; James Weldon Johnson Papers,

Beineke Library, Yale University; Norman E. Yetman, *Life Under the Peculiar Institution* (New York, 1971), 167; Benjamin A. Botkin, ed., *Lay My Burden Down: A Folk History of Slavery* (Chicago, 1945), 146. "Been in the Storm So Long: Spirituals, Folk Tales, and Children's Games from John's Island, South Carolina," Smithsonian Folkways CFS 40031; William F. Allen, Charles P. Ware, and Lucy M. Garrison, *Slave Songs of the United States* (Boston, 1867); Guy and Candie Carawan, *Ain't You Got a Right to the Tree of Life? The People of Johns Island, South Carolina* 2d ed., rev. (Athens, Ga., 1989).

22. The example given is an "antem" from the Bahamas. It was reported by L.D. Powles in *The Land of the Pink Pearl or Recollections of Life in the Bahamas* (London, 1888), 158–59. An almost identical spiritual was collected from Gullah singers on St. Helena Island in South Carolina in the 1860s. See William Francis Allen, Charles P. Ware, and Lucy McKim Garrison, eds., *Slave Songs of the United States* (New York, 1867), xiv; Thomas Wentworth Higginson, "Negro Spirituals," *Atlantic Monthly*, 19 (1867), 685–94, and his *Army Life in a Black Regiment* (Boston, 1870), 197–98; Elizabeth Ware Pearson, ed., *Letters from Port Royal* (Boston, 1906), 22–28; Rupert S. Holland, ed., *Letters and Diary of Laura M. Towne: Written from the Sea Islands of South Carolina, 1862–1884* (Cambridge, Mass., 1912), 20–23; Society for the Preservation of Spirituals, *The Carolina Low Country* (New York, 1931), 198–201; and Charles Joyner, *Folk Song in South Carolina* (Columbia, 1971), 86; Thurlow Weed, *Letters from Europe and the West Indies, 1843–1852* (Albany, 1866), in Tyson and Highfield, eds. *Kamina Folk*, 213–16.

23. Philip D. Curtin, *Two Jamaicas: The Role of Ideas in a Tropical Colony, 1830–65* (Cambridge, 1955), 29–32, 158–77; Orlando Patterson, *The Sociology of Slavery* (London, 1967), 185–95; Beckwith, *Black Roadways*; George E. Simpson, *The Shango Cult in Trinidad* (Puerto Rico, 1965). Joyner, *Down by the Riverside*, 144–53; "Truss Gawd or Ad's Plat Eye," collected by Genevieve Willcox Chandler, Murrells Inlet, South Carolina, WPA MSS, South Caroliniana Library, University of South Carolina, Columbia. "Memories of an Island," 90–94; "Conjure Horses Have Passed," "Edisto Treasure Tales Unfruitful," "Negroes Plagued by Edisto Ghosts," "Boo-Hags," "Conjer-Horses," and "Edisto Reveres Old Time Magic," in Chalmers S. Murray Papers, South Carolina Historical Society; MS vol., 10–17, 60–76, in John Bennett Papers, South Carolina Historical Society; Ben Washington, Eulonia, Georgia, in *Drums and Shadows*, 136; Henry C. Davis, "Negro Folk-Lore in South Carolina," *Journal of American Folklore*, 27 (1914), 247–248; Newbell Niles Puckett, *Folk Beliefs of the Southern Negro* (Chapel Hill, 1926), 130, 147; Ambrose E. Gonzales, *The Black Border: Gullah Stories of the Carolina Coast* (Columbia, 1922), 33; and William R. Bascom, "Acculturation Among the Gullah Negroes," *American Anthropologist*, 43 (1941), 49. Cf. E.E. Evans-Pritchard, *Theories of Primitive Religion* (London, 1965), 17; Bastide, *African Civilisations in the New World*, 108–10; Levine, *Black Culture and Black Consciousness*, 55–80. The term *zombi* in Haiti designates the "living dead," those whose souls have been eaten by sorcerers. The name comes from the Kongo *zumbi*, a revenant, or spirit of the dead, in a sense closer to the Gullah than to the Haitian usage. See Bastide, *African Civilisations in the New World*, 110.

24. Schuler, "*Alas, Alas, Kongo*". See also "Voodoo Survivals Traced on Edisto," "Tom-toms Sound for Edisto Rites," and "Edisto Reveres Old Time Magic," in Murray Papers, South Carolina Historical Society; James R. Sparkman, "The Negro," in Sparkman Family Papers, South Caroliniana Library, University

of South Carolina, Columbia (hereinafter abbreviated SCL). For a similar fragmentation of African religion in Jamaica, see Bastide, *African Civilisations in the New World*, 103. That all three streams should be considered aspects of slave religion is suggested by Anthony F.C. Wallace's definition of religion as "that kind of behavior which can be classified as belief and ritual concerned with supernatural beings, powers, and forces" in his *Religion: An Anthropological View* (New York, 1966), 5 and by Mary Douglas, in her *Edward Evans-Pritchard* (New York, 1980), 25–26.

25. Matthew Gregory Lewis, *Journal of a West India Proprietor, 1815–17*, (London, 1834, 1929), 85–86, 89–90, 286–87; Edwards, *History*, 2:84, 90, 95ff; Brathwaite, *Development of Creole Society*, 219; Handler, *Unappropriated People*, 154; Craton, *Sinews of Empire*, 366, 218; Patterson, *Sociology of Slavery*, 185–95; Mintz, *Caribbean Transformations*, 167–69. Historian Monica Schuler distinguishes between malign conjuration (obeah) and benign conjuration aimed at eradicating evil (myalism). See her *"Alas, Alas, Kongo"*, 41–42. Richard Price discusses benign conjuration to purify the community and protect it from evil among the Saramaka in his, *Alabi's World*, 36.

26. Michael Mullin argues that "Obeahmen and women were doctors in the Western sense of those who cured ostensibly by putting medicines on or in the body." See his *Africa in America: Slave Acculturation and Resistance in the American South and the British Caribbean, 1736–1831*, Blacks in the New World, ed. August Meier and John H. Bracey (Urbana, 1992), 175–76. See also Brathwaite, *Development of Creole Society in Jamaica*, 219, 252–65; George Eaton Simpson, *The Shango Cult in Trinidad* (Rio Piedras, Puerto Rico, 1965); Craton, *Sinews of Empire*, 218; Bastide, *African Civilisations in the New World*, 103.

27. Charles Leslie, *A New and Exact Account of Jamaica*, 3rd ed. (Edinburgh, 1740), 326–27; Sylvester Hovey, *Letters from the West Indies: relating especially to the Danish Island of St. Croix and to the British Islands of Antigua, Barbadoes and Jamaica* (New York, 1838), in Tyson and Highfield, eds. *Kamina Folk*, 191; Sir Hans Sloane, *A Voyage to the Islands: Madera, Barbados, Nieves, S. Christophers and Jamaica*, 2 vols. (London, 1707–1725), xlvii; William Beckford, *A Descriptive Account of the Island of Jamaica*, 2 vols. (London, 1790), 216–18; Carstens, *En Almindelig Beskrivelse om Alle de Danske, Americanske eller West-Indiske EyLande*, 14; Oldendorp, *Geschichte der Mission der evangelischen Bruder*, 89; Frances Anne Kemble, *Journal of a Residence on a Georgian Plantation in 1838–1839* (New York, 1863; Brown Thrasher ed., Athens, Ga., 1984), 141–42, 259–60; Savannah Unit, Federal Writers Project, *Drums and Shadows: Survival Studies Among the Georgia Coastal Negroes* Brown Thrasher ed. (Athens, 1940, rpt. 1987); Alexander Barclay, *A Practical View of the Present State of Slavery in the West Indies* (London, 1827), 10; Hall, *Slave Society in the Danish West Indies*, 115–19; Johan Christian Schmidt, "Blandede Anmaerkninger, samlede paa og over St. Croix i Amerika," *Samleren*, 2 (1788), in Tyson and Highfield, eds. *Kamina Folk*, 114–15; Reimert Haagensen, *Beskrivelse over Eylandet St. Croix i America i VestIndien* (Copenhagen, 1758), in Tyson and Highfield, eds. *Kamina Folk*, 46.

28. Diary of John Becker, December 25, 1812, quoted in Brathwaite, *Development of Creole Society in Jamaica*, 227; James Smith, *Winter of 1840 in St. Croix with an Excursion to Tortola and St. Thomas* (New York, 1840), in Tyson and Highfield, eds. *Kamina Folk*, 202; Craton, *Sinews of Empire*, 220; Dunn, *Sugar and Slaves*, 250; Price, *Alabi's World*, 308–9. The symbolic significance of drums

to both blacks and whites in South Carolina is illustrated in Edward G. Mason, "A Visit to South Carolina in 1860," *Atlantic Monthly*, 53 (1884), 244.

29. Denise Paulme, "Literature orde et comportements sociaux en Afrique noire," *L'homme*, 1 (1961), 37–49; Ruth Finnegan, *Oral Literature in Africa* (Oxford, 1970), 344–45; Bastide, *African Civilisations in the New World*, 61, 65, 179–80, 252.

30. Richard Robert Madden, *A Twelve Month's Residence in the West Indies, during the transition from slavery to apprenticeship*, 2 vols. (London, 1835), 2:153. The popularity of Anancy tales among African-Americans in the Caribbean is attested by Martha Beckwith, *Jamaica Anancy Stories* (New York, 1924), 219; Rev. Charles Daniel Dance, *Chapters from a Guianese Log-Book* (Demerara, 1881), 85–90; Walter Jeckyll, *Jamaica Song and Story* (London, 1907), 1–5; Mrs. Lanigan, *Antigua and the Antiguans* (London, 1844), 2, 115; Lewis, *Journal of a West India Proprietor*, 253–59, 290–96, 301–307; Mrs. Henry [Theodora] Lynch, *The Wonders of the West Indies* (London, 1856), 170–73; Henry G. Murray, *Manners and Customs of the Country a Generation Ago, Tom Kittles Wake* (Kingston, Jamaica, 1877), 25–29; Charles Rampini, *Letters from Jamaica: "The Land of Streams and Woods"* (Edinburgh, 1873), 115–28. See also Charles Joyner, "The Trickster and the Fool: Folktales and Identity among Southern Plantation Slaves," *Plantation Society in the Americas*, 2 (1986), 149–56; Charles Joyner, " 'ALL the Best Stories': Narrative and Identity on the Slave Plantation," in Reimund Kvideland and Torunn Selberg, eds., *The Eighth Congress of the International Society for Folk Narrative Research* (Bergen, Norway, 1984), I, 299–307; Joyner, *Down by the Riverside*, 30, 172–95; Roger D. Abrahams, "Trickster: The Outrageous Hero," in Tristram Potter Coffin, ed., *Our Living Traditions* (New York, 1968), 170; Levine, *Black Culture and Black Consciousness*, 81–135; Finnegan, *Oral Literature in Africa*, 81–135; Frederic G. Cassidy, *Jamaica Talk* (London, 1961), 275–76; Daniel J. Crowley, *I Could Talk Old-Story Good: Creativity in Bahamian Folklore* (New York, 1966), and Daniel J. Crowley, ed. *African Folklore in the New World* (Austin, 1977); Brathwaite, *Development of Creole Society in Jamaica*, 239; and Patterson, *Sociology of Slavery*, 249.

31. Richard Ligon, *A True and Exact History of the Island of Barbados* (London, 1657, 1673), 27, 31–33, 36; Edwards, *History*, 2: 164; Brady, *Observations Upon the State of Negro Slavery*, 161- 63; Haagensen, *Beskrivelse over Eylandet St. Croix*, 39; Oldendorp, *Geschichte der Mission der evangelischen Bruder*, 73; Hans West, *Bidrag til Beskrivelse over Ste. Croix med en Kort Udsigt over St. Thomas, St. Jean, Tortola, Spanishtown og Crabeneiland* (Copenhagen, 1793), in Tyson and Highfield, eds. *Kamina Folk*, 132–35; Charles Boudens, Vicomte de Vanderbourg, "Rapport sur l'etat present des Negres et sur les moyens de l'ameliorer," *Dokumenter vedrorende Kommissionen for Negerhandler Bedre Indretning og Ophoevelse, 1783–1806*, in Tyson and Highfield, eds. *Kamina Folk*, 154–56; A.J. Graham Knox, "Opportunities and Opposition: The Rise of Jamaica's Black Peasantry and the Nature of Planter Resistance," *Caribbean Review of Sociology and Anthropology*, 14:4 (1977), 386–7; da Costa, *Crowns of Glory, Tears of Blood*, 52–54; Hall, *Slave Society in the Danish West Indies*, 79–80, 121; Richard Orraca-Tetteh, Chair, Department of Nutrition, University of Ghana, to Charles Joyner, personal communication, May 30, 1991; Joyner, *Down by the Riverside*, 90–106; Charles Joyner, "Soul Food and the Sambo Stereotype: Foodlore from the Slave Narrative Collection," *Keystone Folklore Quarterly*, 16 (1971), 171–78; Bastide, *African Civilisations in the New World*, 90; Brathwaite, *Development of Creole*

Society in Jamaica, 235; Mintz, *Caribbean Transformations*, 11; Mintz and Price, *Birth of African-American Culture*, 33.

32. Edwards, *History*, 2: 163–64; Report of Sampson Wood, 1796, quoted in Jerome S. Handler and Frederick W. Lange, *Plantation Slavery in Barbados: An Archaeological and Historical Investigation* (Cambridge, Mass., 1978), 96–97; Oldendorp, *Geschichte der Mission der evangelischen Bruder*, 72–73; West, *Bidrag til Beskrivelse over Ste. Croix*, 139; Boudens, "Rapport sur l'etat present des Negres," 151; Brady, *Observations Upon the State of Negro Slavery*, 159–61; da Costa, *Crowns of Glory, Tears of Blood*, 151; Richard B. Sheridan, *Doctors and Slaves: A Medical and Demographic History of Slavery in the British West Indies, 1680–1834* (Cambridge, Eng., 1985), ch. 3; Hall, *Slave Society in the Danish West Indies*, 76–79; Mullin, *Africa in America*, 96–97. The "resilient stick and thatch construction" of the seventeenth-century huts, according to Richard Dunn, "enabled them to escape destruction in the catastrophic Port Royal earthquake of 1692. See his *Sugar and Slaves*, 186. On the creolization of slave architecture, see Joyner, *Down by the Riverside*, 117–26; John Michael Vlach, *Back of the Big House: The Architecture of Plantation Slavery* (Chapel Hill, 1993); George W. McDaniel, *Hearth and Home: Preserving a People's Culture* (Philadelphia, 1982); Leland Ferguson, *Uncommon Ground: Archaeology and Early African America* (Washington, D.C., 1992); Douglas V. Armstrong, *The Old Village and the Great House: An Archaeological and Historical Examination of Drax Hall Plantation, St. Ann's Bay, Jamaica*, a volume in the series Blacks in the New World, edited by August Meier (Urbana, 1991); Theresa A. Singleton, *The Archaeology of Slavery and Plantation Life* (Orlando, Fla., 1985); and her "The Archaeology of Slave Life", in *Before Freedom Came: African-American Life in the Antebellum South*, eds. Edward D.C. Campbell, Jr., and Kym S. Rice (Charlottesville, 1991), 155–75; and James L. Michie, *Richmond Hill Plantation, 1810–1868: The Discovery of Antebellum Life on a Waccamaw Plantation* (Spartanburg, S.C., 1990).

33. Carstens, *En Almindelig Beskrivelse om Alle de Danske, Americanske eller West Jndiske Ey-Lande*, 10; Joyner, *Down by the Riverside*, 90–126; *Richmond Hill Plantation*; John Michael Vlach, *By the Work of Their Hands: Studies in Afro-American Folklife* (Charlottesville, Va., 1991); Vlach, *Afro-American Tradition*, passim; Nan Tournier, "Sea Island Black Quilters," in Laurel Horton and Lynn T. Myers, eds., *Social Fabric: South Carolina's Traditional Quilts* (Columbia, 1984), 41–46; Maude Southwell Wahlman and Ella King Torrey, *Ten Afro-American Quilters* (Oxford, 1983); Dale Rosengarten, *Row Upon Row: Sea Grass Baskets in the South Carolina Lowcountry* (Columbia, 1986); Gerald L. Davis, "Afro-American Coil Basketry in Charleston County, South Carolina," in Don Yoder, ed., *American Folklife* (Austin, 1976), 151–84; Theresa Singleton, ed., *The Archaeology of Slavery and Plantation Life* (Orlando, Fl., 1985); Leland F. Ferguson, "Looking for the Afro- in Colono-Indian Pottery," *Conference on Historic Site Archaeology Papers*, 12 (1978), 68–86; and his *Uncommon Ground*; Jerome Handler and Frederick Lange, *Plantation Slavery in Barbados: An Archaeological and Historical Investigation* (Cambridge, Mass., 1978); Armstrong, *The Old Village and the Great House*.

34. James Weldon Johnson Papers, Beineke Library, Yale University; Mintz and Price, *Birth of African-American Culture*, 39; Bastide, *African Civilisations in the New World*, 88.

35. Ian Forster, *Guilty, No Chattels, To Be Hanged: the Story of Ann Forbes, First Fleet Convict* (Northbridge, NSW: 1991), 13–19.

Notes to THE PROBLEM OF RACE IN CUBA AND THE UNITED STATES
by Aline Helg

I would like to thank Diane M. Sommerville, Michael Hanchard, James Sid-
bury, Stanley L. Engerman, Daniel C. Littlefield, Marc C. McLeod, Omar Farouk
Roque, Milton Jamail, and Isabelle Leconte for their very helpful comments on
earlier drafts of this essay.

1. *La Discusión* (Havana), 28 June 1919.

2. *El Día* (Havana), 29 June 1919. See also *El Imparcial* (Havana), 28 June
1919; *El Mundo* (Havana), 29 June 1919. Not all Havana newspapers supported
the lynching: the pro-Spanish *Diario de la Marina* (Havana), for example, hoped
that for the sake of Cuban national honor, such an incident would not be repeated
(30 June 1919).

3. For estimates of lynching for alleged rape and sexual affront, see Ida B.
Wells, "A Red Record," in Ida B. Wells, *On Lynchings: Southern Horrors; A Red
Record; Mob Rule in New Orleans* (reprint; New York: Arno Press, 1969); National
Association for the Advancement of Colored People, *Thirty Years of Lynching in
the United States, 1889–1918* (New York: National Association for the Advancement of Colored People, 1919), 36; Stewart E. Tolnay and E. M. Beck, *A Festival
of Violence. An Analysis of Southern Lynchings, 1882–1930* (Urbana and Chicago:
University of Illinois Press, 1995), according to which, out of a total of 2,314 black
victims across the South in 1880–1930, 33.6 percent were lynched for alleged
sexual norm violation; 1.9 percent for alleged rape and murder; 37.3 percent for
presumed murder; 9.8 percent for presumed nonsexual assault; and 17.4 percent
for minor offenses or crossing the racial etiquette (pp. 48–49). Lynching in the
South was a very diverse phenomenon: for a discussion of regional differences
and time variations of lynching, see ibid., pp. 37–49; for a taxonomy of lynching,
see W. Fitzhugh Brundage, *Lynching in the New South. Georgia and Virginia,
1880–1930* (Urbana and Chicago: University of Illinois Press, 1992), pp. 19–44.

4. Estimates of the number of Afro-Cuban dead vary according to sources.
Official Cuban sources put it at more than 2,000. U.S. citizens living in Oriente
estimated it at 5,000 to 6,000. One Afro-Cuban survivor spoke of 5,000 dead (Ar-
royo to ministro de estado, 31 July 1912, Ministerio de Asuntos Exteriores, Madrid, Sección Histórica, legajo (herafter leg.) 1431; M. H. Lewis to Philander
Knox, 29 July 1912, National Archives of the United States, Washington, D.C.,
Record Group 59 [hereafter USNA, RG 59], 837.00/913; C. B. Goodrich to Lewis,
20 July 1912, USNA, RG 59, 837.00/911; Guillermo Laza to *La Discusión*, 3 August 1912. In contrast, the official figure for the total dead in the armed forces was
16, a figure that included 8 Afro-Cubans murdered by their white mates and some
shot by friendly fire (Rafael Conte, and José M. Capmany, *Guerra de razas (Negros
y blancos en Cuba)* [Havana: Imprenta Militar Antonio Pérez, 1912], pp. 100–01.

5. Most of the existing literature on Cuba and the United States analyzes
how Cuban relations with the United States worked to shape Cuban history. Although several studies compare the U.S. South with Brazil in order to understand
processes in slave and postslavery societies, very few compare the South with
Cuba. One exception is Rebecca J. Scott, "Defining the Boundaries of Freedom
in the World of Cane: Cuba, Brazil, and Louisiana after Emancipation," *American
Historical Review* 99 (February 1994), 70–102.

6. In the cases of Cuba and the U.S. South at the turn of the century, stereotyping corresponded to power relationships between whites and blacks expressed principally in racial terms, which explains my focus on racial stereotyping of blacks by whites. However, I do not deny that stereotyping is a fundamental process of human cognition and communication. I am aware that the dominated or the "others" also use stereotypes—often based on similar images—to represent the dominant group (but, because domination also means cultural power, these images are not allowed to prevail). I also acknowledge that the same stereotypes can be found to differentiate people belonging to the same "race," or sharing the same "skin color." Moreover, the same image can have different meanings and purposes over time. In fact, what is interesting about stereotypes is that they are not strictly determined by race, but rather by a conjunction of socioeconomic, cultural, and psychological factors that make them effective. For a theoretical discussion of stereotyping, see Jan Nederveen Pieterse, *White on Black. Images of Africa and Blacks in Western Popular Culture.* Translated from Dutch (New Haven and London: Yale University Press, 1992); J. William Harris, "Etiquette, Lynching, and Racial Boundaries: A Mississippi Example," *American Historical Review* 100 (April 1995), pp. 387–90; Sander L. Gilman, *Difference and Pathology. Stereotypes of Sexuality, Race, and Madness* (Ithaca: Cornell University Press, 1985), pp. 16–18.

7. These stereotypes came also with their antidotes: the stereotypes of the "good black." In contrast to the "bad black," he or she was joyful, childish, lazy but obedient and faithful. In the U.S. South he or she was incarnated in the desexualized characters of Rastus, Coon, Uncle, and Mammy; in Cuba in the "negrito" (the comic black), the "negro catedrático," (the pretentious, semi-educated black), the carnivalesque Congo, and the sensual and tragic "mulata." Although not analyzed here, these comforting stereotypes, which represented whites' idealized vision of racial domination, complemented the icons of fear of the black rapist and the black witch. See George M. Fredrickson, *The Black Image in the White Mind. The Debate on Afro-American Character and Destiny, 1817–1914* (1971; reprint, Middletown, CT: Wesleyan University Press, 1987), pp. 206–9, 285- 91; Donald Bogle, *Toms, Coons, Mulattoes, Mammies, and Bucks* (New York: Viking Press, 1973); Pieterse, *White on Black*, pp. 152–56; Vera M. Kutzinski, *Sugar's Secrets: Race and the Erotics of Cuban Nationalism* (Charlottesville, VA: The University Press of Virginia, 1993), pp. 42–44; Robin Dale Moore, "Nationalizing Blackness. Afrocubanismo and Artistic Revolution in Havana, 1920–1935 (Ph.D. diss., University of Texas, Austin, 1995), pp. 49–50; Rine Leal, *La selva oscura de los bufos a la neocolonia (Historia del teatro cubano de 1868 a 1902)* (Havana: Editorial Arte y Literatura, 1982), pp. 469–70, 476.

8. Laënnec Hurbon, *Le barbare imaginaire* (Paris: Editions du Cerf, 1988), pp. 84–98. For pre-nineteenth century U.S. beliefs about black male sexuality, see Winthrop D. Jordan, *White over Black. American Attitudes toward the Negro, 1550–1812* (Chapel Hill, NC: University of North Carolina Press, 1968), pp. 150–60.

9. Brundage, *Lynching in the New South*, pp. 82–83.

10. Brundage, *Lynching in the New South*, pp. 60–61, 71–72; Joel Williamson, *The Crucible of Race: Black-White Relations in the American South since Emancipation* (New York: Oxford University Press, 1984), pp. 111–39; Glenda Elizabeth

180 Notes to Pages 52–54

Gilmore, *Gender and Jim Crow: Women and the Politics of White Supremacy in North Carolina, 1896–1920* (Chapel Hill, NC: University of North Carolina Press, 1996), pp. 82–87; Gregory Lamont Mixon, "The Atlanta Riot of 1906" (Ph. D. diss., University of Cincinnati, 1989), pp. 463–509; Diane Miller Sommerville, "The Rape Myth in the Old South Reconsidered," *Journal of Southern History* 61 (August 1995): 486–87, 517–18.

11. Causa 139/1904, in Archivo Nacional de Cuba, Audiencia de la Havana (hereafter ANC, AH), leg. 627–10 (the file is incomplete and only contains fols. 1 and 200 to 700), fols. 214, 286, 295–98; *El Mundo*, 14 November 1904 to 1 December 1904. For a more detailed discussion of the case, see Aline Helg, *Our Rightful Share. The Afro-Cuban Struggle for Equality, 1886–1912* (Chapel Hill, NC: University of North Carolina Press, 1995), pp. 109–11.

12. Fernando Ortiz, *Hampa afrocubana. Los negros brujos (apuntes para un estudio de etnología criminal)* (1906; reprint, Madrid: Editorial América, [1917?]), pp. 355–57, 368- 402; Fernando Ortiz, "La tremenda expiación de un crimen," *El Mundo*, 5 January 1906. For an analysis of Fernando Ortiz's early racial thought see Aline Helg, "Race in Argentina and Cuba, 1880–1930: Theory, Policies, and Popular Reaction," in Richard Graham, ed., *The Idea of Race in Latin America, 1870–1940* (Austin, TX: University of Texas Press, 1990), pp. 52–53.

13. Cuba, *Jurisprudencia del Tribunal Supremo en materia criminal de 1o de julio a 31 de diciembre de 1905* (Havana: Imprenta y Papelería de Ramble, Bouza y Cía., 1913), pp. 290–304; *El Mundo*, 6 January 1906.

14. *El Mundo*, 13 December 1904. See also *La Discusión*, quoted in Ortiz, *Hampa afrocubana*, pp. 321–23. On the myth of cannibalism in Africa, see W. Arens, *The Man- Eating Myth. Anthropology and Anthropophagy* (New York: Oxford University Press, 1979), pp. 83–96; on European witchcraft and cannibalism, see H. R. Trevor-Roper, *The European Witch-Craze of the Sixteenth and Seventeenth Centuries and Other Essays* (New York: Harper & Row Publishers, 1969).

15. Author's interviews with late anthropologist Argelier León, Havana, 22 June 1987, and historian Enrique Sosa, Havana, 7 April 1988. See also the interesting discussion of the phenomenon by Ernesto Chávez Alvarez, who grew up in terror of the black witch, in his *El crimen de la niña Cecilia. La brujería en Cuba como fenómeno social (1902–1925)* (Havana: Editorial de Ciencias Sociales, 1991), pp. 1–4. For primary sources, see *La Discusión*, notably, 23 October 1909, 9 November 1909, late June 1919 to mid-August 1919; O. J. Sweet to the adjutant general, 13 October 1908, USNA, Records of the Provisional Government of Cuba, Record Group 199, entry 5, no. 248; León Primelles, *Crónica cubana 1919–1922. Menocal y la Liga nacional. Zayas y Crowder. Fin de la danza de los millones y reajuste* (Havana: Editorial Lex, 1957), pp. 134–37.

16. Finally, the schoolteacher herself put an end to the false reports in a public letter to newspaper editors (*La Discusión*, 26 May 1912 and 7 June 1912; *La Lucha* (Havana), 26 May 1912; *El Mundo*, 7 June 1912; *El Día*, 10 June 1912; Cuba, *Diario de Sesiones del Congreso. Cámara de Representantes* [9 June 1912], 2).

17. See, for example, *La Prensa* (Havana), 10 September 1915 to 5 October 1915; José Armando Plá, "El problema negro en su aspecto político," *La Antorcha* (Havana), 20 August 1918.

18. On the frequency of rapes, see Brundage, *Lynching in the New South*, pp. 61–62; Neil R. McMillen, *Dark Journey. Black Mississippians in the Age of Jim Crow* (Urbana and Chicago: University of Illinois Press, 1989), pp. 235–36; Gil-

more, *Gender and Jim Crow*, pp. 83–84, 86; Mixon, "The Atlanta Riot of 1906," pp. 476–80; Edward L. Ayers, *Vengeance and Justice. Crime and Punishment in the 19th-Century American South* (New York: Oxford University Press, 1984), p. 238; also Wilbur J. Cash, *The Mind of the South* (1941; reprint Garden City, NY: Doubleday and Company, Inc., 1954), pp. 124–25. On witchcraft-related crimes, see Helg, *Our Rightful Share*, p. 115. On witchcraft-related child murders, see Chávez, *El crimen de la niña Cecilia*, pp. 25–28; Chávez found eight cases of ritual child murders between 1902 and 1923; out of these, three were rapidly dismissed for being disguised into witchcraft rituals by murderous or negligent parents, three led to a verdict of not guilty for the alleged witches, one led to the massacre of all the alleged witches before trial (the case of Cecilia examined here), and one led to the legal execution of two alleged witches (the case of Zoila examined here). Nevertheless, the two last cases fueled fear of black murderous witchcraft among whites until at least the 1930s.

19. Richard Konetzke, ed., *Colección de documentos para la historia de la formación social de Hispanoamérica, 1493–1810*, 3 vols. (Madrid: Consejo Superior de Investigaciones Científicas, 1953), pp. 3:558, 572, 648. The Spanish legislation, however, authorized mutilation and castration, especially to punish runaway slaves (idem; and William F. Sharp, *Slavery on the Spanish Frontier. The Colombian Chocó, 1680–1810* [Norman, OK: University of Oklahoma Press, 1976], pp. 127–28). Translation of the penal code in force in Cuba and Puerto Rico, in USNA, Records of the Bureau of Insular Affairs, Record Group 350, entry 5, no. 3645.

20. Diane Miller Sommerville, "Rape, Race, and Castration in Slave Law in the Colonial and Early South," in Catherine Clinton and Michele Gillespie, eds., *The Devil's Lane. Sex and Race in the Early South* (New York: Oxford University Press, 1997), pp. 74–89; James Hugo Johnston, *Race Relations in Virginia and Miscegenation in the South, 1776–1860* (Amherst: University of Massachusetts Press, 1970), pp. 20–41, 257–63. For a different view, see Jordan, *White over Black*, pp. 154–58, 398.

21. George C. Wright, *Racial Violence in Kentucky, 1865–1940. Lynchings, Mob Rule, and "Legal Lynchings"* (Baton Rouge: Louisiana State University Press, 1990), pp. 43–46; Allen W. Trelease, *White Terror. The Ku Klux Klan Conspiracy and Southern Reconstruction* (New York: Harper and Row, Publishers, 1971), pp. xx–xxi, 322; Diane Miller Sommerville, "The Rape Myth Reconsidered: The Intersection of Race, Class and Gender in the American South, 1800–1877" (Ph. D. diss., Rutgers University, 1995), chapters 5 and 6; Laura F. Edwards, "Sexual Violence, Gender, Reconstruction, and the Extension of Patriarchy in Granville County, North Carolina," *The North Carolina Historical Review* 58:3 (July 1991): 237–60; Martha Hodes, "The Sexualization of Reconstruction Politics: White Women and Black Men in the South after the Civil War," in Johns C. Fout, and Maura Shaw Tantillo, eds., *American Sexual Politics. Sex, Gender, and Race since the Civil War* (1990; reprint, Chicago: University of Chicago Press, 1993), p. 73.

22. Bernabé Boza, *Mi diario de la guerra desde Baire hasta la intervención americana* (Havana: Imprenta La Propagandista, 1900), p. 85; Grover Flint, *Marching with Gómez. A War Correspondent's Filed Note-Book Kept During Four Months with the Cuban Army* (Boston: Lamson, Wolffe, and Co., 1898), pp. 47–48.

23. See Anne Llewellyn Barstow, *Witchcraze. A New History of the European Witch Hunts* (San Francisco: Pandora/Harper San Francisco, 1994), 78; Michael Taussig, *The Devil and Commodity Fetishism in South America* (Chapel Hill, NC, University of North Carolina Press, 1980), pp. 41–52; Lawrence W. Levine, *Black*

Culture and Black Consciousness. Afro-American Folk Thought from Slavery to Freedom (New York: Oxford University Press, 1978), pp. 55–80; Michael Mullin, *African in America. Slave Acculturation and Resistance in the American South and the British Caribbean, 1736–1831* (Urbana and Chicago: University of Illinois Press, 1992), pp. 185–86. In fact, in the sixteenth- and seventeenth-century Americas, the repression of witches was benign compared with the Central European witchhunt that brought thousands (most of them poor women) to the stake. In Spain itself, although thousands of alleged witches were persecuted by the Inquisition, only a handful were executed, a fact that contributes to explain the low level of witch repression in Spanish America (Barstow, *Witchcraze*; Julio Caro Baroja, *El mundo de las brujas* [Madrid: Revista de Occidente, 1961]; Brian Easlea, *Witch Hunting, Magic and the New Philosophy: An Introduction to Debates of the Scientific Revolution 1450–1750* [London: Harvester Wheatsheaf, 1980]; Brian P. Levack, *The Witch-Hunt in Early Modern Europe* [London and New York: Longman, 1987]; and Trevor-Roper, *The European Witch-Craze*).

24. Cuban newspapers in 1890–1897 seldom mention witchcraft and only about harmless cases. There is no mention of witchcraft and African traditions in United States, *Civil Report of Mayor General John R. Brooke, U.S. Army, Military Governor, Island of Cuba*, 3 vols. (Havana: n.p., 1899), and in United States, *Civil Report of Brigadier General Wood, Military Governor of Cuba, for the Period from January 1 to May 20, 1902*, 6 vols. (Washington, DC: Government Printing Office, 1902). See also Chávez, *El crimen de la niña Cecilia*, p. 26.

25. Robert L. Paquette, *Sugar Is Made with Blood: The Conspiracy of La Escalera and the Conflict between Empires over Slavery in Cuba* (Middletown, CT: Wesleyan University Press, 1988), pp. 229, 242–43.

26. J. W. Harris, "Etiquette, Lynching, and Racial Boundaries," p. 390.

27. James Elbert Cutler, *Lynch-Law. An Investigation into the History of Lynching in the United States* (1905; reprint, Montclair, NJ: Patterson Smith, 1969), pp. 41–154; Bertram Wyatt-Brown, *Southern Honor: Ethic and Behavior in the Old South* (New York: Oxford University Press, 1982), pp. 425–93; Jacquelyn Dowd Hall, *Revolt against Chivalry: Jessie Daniel Ames and the Women's Campaign against Lynching* (New York: Columbia University Press, 1979), pp. 130–31; Sommerville, "The Rape Myth Reconsidered," pp. 413–16, 475–77.

28. Tolnay and Beck, *A Festival of Violence*, p. 23.

29. Brundage, *Lynching in the New South*, p. 36. For other descriptions of gruesome lynchings, see Wells, "A Red Record"; NAACP, *Thirty Years of Lynching*, pp. 11–28; Wright, *Racial Violence in Kentucky*, pp. 80–81, 90–95; Trudier Harris, *Exorcising Blackness. Historical and Literary Lynching and Burning Rituals* (Bloomington, IN: Indiana University Press, 1984), p. 2; Williamson, *The Crucible of Race*, pp. 185–86.

30. Brundage, *Lynching in the New South*, pp. 37–38; Gilmore, *Gender and Jim Crow*, pp. 82–89; Wright, *Racial Violence in Kentucky*, pp. 82–95; Jacquelyn Dowd Hall, " 'The Mind That Burns in Each Body': Women, Rape, and Racial Violence," in Ann Snitow, Christine Stansell, and Sharon Thompson, eds., *Powers of Desire. The Politics of Sexuality* (New York: Monthly Review Press, 1983), p. 330.

31. Brundage, *Lynching in the New South*, p. 18; also ibid., p. 39.

32. See Tolnay and Beck, *A Festival of Violence*, p. 23; Wright, *Racial Violence in Kentucky*, pp. 90–95; Williamson, *The Crucible of Race*, pp. 188–89. For a

general discussion of mass mob lynching, see Tolnay and Beck, *A Festival of Violence*, pp. 36–44.

33. Mixon, "The Atlanta Riot of 1906," pp. 486, 529. On the role of the white press in the 1898 Wilmington riot, see H. Leon Prather, Sr. *We Have Taken a City. Wilmington Racial Massacre and Coup of 1898* (Rutherford: Associated University Press, Inc., 1984), pp. 52–55, 68, 81, 107.

34. Paul A. Gilje, *Rioting in America* (Bloomington, IN: Indiana University Press, 1996), pp. 89–115; Williamson, *The Crucible of Race*, pp. 189–223; Mixon, "The Atlanta Riot of 1906," pp. 531–32, 483–86, 523–36; Prather, *We Have Taken a City*; Wright, *Racial Violence in Kentucky*, pp. 10–11, 137–54.

35. For the repression against the Independent Party of Color before 1912, see Helg, *Our Rightful Share*, chapter 6. For casual reports of alleged interracial rape and sex, see *La Discusión*, June-July 1902. During the height of the repression against the Independent Party of Color, however, several minor incidents between black men and white women could be perceived as an assault against white women. In summer 1912, for example, one "insolent black" was sentenced to 180 days' imprisonment because "he managed to press his thick lips on the rosy cheeks" of a white girl (Causa 602/1912, ANC, AH, leg. 216–1; Causa 613/1912, ANC, AH, leg. 216–1; Causa 45/1912, ANC, AH, leg. 476–4; *La Discusión*, 24 July 1912, p. 2, 25 July 1912, p. 1, 27 July 1912, p. 1).

36. Armed protest was used as a means of forcing the government into concessions by several other political groups in early independent Cuba, notably by the National Council of Veterans (of the War for Independence) in 1911 (see Bartolomé Sagaró Benítez, in Cuba, *Diario de Sesiones del Congreso. Cámara de Representantes* [30 April 1913], 21–22; also Helg, *Our Rightful Share*, pp. 188–89, 232–34).

37. Francisco M. Duque, *Historia de Regla. Descripción política, económica y social, desde su fundación hasta el día* (Havana: Imprenta y Papelería de Rambla, Bouza y Cía., 1925), pp. 127–128.

38. *La Discusión*, 19 June 1912.

39. For graphic descriptions of the racist massacre of 1912 by foreign observers, see Mason to Leech, 12 June 1912, Public Record Office, London, Foreign Office Papers (herafter noted PRO, FO) 277/183, no. 95; Henri Bryois to de Clercq, 12 and 14 June 1912, Ministère des Affaires Etrangères, Paris, Archives Diplomatiques, Cuba, Nouvelle Série, Box 27, Indemnités cubaines, 1908–1918, Dossiers particuliers; Rand to Department of State, 10 June 1912, USNA, RG 59, 837.00/728; G. C. Peterson to M. H. Lewis, 14 June 1912, USNA, RG 59, 837.00/834; Bayliss to Beaupré, 15 June 1912, USNA, RG 59, 837.00/827, encl. no. 2; C. B. Goodrich to Lewis, 21 June 1912, USNA, RG 59, 837.00/848; Commanding officer USS Petrel to secretary of the navy, 17 July 1912, USNA, RG 59, 837.00/908. On the army testing of new armament, see *La Discusión*, 28 and 29 May 1912, 1 and 2 June 1912; Mason to Leech, 1 June 1912, PRO, FO 277/183, no. 74; Beaupré to secretary of state, 4 June 1912, USNA, RG 59, 837.00/711.

40. *La Discusión*, 7 June 1912. See also ibid., 6 to 11 June 1912.

41. Ibid., 14 June 1912.

42. *El Día*, 8 July 1912. For another bloody cartoon, see *La Política Cómica* (Havana), 14 July 1912.

43. *La Discusión*, 28 May 1912, p. 2, and 4 June 1912, p. 1. Also Brooks to Leech, 23 May 1912, PRO, FO 277/183, no. 63. For a similar accusation during

the 1910 repression against the party, see *Diario de la Marina* quoted in Causa 321/1910, ANC, AH, leg. 228–1, fol. 1234.

44. In this article witchcraft (in Spanish: *brujería*) is defined as the complex use of plants and animals, incantation, and/or the exercise of supernatural powers to heal, protect, or harm people.

45. See for example X.X.X., *La brujería y los brujos de Cuba* (Havana: Imprenta de "El Cubano," 1900); Ortiz, *Hampa afrocubana*; and cases in the Havana newspapers *El Mundo, La Discusión,* and *La Lucha.*

46. Chávez, *El crimen de la niña Cecilia*, pp. 16–32. According to Chávez, there were then and still continue to be two versions of the crime: a white version discussed here, according to which Cecilia was killed by black witches, and a black version, according to which the almost white Cecilia was not the daughter of her mulatto father, but the illegitimate child of her mulatto mother and her Spanish lover. Cecilia had not been killed but secretly taken to Spain by her biological father in order to avoid scandal. The black version, informed by slavery and postslavery exploitative sexual relationships, deserves further analysis.

47. *El Día,* 24 to 30 June 1919; *La Discusión,* 28 and 30 June 1919, 8 July 1919. See also Chávez, *El crimen de la niña Cecilia*, pp. 16–32.

48. *La Discusión,* 30 June 1919. See also *El Día,* 28 June 1919. For a similar message written in the wake of Zoila's murder, see *El Mundo,* 2 December 1904.

49. See *El Día,* 28 June 1919 and 1 July 1919; *La Discusión,* 30 June 1919. On the antiblack terror in Matanzas after the disappearance of Cecilia, see Chávez, *El crimen de la niña Cecilia*, pp. 59–192.

50. Among the eight cases of alleged witchcraft-related child murders found by Chávez, the last two, in 1922–23, targeted Afro-Caribbean alleged witches in the province of Camagüey, where Afro-Caribbean migration of seasonal sugar workers was particularly numerous (Chávez, *El crimen de la niña Cecilia*, pp. 37–38; see also note 17).

51. It is remarkable, in particular, that after the discovery of the body of Zoila in 1904, the local whites, furious that the "witches" they held responsible for the murder had been first released from prison for lack of evidence, did not take justice into their hands. Instead, they sent a 50-man commission on horseback to the district court to demand that a special judge be assigned to the case, which was granted to them (*El Mundo,* 30 November 1904).

52. Helg, *Our Rightful Share*, pp. 114–15.

53. After independence in Cuba, the Spanish penal code, which increased liability when a crime was committed by a person of color against a white, remained in force, but there is no historical study that documents the racial biases of Cuban justice. In the postbellum South, the Black Codes that included different capital statuses for blacks and whites disappeared, but many southern states broadened their capital statuses to include crimes that had previously been capital offenses only for blacks. This provided a legal framework in which differential application of the death penalty could continue. For example, in some states, the punishment for rape or attempted rape ranged from a five-year prison term to death, but the latter was almost exclusively applied to black men accused of raping or attempting to rape white women (William J. Bowers, *Legal Homicide: Death as Punishment in America, 1864–1982* [Boston: Northeasten University Press, 1984], pp. 67–87; Sommerville, "The Rape Myth Reconsidered," pp. 403–407. A few figures illustrate the racial biases of Southern justice: between 1882 and 1930, 1,977 blacks—in comparison with 451 whites—were legally executed in the South

(Tolnay and Beck, *A Festival of Violence*, 100). See also Donald H. Partington, "The Incidence of the Death Penalty for Rape in Virginia," *Washington and Lee Law Review* 22 (1965), pp. 43, 52–54. In 1890, the Convict Lease System comprised a total of about 27,000 inmates, in their overwhelming majority blacks (Ayers, *Vengeance and Justice*, pp. 197–99, 212).

54. Michel Foucault, *Discipline and Punish. The Birth of the Prison*. Transl. from the French by Alan Sheridan (1977; reprint, New York: Vintage Books, 1979), p. 11; also p. 73.

55. See Ayers, *Vengeance and Justice*.

56. Ibid., pp. 49–56; Hall, *Revolt against Chivalry*, p. 136; Harris, *Exorcising Blackness*, pp. 2, 8–9; McMillen, *Dark Journey*, pp. 233–34; Tolnay and Beck, *A Festival of Violence*, p. 23; Williamson, *The Crucible of Race*, pp. 183–89.

57. *La Discusión*, 1 June 1912.

58. As the already cited editorialist of the murder of Cecilia put it, the lynching of the alleged witches would be "a 'cleaning stain' " necessary to reconstitute "our national ensign ("*La Discusión*, 30 June 1919). Similarly, in 1912 the Cuban president called on volunteers to "fight the rebellion of the liberticides who dishonor the republic," and editorialists and cartoonists justified the unrestricted use of violence to defend the Cuban "national contribution and heritage against [the Independents'] atavistic upsurge of savage instincts and inclinations" (*La Discusión*, 8 June 1912; *El Día*, 26 May 1912).

59. For a discussion of Cuba's two-tier racial system as a singularity in Latin America and the Caribbean, see Aline Helg, "Race and Black Mobilization in Colonial and Early Independent Cuba: A Comparative Perspective," in *Ethnohistory* 44 (Winter 1997): 53–74.

60. Wells, "A Red Record"; Brundage, *Lynching in the New South*, pp. 49, 80–82; McMillen, *Dark Journey*, 29–31, 229, 236; Tolnay and Beck, *A Festival of Violence*, pp. 19–21.

61. Helg, *Our Rightful Share*, pp. 212–18.

62. See for example the following judicial cases against alleged witches in ANC, AH, Causa 258/1902, leg. 214–5; Causa 628/1902, leg. 734–2; Causa 256/1903, leg. 703–4; Causa 21/1906, leg. 459–5; Causa 468/1909, leg. 213–5; Causa 261/1910, leg. 205–10; Causa 170/1911, leg. 459–4; Causa 1009/1913, leg. 716–15; Causa 310/1915, leg. 781–9; *La Discusión*, 16 February 1911; cases recorded throughout Cuba between September 1902 and September 1905 in Ortiz, *Hampa afrocubana*, pp. 300, 310, 318, 327, 333, 341, 346–47; Cuba, *Jurisprudencia*, pp. 302–04.

63. Ayers, *Vengeance and Justice*, p. 237; Helg, *Our Rightful Share*, pp. 105–6. See also Lawrence J. Friedman, *The White Savage. Racial Fantasies in the Postbellum South* (Englewood Cliffs, NJ: Prentice-Hall, Inc., 1970), p. v.

64. Prather, *We Have Taken a City*, pp. 22–26; Mixon, "The Atlanta Riot of 1906," pp. 29–31, 46, 59–60, 97; Gilmore, *Gender and Jim Crow*, pp. 4–18.

65. See, for example, the Afro-Cuban newspapers *El Nuevo Criollo* (Havana), *Previsión*, and *La Antorcha* (Havana). Also Helg, *Our Rightful Share*, pp. 118–24; Thomas T. Orum, "The Politics of Color: The Racial Dimension of Cuban Politics During the Early Republican Years, 1900–1912" (Ph.D. diss., New York University, 1975), pp. 71–72, 76, 81–86.

66. Ayers, *Vengeance and Justice*, p. 250; Mixon, "The Atlanta Riot of 1906," pp. 59–61.

67. Mixon, "The Atlanta Riot of 1906," pp. 125–26, 140–41.

68. Gilmore, *Gender and Jim Crow*, p. 83. See also Nancy MacLean, *Behind the Mask of Chivalry. The Making of the Second Ku Klux Klan* (New York: Oxford University Press, 1994), pp. 141–44.

69. Helg, *Our Rightful Share*, pp. 49–51, 78–82.

70. For a discussion of racial inequality in postindependence Cuba, see Helg, *Our Rightful Share*, pp. 98–103. For a discussion of the party's importance, see ibid., pp. 147–59.

71. Acto de procesamiento del 25 abril 1910, Causa 321/1910, ANC, AH, leg. 228–1, fol. 427; K. Rillo, "Cuando un negro monta en coche," *Previsión* (Havana), 20 February 1910; "Cinematógrafo cubano," ibid., 25 February 1910; "Somos racistas de amor," ibid., 5 November 1909; "Baterías de rebote," ibid., 30 September 1908.

72. Mixon, "The Atlanta Riot of 1906," p. 375; Hall, " 'The Mind That Burns in Each Body'," p. 334; Helg, *Our Rightful Share*, pp. 135–37.

73. Tolnay and Beck, *A Festival of Violence*, pp. 32–34, 111–13, 157–60.

74. McMillen, *Dark Journey*, pp. 3–5, 10, 12, 29, 127, 203.

75. Cuba, *Diario de Sesiones del Senado* (sessions from 19 September 1904 to 19 October 1904) 5, nos. 21–28 (January 1909); Louis A. Pérez, Jr., *Cuba under the Platt Amendment, 1902–1934* (Pittsburgh: University of Pittsburgh Press, 1986), p. 78.

76. Helg, *Our Rightful Share*, pp. 224–25.

77. Williamson, *The Crucible of Race*, pp. 249–58; McMillen, *Dark Journey*, pp. 3–5; Ted Ownby, *Subduing Satan. Religion, Recreation, and Manhood in the Rural South, 1865–1920* (Chapel Hill, NC: University of North Carolina Press, 1990), pp. 136–37. For a socioeconomic perspective, see Jay R. Mandle, "Black Economic Entrapment after Emancipation in the United States," in Frank McGlynn and Seymour Drescher, eds., *The Meaning of Freedom. Economics, Politics, and Culture after Slavery* (Pittsburgh: University of Pittsburgh Press, 1992), pp. 69–84.

78. Helg, *Our Rightful Share*, pp. 99–103.

79. Cash, *The Mind of the South*, p. 126; Friedman, *The White Savage*, pp. 78–97; Nell Irvin Painter, " 'Social Equality,' Miscegenation, Labor, and Power," in Numan V. Bartley, ed., *The Evolution of Southern Culture* (Athens and London: University of Georgia Press, 1988), pp. 53–54; Robert C. McMath, Jr., *American Populism. A Social History, 1877–1898* (New York: Hill and Wang, 1993), pp. 92–93, 171–74; Gerald H. Gaither, *Blacks and the Populist Revolt. Ballots and Bigotry in the "New South"* (University, AL: The University of Alabama Press, 1977), pp. 67–71, 75–76; Mcmillen, *Dark Journey*, p. 8. For a less critical view on Populism, see Vann C. Woodward, *Origins of the New South, 1877–1913* (1951; reprint, Baton Rouge, LA: Louisiana State University Press, 1980).

80. Cuba, *Diario de Sesiones del Congreso de la República de Cuba. Senado* 15:32 (16 February 1910), 3–7.

81. McMillen, *Dark Journey*, pp. 134–35, 172–94, 288–94, 302–08, 314; Brundage, *Lynching in the New South*, pp. 183–86, 203–06, 225–31; Wright, *Racial Violence in Kentucky*, pp. 169–72.

82. See *Previsión*, "El nivel intelectual de los negros cubanos y americanos," 28 October 1909; "Linchamiento moral," ibid., 25 November 1909; "Como llegan, como nos empujan," ibid., 15 December 1909. Some Afro-Cuban leaders were in contact with their peers in the U.S. South; several members of Durham black

bourgeoisie, for example, visited *Previsión* during a leisure trip to Havana ("Agradable visita," ibid., 25 January 1910).

83. Gilmore, *Gender and Jim Crow*, pp. 94–96.

84. Juan Pérez de la Riva, "Cuba y la migración antillana, 1900–1931," in *La república neocolonial. Anuario de estudios cubanos* 2 (Havana: Editorial de Ciencias Sociales, 1979); Juan Pérez de la Riva, "Los recursos humanos de Cuba al comenzar el siglo: inmigración, economía y nacionalidad (1899–1906)," in *La república neocolonial. Anuario de estudios cubanos* 1 (Havana: Editorial de Ciencias Sociales, 1975).

85. United States, War Department, *Censo de la república de Cuba bajo la administración provisional de los Estados Unidos, 1907* (Washington, DC: Government Printing Office, 1908).

86. Gilmore, *Gender and Jim Crow*, pp. 22–24, 72, 95, 131–33; Nancy Mac-Lean, "The Leo Frank Case Reconsidered: Gender and Sexual Politics in the Making of Reactionary Populism," *Journal of American History* 78:3 (December 1991): 921–22; Ayers, *Vengeance and Justice*, pp. 185–222; Mixon, "The Atlanta Riot of 1906," p. 105; Tolnay and Beck, *A Festival of Violence*, pp. 213–14; Brundage, *Lynching in the New South*, pp. 113–15, 123; Steven Hahn, *The Roots of Southern Populism. Yeoman Farmers and the Transformation of the Georgia Upcountry, 1850–1890* (New York: Oxford University Press, 1983), pp. 178–79.

87. Gilmore, *Gender and Jim Crow*, pp. 65–67, 94–96; Brundage, *Lynching in the New South*, pp. 5, 59; McMillen, *Dark Journey*, pp. 234–35.

88. Miguel Barnet, *Gallego* (Havana: Letras Cubanas, 1983). On Argentina, see Helg, "Race in Argentina and Cuba," p. 46.

89. Gilmore, *Gender and Jim Crow*; Hall, *Revolt against Chivalry*, pp. 78–82; Hall, "'The Mind That Burns in Each Body'," pp. 332–33; United States, War Department, *Censo de la república de Cuba, 1907*; "El trato social. La mujer," *Previsión*, 20 December 1909; Helg, *Our Rightful Share*, p. 132.

90. See Hall, *Revolt against Chivalry*; Wyatt-Brown, *Southern Honor*. For a criticism of these works, see Ayers, *Vengeance and Justice*, pp. 241, 250; Brundage, *Lynching in the New South*, pp. 11–12.

91. See Verena Martinez-Alier, *Marriage, Class and Colour in Nineteenth-Century Cuba. A study of Racial Attitudes and Sexual Values in a Slave Society* (1974; reprint: Ann Arbor, MI: University of Michigan Press, 1989).

92. According to this line of interpretation, the roots of lynching and the myth of the black rapist reside in whites' sexual tensions. Whites projected forbidden sexual fantasies onto blacks by creating the image of the black rapist. Black males embodied the sexual liberation white males could not achieve without guilt, and in the lynching of black men, white males symbolically killed their frustrated fantasies (see Williamson, *The Crucible of Race*, p. 308; T. Harris, *Exorcising Blackness*, pp. 19–24).

93. Hazel V. Carby, "'On the Threshold of Woman's Era': Lynching, Empire, and Sexuality in Black Feminist Theory," in Henry Louis Gates, Jr., ed. *"Race," Writing, and Difference* (Chicago: University of Chicago Press, 1986), pp. 307–09; Helg, *Our Rightful Share*, pp. 18, 27; Martinez-Alier, *Marriage, Class and Colour*, pp. 115–18; Kutzinski, *Sugar's Secrets*, pp. 17–80.

94. Hodes, "The Sexualization of Reconstruction Politics," p. 70; McMillen, *Dark Journey*, p. 16; Trelease, *White Terror*, pp. 322–23; Sommerville, "The Rape Myth Reconsidered," pp. 378–83.

95. United States, War Department, *Censo de la república de Cuba, 1907*, pp.

419–51. On continuing literary representations of women of African descent as sexual objects and the construction of Cuba's ideology of *mestizaje* (racial mixture) after the 1920s, see Kutzinski, *Sugar's Secrets*, pp. 163–92.

96. Barnet, *Gallego*. The parish of Bejucal near Havana, for example, kept separate marriage registers for whites and persons of color until 1929, and the parish of Nuestra Señora del Pilar in Havana did so until 1917; both included marriages of Spaniards with Afro-Cuban women in the registers for persons of color (Archivo parroquial de Bejucal, Libro tercero de matrimonios de pardos y morenos, 1888–1929; Archivo parroquial de Nuestra Señora del Pilar, Barrio del Pilar, La Habana, Libro primero de matrimonios de personas de color, 1889–1917).

97. Hodes, "The Sexualization of Reconstruction Politics," pp. 59–60; Sommerville, "The Rape Myth Reconsidered," pp. 459–64; Martinez-Alier, *Marriage, Class and Colour*, pp. 14–19, 22–26.

98. Hodes, "The Sexualization of Reconstruction Politics," pp. 60–61; qualified by Sommerville, "The Rape Myth Reconsidered," pp. 460–61, 477–81.

99. Hodes, "The Sexualization of Reconstruction Politics," pp. 60–61, 67; J. W. Harris, "Etiquette, Lynching, and Racial Boundaries," p. 392; Mcmillen, *Dark Journey*, 14–19; Brundage, *Lynching in the New South*, p. 62.

100. Mcmillen, *Dark Journey*, pp. 8, 15.

101. Causa 170/1911, ANC, AH, leg. 459–4; Ortiz, *Hampa afrocubana*, p. 328; *La Lucha*, 7 and 28 July 1902; *La Discusión*, 5 July 1902.

102. On African-American attitudes toward racial mixture, see Eric Anderson, *Race and Politics in North Carolina, 1872–1902* (Baton Rouge: Louisiana State University Press, 1981), p. 281; Friedman, *The White Savage*, p. 141; Gilmore, *Gender and Jim Crow*, pp. 70–71. On Afro-Cubans, see Helg, *Our Rightful Share*, pp. 18, 27; Martinez-Alier, *Marriage, Class and Colour*, pp. 115–18.

103. In 1898, for example the claim by a local African-American journalist that lynching was caused by white women being attracted to black men served as the catalyst of the riot against blacks in Wilmington, North Carolina (Prather, *We Have Taken a City*, pp. 68–86). The 1921 riot in Tulsa, Oklahoma was ignited by an inflammatory editorial on a trivial incident involving a white woman and a black man (ibid., pp. 168–69).

104. Representative of Cuban attitude toward sexual relationships between black men and white women, in Matanzas the grandmother of a white teenage girl who was the lover of a man of color did not kill the black man but strangled the baby born out of their union (*La Lucha*, 7 July 1902).

105. Hahn, *The Roots of Southern Populism*, pp. 153–55, 169–76; McMath, *American Populism*, pp. 30–33.

106. Jorge Ibarra, *Cuba: 1898–1921. Partidos políticos y clases sociales* (Havana: Editorial de Ciencias Sociales, 1992), pp. 66–108.

107. Eric Foner, *Reconstruction. America's Unfinished Revolution, 1863–1877* (New York: Harper & Row, Publishers, 1988), pp. 303–07; Hahn, *The Roots of Southern Populism*, pp. 108–10, 123–32; Leon F. Litwack, *Been in the Storm so Long: The Aftermath of Slavery* (New York: Knopf, 1979), pp. 489, 546; Williamson, *The Crucible of Race*, pp. 79–80.

108. Louis A. Pérez, Jr., *Cuba between Empires, 1878–1902* (Pittsburgh: University of Pittsburgh Press, 1983).

109. Hahn, *The Roots of Southern Populism*, pp. 212–13; Tolnay and Beck, *A*

Festival of Violence, pp. 6–14, 170–80; Gaither, *Blacks and the Populist Revolt*, pp. 66–78; Friedman, *The White Savage*, pp. 78–97.

110. Gilmore, *Gender and Jim Crow*, pp. 91–92, 98. Also Cash, *The Mind of the South*, pp. 175–79.

111. Symptomatic of white Northerners' receptivity to southern views of blacks as brutes and rapists was the former's enthusiastic reception of the film *The Birth of a Nation* in 1915 (Thomas Cripps, *Slow Fade to Black. The Negro in American Film, 1900–1942* [New York: Oxford University Press, 1977], pp. 41–69).

112. Brundage, *Lynching in the New South*, p. 10; Hall, *Revolt against Chivalry*, pp. 132–36; J. W. Harris, "Etiquette, Lynching, and Racial Boundaries," pp. 393–94; Mixon, "The Atlanta Riot of 1906," pp. 367–68; Mcmillen, *Dark Journey*, pp. 238–39, 245–49; Tolnay and Beck, *A Festival of Violence*, pp. 27, 32–34, 111–13, 157–60. See also Woodward, *Origins of the New South*; McMath, *American Populism*.

113. Gustavo Enrique Mustelier, *La extinción del negro. Apuntes político-sociales* (Havana: Imprenta y Papelería de Rambla, Bouza y Cía., 1912), pp. 63, 65. For a similar opinion see José Sixto de Sola, "El pesimismo cubano," *Cuba Contemporánea* 3 (December 1913): 273–303; Pelayo Pérez, "El peligro amarillo y el peligro negro," *Cuba Contemporánea* 9 (November 1915): 258–50.

114. Helg, *Our Rightful Share*, pp. 213–18, 222, 228.

115. Ibid., pp. 96, 99–102, 127–28, 188.

116. On Cuban white elite perception of North Americans see Fernando Ortiz, "Las dos barajas," in Fernando Ortiz, *Entre cubanos* (1914[?]; reprint, Havana: Editorial de Ciencias Sociales, 1987), pp. 102–04; Fernando Ortiz, *La crisis política (sus causas y remedios)* (Havana: Imprenta y Papelería "La Universal," 1919), pp. 16–20; José Antonio Ramos, *Entreactos* (Havana: R. Veloso Editores, 1913), p. 111; José Sixto de Sola, "Los extranjeros en Cuba," *Cuba Contemporánea* 8 (June 1915): 105–09. See also Ann Wright, "Intellectuals of an Unheroic Period of Cuban History, 1913–1923. The 'Cuba Contemporánea' Group," *Bulletin of Latin American Research* 7 (1988): 109–22.

117. See for example Andrew S. Draper, *The Rescue of Cuba. An Episode in the Growth of Free Government* (New York: Silver, Burdett and Co., 1899), pp. 176–80; Leland Hamilton Jenks, *Our Cuban Colony. A Study in Sugar* (New York: Vanguard Press, 1928), pp. 62, 65; Irene A. Wright, *Cuba* (New York: Macmillan, 1910), pp. 83, 88.

118. Conte and Capmany, *Guerra de razas*, pp. 11, 119.

119. See, for example, in chronological order, *El Mundo*, 18 December 1904; *El Día*, 27 May 1912; Conte and Capmany, *Guerra de razas*, p. 119; Carlos de Velasco, "El problema negro," *Cuba Contemporánea* 1 (February 1913), 79; Sola, "El pesimismo cubano," 294, 301; Mario Guiral Moreno, "Nuestros problemas políticos, económicos y sociales," *Cuba Contemporánea* 5 (August 1914), 418–19; *La Discusión*, 30 June 1919, 1 July 1919; Julio Pérez Goñi, "La ley de Lynch bárbara y humanitaria," in *La Discusión*, 2 July 1919; Enrique José Varona to *El Día*, 4 July 1919; Julio Villoldo, "El lynchamiento, social y jurídicamente considerado," *Cuba Contemporánea* 21 (September 1919), 18–19.

120. See Helg, *Our Rightful Share*, pp. 242–43.

121. On the uniqueness of southern lynching, see Brundage, *Lynching in the New South*, 3; p. T. Harris, *Exorcising Blackness*, pp. 12–15.

122. Ortiz, *Hampa afrocubana*, pp. 355–57, 366; "La ponencia del Dr. Fernando Ortiz sobre la brujería," *La Discusión*, 11 July 1919; Cuba, *Diario de Sesi-*

ones del Congreso. Cámara de Representantes 30, no. 30 (4 July 1919), 18–21; ibid., no. 36 (13 July 1919), 11–13.

123. Tolnay and Beck, *A Festival of Violence*, pp. 239–46, 255–56; Robert L. Zangrando, *The NAACP Crusade against Lynching, 1909–1950* (Philadelphia: Temple University Press, 1980); MacLean, *Behind the Mask of Chivalry*, pp. 25–30; David L. Chappell, *Inside Agitators. White Southerners in the Civil Rights Movement* (Baltimore, MD: Johns Hopkins University Press, 1996), pp. 23–39; Gilmore, *Gender and Jim Crow*, pp. 203–24; Hall, *Revolt against Chivalry*; Wright, *Racial Violence in Kentucky*, pp. 200–13. See also Arthur Raper, *The Tragedy of Lynching* (Chapel Hill, NC: University of North Carolina Press, 1933); Cash, *The Mind of the South*, pp. 301–10.

124. In the U.S. South, in particular, the decline of lynching coincided with a sharp increase of legal executions of alleged black criminals and with the rebirth and rapid expansion of the Ku Klux Klan (Bowers, *Legal Homicide*, pp. 57–60, 79–80; MacLean, *Behind the Mask of Chivalry*). For an analysis of the contradictions between women's suffrage and entry into the Klan in the 1920s and the images of white female vulnerability and white male supremacy inherent to the myth of the black rapist, see Kathleen M. Blee, *Women of the Klan: Racism and Gender in the 1920s* (Berkeley: University of California Press, 1991), pp. 42–69.

Notes to COMMENTARY
by Daniel C. Littlefield

1. Ruth Pike, "Sevillian Society in the Sixteenth Century: Slaves and Freedmen," *Hispanic American Historic Review* XLVII (August 1967), 359.

2. F. James Davis, *Who Is Black: One Nation's Definition* (University Park, Pa., 1991), 7.

3. Thomas Nelson Page, *The Old South: Essays Social and Political* (New York, 1968: originally published 1892), 339.

4. ———, *Mediterranean Winter—1906: Journal and Letters*, edited by Harriet R. Holman (Coconut Grove, Miami, 1971), 6.

5. ———, *The Negro: The Southerner's Problem* (New York, 1904), 95.

6. Quoted in Verena Martinez-Alier, *Marriage, Class and Colour in Nineteenth-Century Cuba: A Study in Racial Attitudes and Sexual Values in a Slave Society* (Cambridge, 1974), 35.

7. *Ibid.*, 36.

8. Simeon Booker, "The Couple That Rocked Courts: Lovings' Fight Brought Supreme Court Decision Against Miscegenation," *Ebony* XXII (September 1967), 79.

Notes to COMMENTARY
by Kenneth Bilby

1. Melville J. Herskovits and Frances S. Herskovits, *Rebel Destiny: Among the Bush Negroes of Dutch Guiana* (New York, 1934).

2. Among the Caribbean areas in which these writers have carried out fieldwork (in addition to their work on U.S. African-American traditions) are the

following: Zora Neale Hurston (Jamaica, Haiti); Katherine Dunham (Jamaica, Haiti, Martinique, Trinidad); Alan Lomax (Bahamas, Tobago, Carriacou, and other parts of the Caribbean); Harold Courlander (Haiti, Cuba); Richard Waterman (Puerto Rico, and also worked with Herskovits' field recordings from Trinidad); Frederic Ramsey (Jamaica); Marshall Stearns (Bahamas, Haiti); Arthur Alberts (Cuba [as well as West Africa]); Samuel Charters (Bahamas [as well as West Africa]); Roger Abrahams (St. Vincent, St. Kitts, Nevis, Tobago); William Ferris (Guyana); John Storm Roberts (Jamaica, Haiti, Dominican Republic, Cayman Islands, Tortola [as well as East Africa]); Morton Marks (Haiti, Puerto Rico, Dominican Republic [as well as Brazil]); Robert Farris Thompson (Haiti, Suriname [as well as West and Central Africa); Donald Hill (Carriacou, Trinidad); Barbara Hampton (Jamaica [as well as West Africa]); Jacqueline DjeDje (Jamaica [as well as West Africa]).

3. Marshall W. Stearns, *The Story of Jazz* (London, 1956), 23–33; Lynne Fauley Emery, *Black Dance in the United States from 1619 to 1970* (Palo Alto, 1972), 30–65; John Lovell, Jr., *Black Song: The Forge and the Flame* (New York, 1972), 49–63; Dena J. Epstein, *Sinful Tunes and Spirituals: Black Folk Music to the Civil War* (Urbana, 1977), xvi–xvii; Albert J. Raboteau, *Slave Religion: The "Invisible Institution" in the Antebellum South* (Oxford, 1978), 35–42.

4. As John Blassingame noted more than two decades ago, "several aspects of West African culture are so distinctive that it is relatively easy to discover their presence or absence among Southern slaves. Dances, folk tales, music, magic, and language patterns are susceptible to this kind of analysis." See John Blassingame, *The Slave Community: Plantation Life in the Antebellum South* (New York, 1972), 19. See also Richard Alan Waterman, "African Influence on the Music of the Americas," in Sol Tax, ed., *Acculturation in the Americas* (Chicago, 1952), 207–217; Gunther Schuller, *Early Jazz: Its Roots and Musical Development* (New York, 1968), 3–62; Alan Lomax, "The Homogeneity of African-Afro-American Musical Style," in Norman E. Whitten, Jr. and John F. Szwed, eds., *Afro-American Anthropology* (New York, 1970), 181–201; David Welch, "West African Cult Music Retentions in Haitian Urban Vaudou: A Preliminary Report," *Essays for a Humanist: An Offering to Klaus Wachsmann* (New York, 1977), 337–349; David Welch, "A Yorùbá/Nagô 'Melotype' for Religious Songs in the African Diaspora: Continuity of West African Praise Songs in the New World," in Irene V. Jackson, ed., *More Than Drumming: Essays on African and Afro-Latin Music and Musicians* (Westport, CT, 1985), 145–162; Hewitt Pantaleoni, "The Possibility of Objective Rhythmic Evidence for African Influence in Afro-American Music," in John Blacking and Joann W. Kealiinohomoku, eds., *The Performing Arts: Music and Dance* (New York, 1979), 287–291; Gerhard Kubik, "Transplantation of African Musical Cultures into the New World: Research Topics and Objectives in the Study of African-American Music," in Wolfgang Binder, ed., *Slavery in the Americas* (Würzburg, 1993), 421–452.

5. The specific Yoruba origins of Cuban *lucumí* music have been recognized by scholars for decades. More than forty years ago, in his article "Estudiemos la Música Afrocubana" (*Estudios Afrocubanos*, 5 [1940–1946], 16), the pioneering Cuban musicologist Fernando Ortiz wrote that "the peoples of the Niger River, particularly the Yorubas or Nagos, known in Cuba as *lucumís*, brought us, along with their complex religious beliefs, the drums, songs and dances of their ancient

rites, which still resound intact under American skies, to implore favors from the divinities of Africa" (my translation). For further details on the Yoruba background of Cuban *batá* drumming, see Fernando Ortiz, "La Música Religiosa de los Yoruba entre los Negros Cubanos," *Estudios Afrocubanos*, 5 (1940–1946), 19–60. Information on Yoruba influence in Afro-Trinidadian religious music may be found in Maureen Warner-Lewis, *Yoruba Songs of Trinidad with Translations* (London, 1994). My statement regarding the specific Akan background of Surinamese Maroon *kumanti* drumming is based on my own ethnographic research among the Aluku Maroons (1983–1987), which included a musicological study of drumming (the results of which have yet to be published); my previous study of a number of cognate Akan drumming styles with Fanti master drummer Abraham Adzenyah at Wesleyan University (1976–77, 1979–80); and my reading of J.H. Nketia, *Drumming in Akan Communities of Ghana* (London, 1963). Many more examples of specific African continuities in Afro-American musical traditions could be added to these.

6. John Storm Roberts, *Black Music of Two Worlds* (New York, 1972), 19–39; Kenneth Bilby, "Drums of Defiance: Maroon Music from the Earliest Free Black Communities of Jamaica," booklet accompanying compact disc, *Drums of Defiance* (Washington, D.C. SF CD 40412, 1992 [1981]), 9; Kenneth Bilby, "The Caribbean as a Musical Region," in Sidney W. Mintz and Sally Price, eds., *Caribbean Contours* (Baltimore, 1985), 183–194.

7. Historians have increasingly become aware of this as well. Two notable recent contributions to the historiography of musical interpenetration and creolization among Africans and their descendants in the Americas are Richard Cullen Rath, "African Music in Seventeenth-Century Jamaica: Cultural Transit and Transition," *William and Mary Quarterly* (3d Series), 50 (1993), 700–726; and Alex van Stipriaan, " 'Een Verre Verwijderd Trommelen . . .': Ontwikkeling van Afro-Surinaamse Muziek en Dans in de Slavernij," in Ton Bevers, Antoon van den Braembussche, and Berend Jan Langenberg, eds., *De Kunstwereld: Produktie, Distributie en Receptie in de Wereld van Kunst en Cultuur* (Hilversum, 1993), 143–173.

8. Roger D. Abrahams, *Singing the Master: The Emergence of African-American Culture in the Plantation South* (New York, 1992).

9. Sidney W. Mintz and Richard Price, *The Birth of African-American Culture: An Anthropological Perspective* (Boston, 1992 [1976]); Sally Price and Richard Price, *Afro-American Arts of the Suriname Rain Forest* (Berkeley, 1980), 194–215; Herbert G. Gutman, *The Black Family in Slavery and Freedom 1750–1925* (New York, 1976); Edward Kamau Brathwaite, *Folk Culture of the Slaves in Jamaica*, second edition (London, 1981), 6–7; Charles Joyner, *Down by the Riverside: A South Carolina Slave Community* (Urbana, 1984), 196–240; Charles Joyner, "Creolization," in Charles Reagan Wilson and William Ferris, eds., *Encyclopedia of Southern Culture* (Chapel Hill, 1989), 147–149; Charles Joyner, "A Single Southern Culture: Cultural Interaction in the Old South," in Ted Ownby, ed., *Black and White: Cultural Interaction in the Antebellum South* (Jackson, 1993), 12–17.

10. The Aluku have a special significance for historians of slavery, as the direct descendants of the "revolted Negroes" against whom the British soldier John Gabriel Stedman fought during the 1770s. The historic struggles of their ancestors are at the center of Stedman's classic account of slavery in Dutch Guiana. See John Gabriel Stedman, *Narrative of a Five Years Expedition against the Revolted*

Negroes of Surinam, Transcribed for the First Time from the Original 1790 Manuscript, ed. by Richard Price and Sally Price (Baltimore, 1988).

11. Such work has been particularly successful in the area of language. See, for instance, David Dalby, "Ashanti Survivals in the Language and Traditions of the Windward Maroons of Jamaica," *African Language Studies,* 12 (1971), 31–51. See also Kenneth Bilby, "The Kromanti Dance of the Windward Maroons of Jamaica," *Nieuwe West-Indische Gids,* 55/1&2 (1981), 52–101. I am currently working on a paper that traces a large number of lexical items from the esoteric Kromanti language of the Jamaican Maroons, gathered during my fieldwork in 1978, to a variety of African languages. I am also compiling a dictionary of the Aluku language, spoken by the Surinamese Maroon people among whom I carried out fieldwork during the 1980s. As part of this project, I have already established hundreds of African etymologies, most of which have never been proposed before.

12. Sally Price and Richard Price, *Afro-American Arts of the Suriname Rain Forest* (Berkeley, 1980), 208–210.

13. The Aluku musical genre called *awawa* is very briefly described in Kenneth Bilby, "La Musique Aluku: Un Héritage Africain," in Marie-Paule Jean-Louis and Gérard Collomb, eds., *Musiques en Guyane* (Cayenne, 1989), 60.

14. For more on traditions of this kind, see Roger D. Abrahams, *Deep Down in the Jungle* (Hatboro, PA, 1964), 47–63; Roger D. Abrahams, *The Man-of-Words in the West Indies* (Baltimore, 1983), 3, 55–76; William Labov, *Language in the Inner City: Studies in the Black English Vernacular* (Philadelphia, 1972), 297–353; Lawrence W. Levine, *Black Culture and Black Consciousness: Afro-American Folk Thought from Slavery to Freedom* (New York, 1977), 344–358. The reference above to a Jamaican Maroon genre of sung criticism called *kyazam* (also known as *benta,* or *banta*) is from my own fieldwork; like many other such traditions in the Caribbean, *kyazam* has yet to be documented in the literature.

15. A similar range of practices and behaviors is found among the Saramaka Maroons, where, for instance, young men often engage in "verbal dueling, involving the improvisation and recital . . . of long strings of imaginative insults"; and where *sêkêti* songs are typically used to air "local scandals, interpersonal disputes, and the joys and sorrows of lovers." See Price and Price, *Afro-American Arts of the Suriname Rain Forest,* 169, 175–176.

16. Kenneth Bilby, "Caribbean Crucible," in Geoffrey Haydon and Dennis Marks, eds., *Repercussions: A Celebration of African-American Music* (London, 1985), 138–140, 149 n 6. For discussions of African-American fife and drum bands in the southern U.S., see David Evans, "Black Fife and Drum Music in Mississippi," *Mississippi Folklore Register,* 6/3 (1972), 94–107; and Alan Lomax, *The Land Where the Blues Began* (New York, 1993), 331–347.

17. For background on the possession dance performed in Montserrat to the sounds of tambourines and a fife, see Jay D. Dobbin, *The Jombee Dance of Montserrat: A Study of Trance Ritual in the West Indies* (Columbus, 1986). The similar "jumbie dance" tradition of Tobago, in which "reel songs" accompanied by fiddle and tambourine-like frame drums are used to invoke spirit possession, is briefly described in J.D. Elder, *Folk Song and Folk Life in Charlotteville* (Port of Spain: Universal Printing, 1972), 31–32; and in Krister Malm, "Music from the West Indies: The Lesser Antilles," booklet accompanying LP album *Västindien Små Antillerna* (Stockholm CAP 2004, 1977), 5. Marie-Céline Lafontaine describes the Guadeloupean *balakadri* in "Unité et Diversité des Musiques Traditionnelles Guadeloupéennes," in *Les Musiques Guadeloupéennes dans le Champ Culturel Afro-*

Américain, au Sein des Musiques du Monde (Paris, 1988), 71–92. See also Carnot and Marie-Céline Lafontaine, *Alors Ma Chère, Moi . . . : Propos d'un Musicien Guadeloupéen* (Paris, 1986).

18. Before my brief fieldwork in 1991 and 1992, no research had been done on the *jonkonnu* tradition in this particular rural Jamaican community, and so there exists no published documentation of it. (I intend to publish the results of my fieldwork there in the near future.) Clearly, in light of this new information, the significance of Jamaican *jonkonnu*, both in the past and present, must be reevaluated. For instance, the leading authority on *jonkonnu*, Judith Bettelheim, has made the generalization that "Jonkonnu is a secular festival . . . [which] does not systematically address gods or spirits in a uniform or codified manner." (See Judith Bettelheim, "Jonkonnu and Other Christmas Masquerades," in John W. Nunley and Judith Bettelheim, eds., *Caribbean Festival Arts* [Seattle and Saint Louis, 1988], 40.) A number of other scholars, however, had earlier argued, on the basis of the brief fieldwork carried out by the folklorist Martha Beckwith and the ethnomusicologist Helen Roberts in Lacovia, Jamaica during the early 1920s, that *jonkonnu* was once associated with African-derived religious rites. (And, in fact, the regional religious variant of *jonkonnu* very briefly described by Beckwith and Roberts in a number of publications, though long assumed to be extinct, has survived in attenuated form to the present, and is closely related to the tradition I encountered in another community in the early 1990s.) See Sylvia Wynter, "Jonkonnu in Jamaica: Towards the Interpretation of Folk Dance as a Cultural Process," *Jamaica Journal*, 4/2 (1970), 40; and Cheryl Ryman, "Jonkonnu: A Neo-African Form, Part II," *Jamaica Journal*, 17/2 (1984), 54–55.

19. In the journal she kept during her fieldwork with Jamaican Maroons, Dunham repeatedly expresses her disappointment at finding that European "set dances" (including the quadrille) appeared to have displaced the more African forms of dance in Accompong. See Katherine Dunham, *Journey to Accompong* (New York, 1946), 22–27; 98–99; 125. The popularity of the quadrille and other set dances in Accompong is also noted in Earl Leaf, *Isles of Rhythm* (New York, 1948), 70–72. A vivid description of the tea meeting as once practiced by the Windward Maroons on the other side of the island is to be found in C.L.G. Harris, *The Maroons of Moore Town (A Colonel Speaks)* (Moore Town, Jamaica . . . , n.d.), 106–108.

20. Kenneth Bilby, " 'Roots Explosion': Indigenization and Cosmopolitanism in Contemporary Surinamese Popular Music" (forthcoming).

21. Dena J. Epstein, "The Folk Banjo: A Documentary History," *Ethnomusicology*, 19 (1975), 359–360; Cecelia Conway, *African Banjo Echoes in Appalachia* (Knoxville, 1995), 57–58.

22. Judith Bettelheim, "The Afro-Jamaican Jonkonnu Festival: Playing the Forces and Operating the Cloth," Ph.D. Diss., Yale University, 1979, 200–261; Elizabeth A. Fenn, " 'A Perfect Equality Seemed to Reign': Slave Society and Jonkonnu," *North Carolina Historical Review*, 65 (1988), 129–130.

23. For recent discussions of the underlying cultural connectedness of Afro-American street festivals in the Caribbean and North America (of which the Asheville *goombay* festival is one of the newest examples), see Rosita M. Sands, "Carnival Celebrations in Africa and the New World: Junkanoo and the Black Indians of Mardi Gras," *Black Music Research Journal*, 11 (1991), 75–92; and Michael P. Smith, "Behind the Lines: The Black Mardi Gras Indians and the New Orleans Second Line," *Black Music Research Journal*, 14/1 (1994), 43–73.

24. In 1993, while visiting Asheville, I spoke with staff members at the YMI Cultural Center, the African-American community organization that sponsors the *goombay* festival. They were surprised to learn of the historical *john kuner* masquerade dance of eastern North Carolina (although they knew of *jonkonnu* in the Caribbean), and they assured me that the original organizers of the festival in Asheville were unaware that such a tradition had ever existed in their own state. Background on *john kuner* in North Carolina may be found in Dougald MacMillan, "John Kuners," *Journal of American Folklore*, 39 (1926), 53–57; Ira De A. Reid, "The John Canoe Festival: A New World Africanism," *Phylon*, 3 (1942), 349–370; Richard Walser, "His Worship the John Kuner," *North Carolina Folklore*, 19/4 (1971), 160–172; Bettelheim, "The Afro-Jamaican Jonkonnu Festival," 253–261; Sterling Stuckey, *Slave Culture: Nationalist Theory and the Foundations of Black America* (New York, 1987), 67–73, 104–111; and Fenn, " 'A Perfect Equality Seemed to Reign'," 127–153.

25. According to one Guadeloupean musicologist, "some Guadeloupean musicians still believe that biguine came from Louisiana, more specifically, New Orleans"; see Édouard Benoit, "Biguine: Popular Music of Guadeloupe, 1940–1960," in Jocelyne Guilbault, with Gage Averill, Édouard Benoit, and Gregory Rabess, *Zouk: World Music in the West Indies* (Chicago, 1993), 242 n 5. For a brief discussion of the early influence of New Orleans jazz on the biguine, and especially on the important Martiniquan clarinettist and band leader Alexandre Stellio, see Jacqueline Rosemain, *Jazz et Biguine: Les Musiques Noires du Nouveau Monde* (Paris, 1993), 143–144. Continuing jazz influence since then is summarized in Maurice Jallier and Yollen Lossen, *Musique aux Antilles* (Paris, 1985), 40–41.

26. The Jamaican "blues dances" of the 1950s, and the role of both jazz and rhythm and blues in the development of Jamaican popular styles, are discussed in Garth White, "The Development of Jamaican Popular Music—Pt. 2: Urbanisation of the Folk: The Merger of the Traditional and the Popular in Jamaican Music," *ACIJ Research Review* (African-Caribbean Institute of Jamaica), 1 (1984), 47–52; 64–76. See also Peter Manuel, Kenneth Bilby, and Michael Largey, *Caribbean Currents: Caribbean Music from Rumba to Reggae* (Philadelphia, 1995), 154–159. Mary Ellison also comments briefly on the contribution of the blues to ska and reggae in her book, *Extensions of the Blues* (London, 1989), 96. Blues and jazz influences remain apparent in Jamaican popular music all the way up to the period of Bob Marley, who, for instance, composed a reggae-blues lament and protest song called "Talking Blues" (featured on the LP album, *Natty Dread* [Island 90037-1, 1974]), and adapted scat singing techniques to his Rastafarian reggae framework.

Notes to THE POLITICAL ECONOMY OF THE CARIBBEAN
by Ralph Lee Woodward, Jr.

1. On international rivalry in early Caribbean history see especially Kenneth R. Andrews, *Elizabethan Privateering: English Privateering During the Spanish War, 1585–1603* (Cambridge, 1964), *The Spanish Caribbean: Trade and Plunder, 1530–1630* (New Haven, 1978), and *Trade, Plunder, and Settlement: Maritime Enterprise and the Genesis of the British Empire* (Cambridge, 1984). See also A. P. Newton, *The European Nations in the West Indies, 1493–1688* (London, 1933) and *The Colonising Activities of the English Puritans* (New Haven, 1914); and Clarence

Haring, *Trade and Navigation Between Spain and the Indies in the Time of the Hapsburgs* (Cambridge, 1918), and *The Buccaneers in the West Indies in the XVII Century* (New York, 1910).

2. On the Dutch in the Caribbean see C. R. Boxer, *The Dutch Seaborne Empire, 1600–1800* (Harmondsworth, 1973); C. C. Goslinga, *The Dutch in the Caribbean and on the Wild Coast, 1580–1680* (Gainesville, 1971), and *The Dutch in the Caribbean and in the Guianas* (Dover, N.H.L Van Gorcum, 1985); Philip H. Hiss, *Netherlands America: The Dutch Territories int he West* (New York, 1943); and Gert Oostindie, ed., *Fifty Years Later: Antislavery, Capitalism and Modernity in the Dutch Orbit* (Leiden, 1995).

3. *Sugar and Slavery: An Economic History of the British West Indies, 1623–1775* (Baltimore, 1973).

4. Howard Johnson, "Richard B. Sheridan: The Making of a Caribbean Economic Historian," in Roderick A. McDonald, editor, *West Indian Accounts: Essays on the History of the British Caribbean and the Atlantic Economy* (Kingston, Jamaica, 1996), p. 15.

5. Ibid., p. 15.

6. Sheridan, *Sugar and Slavery*, p. 448.

7. R. P. Thomas and R. N. Bean, "The Fishers of Men: The Profits of the Slave Trade," *Journal of Economic History* 34 (1974): 914, cited by Ralph A. Austen and Woodruff D. Smith, "Private Tooth Decay as Public Economic Virtue: The Slave-Sugar Triangle, Consumerism, and European Industrialization," in Joseph E. Inikori and Stanley L. Engerman, *The Atlantic Slave Trade: Effects on Economies, Societies, and Peoples in Africa, the Americas, and Europe* (Durham, NC, 1992), p. 183. The role of sugar especially in promoting the industrial revolution in Europe is further developed by Austen and Smith in this article, pp. 183–203.

8. Douglas C. North made this argument persuasively in his *The Economic Growth of the United States, 1790–1860* (Englewood Cliffs, NJ, 1961). One aspect of this process has been described by Ronald Bailey, "The Slave(ry) Trade and the Development of Capitalism in the United States: The Textile Industry in New England," in Joseph E. Inikori and Stanley L. Engerman, *The Atlantic Slave Trade: Effects on Economies, Societies, and Peoples in Africa, the Americas, and Europe* (Durham, NC, 1992), pp. 205–46.

9. William Darity, Jr., "British Industry and the West Indian Plantations," in Joseph E. Inikori and Stanley L. Engerman, *The Atlantic Slave Trade: Effects on Economies, Societies, and Peoples in Africa, the Americas, and Europe* (Durham, NC, 1992), pp. 247–79. Quotations from p. 273.

10. Clarence J. Munford and Michael Zeuske, "Black Slavery, Class Struggle, Fear and Revolution in St. Domingue and Cuba, 1785–1795," *Journal of Negro History* 53 (1988): 12–13.

11. Arthur L. Stinchcombe, *Sugar Island Slavery in the Age of the Enlightenment: The Political Economy of the Caribbean World* (Princeton, 1995), p. 22.

12. Ibid., p. 4.

13. Ibid., p. 9.

14. David Eltis, *Economic Growth and the Ending of the Transatlantic Slave Trade* (New York, 1987), p. 4.

15. Ibid. For a fine collection of articles on the impact of the evolution of the abolition of the slave trade see also, David Eltis and James Waivin, eds., *The*

Abolition of the Atlantic Slave Trade; Origins and Effects in Europe, Africa, and the Americas (Madison, 1981).

16. On the migration from Haiti to Louisiana, I am very much indebted to an unpublished paper by Michael Mizell-Nelson, "From Saint Domingue to New Orleans, 1792–1809," New Orleans, 1966. See also the edited anthology of Carl A. Brasseaux and Glenn R. Conrad, *The Road to Louisiana: The Saint-Domingue Refugees, 1792–1809* (Lafayette, La., 1992).

17. Ramiro Guerra, *Sugar and Society in the Caribbean: An Economic History of Cuban Agriculture* (New Haven, 1964); Fernando Ortiz Fernández, *Cuban Counterpoint: Tobacco and Sugar* (New York, 1947); Félix Goizueta-Mimó, *Bitter Cuban Sugar: Monoculture and Economic Dependence from 1825–1899* (New York, 1987).

18. Louis A. Pérez, Jr. *Cuba and the United States: Ties of Singular Intimacy* (Athens, 1990).

19. Robert F. Smith, *The United States and Cuba: Business and Diplomacy, 1917–1960* (New York, 1960).

20. On rural aspects of the Cuban revolutionary experience, see Thomas C. Dalton, *Everything Within the Revolution: Cuban Strategies for Social Development Since 1960* (Boulder, 1993); Carmelo Mesa-Lago, *The Cuban Economy in the First Two Decades of the Revolution: Policies and Performances* (Tokyo, 1982); Edward Boorstein, *The Economic Transformation of Cuba* (New York, 1968); Brian M. Pollitt, *Revolution and the Mode of Production in the Sugar-Cane Sector of the Cuban Economy, 1959–1980: Some Preliminary Findings* (Glasgow, 1981); Dhram P. Ghai, Cristobal Kay, and Peter Peek, *Labour and Development in Rural Cuba* (New York, 1988); Mariana Ravenet Ramírez and Jorge Hernández Martínez, *Estructura social y transformaciones agrarias en Cuba* (La Habana: Editorial de Ciencias Sociales, 1984).

21. Laird W. Bergad, *Cuban Rural Society in the Nineteenth Century: The Social and Economic History of Monoculture in Matanzas* (Princeton, 1990), demonstrates this tendency using the example of Matanzas Province, Cuba.

22. See E. Bradford Burns, *The Poverty of Progress: Latin America in the Nineteenth Century* (Berkeley, 1980) for a provocative statement of this argument in Latin America during the nineteenth century.

Notes to COMMENTARY
by David Eltis

1. For the data supporting this paragraph, see David Eltis, "The Slave Economies of the Caribbean: Structure, Performance, Evolution and Significance," *The UNESCO General History of the Caribbean*, 5 vols., 3 *The Slave Societies* (Macmillan, forthcoming).

Notes to BASEBALL IN SOUTHERN CULTURE, AMERICAN CULTURE, AND THE CARIBBEAN
by Milton Jamail

1. Robert González Echevarría, "The '47 Dodgers in Havana: Baseball at a Crossroads," *1996 Spring Training Baseball Yearbook*, vol. 9 (Spring 1996), p. 62.

See also Louis A. Pérez, Jr., "Between Baseball and Bullfighting: The Quest for Naturality in Cuba, 1868–1898," *Journal of American History*, 81 (September 1994): pp. 493–507.

2. Gilbert Joseph, "Forging the Regional Pastime: Baseball and Class in Yucatán," in *Sport and Society in Latin America*, ed. Joseph L. Arbena (Westport, Conn., 1988), p. 35.

3. Ibid., p. 35, 54–55.

4. Jackie Robinson, as told to Alfred Duckett, *I Never Had It Made* (New York, 1972), p. 68.

5. González Echevarría, "The '47 Dodgers in Havana," p. 24; Jules Tygiel, *Baseball's Great Experiment: Jackie Robinson and His Legacy* (New York, 1983), p. 17.

6. David Halberstam, *Summer of '49* (New York, 1989), p. 183; Tygiel, *Baseball's Great Experiment*, pp. 295–97.

7. David Halberstam, *October 1964* (New York, 1994), pp. 232–33.

8. Jack Orr, "Were the Yankees Wrong on Vic Power?," *Sport* (September 1954), p. 74; Halberstam, *Summer of '49*, pp. 183–184; Danny Peary, "Vic Power," in *Cult Baseball Players*, ed. Danny Peary (New York, 1990), p. 355.

9. Interview with Victor Pellot Power, November 3, 1988, La Romana, Dominican Republic. The other sources are: Peary, "Vic Power," p. 357; Leonard Schecter, "Vic Power's New, Wonderful World," *Sport* (May 1963), p. 65; Peter Bjarkman, *Baseball With a Latin Beat* (Jefferson, North Carolina, 1994), p. 93; and Tygiel, *Baseball's Great Experiment*, p. 315. Last quote is Ibid., p. 357.

10. Peary, "Vic Power," p. 357.

11. Curt Flood, with Richard Carter, *The Way It Is* (New York, 1971).

12. Interview with Curt Flood, February 2, 1989, Atlanta, Georgia.

13. Interviews with Ruben Amaro, March 26, 1989, Lakeland, Florida, and April 1995, Nueva Laredo, Mexico.

14. Interview with Santos Amaro, November 2, 1989, Veracruz, Mexico.

15. Interview with Ruben Amaro, March 26, 1989, Lakeland, Florida.

16. Interview with Ruben Amaro, March 26, 1989, Lakeland, Florida; Interview with Santos Amaro, November 2, 1989, Veracruz, Mexico.

17. Interview with Juan Marichal, November 4, 1988, Santo Domingo, Dominican Republic.

18. Interview with Juan Marichal, November 4, 1988, Santo Domingo, Dominican Republic.

19. Felipe Alou, with Arnold Hano, "Latin -American Ballplayers Need a Bill of Rights," *Sport* (November 1963), p. 78.

20. Ibid, pp. 78–79.

21. Interview with Felipe Alou, May 20, 1995, Houston, Texas.

22. Felipe Alou, with Herm Weiskopf, *My Life and Baseball* (Waco, Texas, 1967), p. 34.

23. Alou, "Latin-American Ballplayers Need a Bill of Rights," p. 79.

Contributors

Roger D. Abrahams is professor of folklore and folklife at the University of Pennsylvania. He has done extensive fieldwork in the cultures of the African diaspora and is the author of *Afro-American Folktales* (1999) and *African Folktales* (1983).

Kenneth Bilby received his doctorate in anthropology from The Johns Hopkins University and has been a research associate at the Smithsonian Institution. He coauthored *Caribbean Currents: Caribbean Music from Rumba to Reggae* (1995).

David Eltis is professor of history at Queen's University in Kingston. He wrote *Economic Growth and the Ending of the Transatlantic Slave Trade* (1987).

Stanley L. Engerman is John H. Munro Professor of Economics and professor of history at the University of Rochester. He is the author or editor of over a dozen books including *Time on the Cross* (with Robert W. Fogel) (1974) and the *Cambridge Economic History of the United States* (with R. E. Gallman) (1996).

Aline Helg is associate professor of history at the University of Texas at Austin. She wrote *Our Rightful Share: The Afro-Cuban Struggle for Equality, 1886–1912* (1995).

Milton Jamail has been associated with the University of Texas at Austin since 1982. The author of over a hundred articles on baseball, he has lectured in the United States, Sweden, Germany, Mexico, and Belize.

Charles Joyner is Burroughs Distinguished Professor of Southern History and Culture at Coastal Carolina University. The author or editor of five books and more than sixty articles and essays, he is best known for his book *Down by the Riverside: A South Carolina Slave Community* (1984).

Daniel C. Littlefield teaches American history at the University of Illinois at Urbana-Champagne. He is the author of *Rice and Slaves: Ethnicity and the Slave Trade in Colonial South Carolina* 1981).

Bonham C. Richardson is professor of geography at Virginia Polytechnic Institute and State University in Blacksburg, Virginia. His book *The Caribbean in the Wider World, 1492–1992* (1992) won the Gordon K. Lewis book award of the Caribbean Studies Association.

Ralph Lee Woodward, Jr. is professor of history at Tulane University. He is the associate editor of the *Encyclopedia of Latin American History and Culture* (1996).

Index

abolition, 57, 135, 136, 146, 147, 148–49
Abrahams, Roger D., 116
accommodation, 23
Adams, Tom, 3
Africa, x, 7, 52, 57, 91, 92, 140, 148;
    African slaves, ix, 10, 26, 28, 57, 129,
    133, 145; cultural continuity with
    African Americans, 21–43, 97–113,
    115–25; West Africa, 37–38, 110. *See
    also* U.S. South
African Americans, 15; and baseball,
    153, 156; compared to Afro-Cubans,
    49–96; cultural continuity with
    Africa, 21–43, 97–113, 115–25
Afro-Caribbean, 11
Afro-Cubans, 49–96, 178 n 4
Alabama, 156
Alberts, Arthur, 116
Alou, Felipe Rojas, xi, 153, 163, 165
Alou, Jesus, 164
Alou, Mateo, 164
Aluku, 120
Amaro, Ruben, xi, 152, 153, 159, 160,
    161, 165
Amaro, Ruben, Jr., 161
Amaro, Santos, 160–61
American League, 157, 160
American Revolution. *See* United
    States, the
Americans. *See* United States, the
Amsterdam, 147
Anansi, 37
Anegada, 134
Anglican, 27, 28, 29
Angola, 24
Anguilla, 18
Antigua, 6, 16, 25, 37, 134
Aparicio, Luis, 155
Arango y Perreno, Fracisco de, 95
Archer, Chalmers, 16
Arizona-Mexico League, 160
art, 40
Aruba, 6, 14, 25
Asheville, N.C., 124

Asia, 166
Association of Southern Women for the
    Prevention of Lynching, 87
Atkins, Cholly, 109
Atlanta, Ga., ix, x, 18, 59, 161
Atlanta Crackers, 152
Austin, Tex., 153
Australia, 41, 42, 45, 140, 166
Avila, Roberto, 160
Awawa, 120

Bahamas, x, 4, 18, 38, 105, 134
balakadri, 122
banana, 18, 137, 138, 143
Banes, Sally, 110
banjo (banjil), 35, 107, 123
Bantu, 38
Barbados, 3, 6, 9, 15, 18, 25, 27, 39, 40,
    134
Barbuda, 16, 134
Barclay, Alexander, 36
Barthelemy, Sidney, 91
baseball, x, xi, 3, 17, 151–65
Baseball Encyclopedia, 165
Baseball Hall of Fame, 155, 162
batá drumming, 117
Bean, R. N., 131
Becker, John, 36
Beckford, George, 16
Beguine, 103
Belafonte, Harry, 17
Belize, 18, 100
Bellan, Esteban, 155
Bermuda, 124
blacks, x–xi, 7, 38, 98, 120, 152, 157–58;
    U.S. blacks, 11, 14, 91, 94; and
    whites, 7, 36, 38, 56–57, 58, 64–65,
    68, 70, 81–87, 98, 102, 107. *See also*
    African Americans; Afro-Cubans;
    baseball
bluegrass, 100
blues, ix, 23, 99, 100, 109, 111, 124, 125
bois stick dance, 100
Bonaire, 6, 25

201

Boni, 120
bossa nova, 23
Boston, Mass., 11
Boucourt, Domingo, 52–53
Bourbon reformers, 140
Bragan, Bobby, 156
Bragaña, Ramón, 160
Braudel, Fernand, ix
Braves (Atlanta and Milwaukee), 11, 165
Brazil: African culture, 23, 25, 32, 100;
    slavery, 9, 22, 26, 41, 47, 89, 144;
    sugar plantations, 13, 128, 140, 144,
    146, 147
breakdown, 103, 107, 109
breakout, 103
Bridenbaugh, Carl and Roberta, 12
British Guiana, 14, 146
British West Indies, 10, 12, 45, 46, 130,
    134, 136, 140
Brooklyn Dodgers, 155–56
Brooklyn, N.Y., 100
Brown, Willard, 153
Brundage, W. Fitzhugh, 59
buccaneer, 128, 129
bum drum (bone drum), 106

cacao, 128, 144
calling, 109
calypso, 3, 23, 109
Canada, 14
Canoers, John, 105
Capetown, 105
Capoeira, 100
Cárdenas, Leo, 159
Caribbean: baseball, 151–66; British, 7,
    10, 146; defined, ix, 4–20, 97; French,
    146, 147; locus of cultural interchange,
    100, 103, 112, 116, 117; political
    economy of, 127–49; and slavery,
    21–43, 137–39
Caribbean Basin Initiative, 3
Caribs, 9
Carioca, 23
Carlyle, Thomas, 7
carnival, 100, 105
Carolinas, the, 22, 26, 28, 32, 38, 41,
    105, 138
Carrasquel, Chico, 155
Carstens, Johan Lorentz, 35
Carty, Rico, 11

Casey, Hugh, 156
Castro, Fidel, 5
Catholic Church, 27, 29
cattle, 129, 134–35, 141
Caymans, 134
Central America, x, 4, 14, 18, 100, 103,
    133, 151
Charleston, S.C., 4
Charters, Samuel, 116
cheering, 108
Cherokees, 9
Chesapeake, 45
Chicago Cubs, 161
Chicago White Sox, 156, 162
chicken wing, 103
Chisholm, Shirley, 17
Choctaws, 9
Christianity, Africans and creolization
    of, 26–33, 34, 91, 172 n 17, 173 n 20
Church Missionary Society, 27
Civil War (U.S.), 44, 55, 56, 70, 80, 82,
    105
Clemente, Roberto, 155
Cleveland, Ohio, 160, 161
CNNization, x, 18
coal, 148
Coca-Cola, 142
Cocoa, Fla., 163
coffee, 130, 135, 136, 141, 144, 146
Colombia, 25
Columbus, Christopher, 8
Commission on Interracial
    Cooperation, 87
condomble, 32
Confederacy, 4, 82
Congo, 24, 32, 109
Conservatives, 70, 85
contraband, 143
Cooperstown, N.Y., 162
Coromantees, 23
Corpus Christi, Tex., 4
Costa Rica, 100, 138
cotton, 46, 101, 130, 136, 137, 138, 147
Courlander, Harold, 116
Cranford, Alfred, 52
creole, x, 4, 24–25, 39–40, 97, 140
creolization, x, 24–25, 26, 30, 34, 37, 38,
    103, 120, 170 n 7, 170 n 9
Crosby, Alfred, 9
Crosby, Ralph, 163

Index

Cuba, 3, 25, 29, 130; and baseball, 154, 155–56, 160, 162, 165; and race, 49–96; and slavery, x, 13–14, 47, 52, 57, 79, 89, 140; and sugar economy, 135, 136, 138, 140–42, 143, 146–47; and War for Independence, 56, 69, 72, 82, 142. *See also* Afro-Cubans; Oriente, Cuba; U.S. South
Curaçao, 6, 14, 25, 129
cutting, 100, 109

Dakar, 41
dance/dancing, 30–31, 36, 100, 103, 107–12, 120, 122–24
Dandridge, Ray, 153, 160
Danish Virgin Islands, 35
Darity, William, Jr., 131
Degler, Carl, 6
Demerara, 39
Democratic Party, 83
Democrats, 70
Denmark, 13
DeSoto, Hernando, 128
Detroit Tigers, 156
Dihigo, Martín, 160
disco, 100
Disco Dancing, 103
Dixie Series, 161
DjeDje, Jacqueline, 116
Dominica, 8, 134
Dominican Republic, ix, 9, 11, 14, 17; and baseball, 154, 155, 156, 158, 160, 162, 163
double-dutch jumping, 108
drum, 36, 122
Du Bois, W. E. B., 17
dub poetry, 23
Dunham, Katherine, 116, 123
Dutch Reformed, 27
Dutch West India Company, 129
Dyewoods, 130

Edwards, Bryan, 22, 33, 39
El Día, 49
El Salvador, 3
El Sporting Club, 154
Eltis, David, 139
encomienda, 132
England. *See* Great Britain
ethnography, 188

Europe, 9, 13, 15, 22, 41, 43, 148, 166; and Europeans, 15, 22, 100, 101, 103, 127
Evangeline League, 163
expressive inventions, 98, 100–02

Fante-Ashanti, 37
Farmer Alliance, 83
Farrakhan, Louis, 11, 17
Ferris, William, 116
feudalism, 127–28
fiddle, 107–08
fife and drum, 121
Fiji, 13
filibusters, 4
Flood, Curt, 158–59, 164
Florida, 5, 11, 156, 158
Florida Marlins, 165
folktales, 36, 43
food, 38, 43
Forbes, Ann, 42
Foucault, Michel, 65, 66
foxtrot, 102
France, 4, 13, 14, 18, 24, 128, 129, 131, 132, 133, 134, 147
French Antilles, 124
French Guiana, ix, 4, 25, 120
French Revolution, 134–35
French West Indies, 45, 130, 134, 136, 139
Fula, 23
Fulani, 23, 28, 29

Gambia, 105
Garvey, Marcus, 17
Genovese, Eugene, 5, 48
gens de couleur, 10
Georgia, 9, 25, 29, 30, 32, 38, 40, 52, 58, 156
Georgia Sea Islands, 102–03, 108
Germany, 100
getting down and jumping up, 110
Ghana, 37
Gibson, Josh, 160
Gilmore, Glenda E., 71
Gladwell, Maxwell, 10
globalism/globalization, 4, 18
Gold Coast, 23
González Echevarría, Roberto, 154
goombay, 35, 124

grammars, 119
Grant, Ulysses, 4
Great Britain, 10, 14, 24, 100, 128, 129,
    135; and Cuba, 135; and economic
    policies, 131–32, 135, 138, 146, 148;
    and slavery, 13, 89, 131, 139–40, 147.
    See also Caribbean
Greater Antilles, 5, 6, 9, 10, 18
Greece, 21
Grenada, 3, 6, 16, 17, 25, 27, 134
Guadeloupe, 9, 18, 25, 122, 124, 134
Guerrero, Mexico, 151
Guiana, 27
Guinea, 24, 39
gullah, 31, 47
gumbe, 122
Guyana, 5, 13, 25

Habanera, 99
hacienda, 133
hags, 32–33
Haiti (St. Domingue), 4, 17, 25, 32, 37,
    116, 134; and revolution, 50, 54, 92;
    and slavery, 10, 27, 45, 135, 136, 140,
    141, 146
Halberstam, David, 157
Hamburg, Germany, 147
Hamilton, Alexander, 17
Hampton, Barbara, 116
Haraksingh, Kusha, 17
Hausa, 37
Havana, Cuba, 52, 60, 135, 140, 156
Hawaii, 141
Hawes, Bess Lomax, 101–02, 103
Hershey Chocolate, 142
Herskovits, Melville, 104, 116, 119
hides, 141
Hill, Donald, 109, 116
hip hop, xi, 103
Hires Root Beer, 142
Hispaniola, 4, 8, 9
hoedown, 107
hoodoo. See voodoo/hoodoo
Hose, Sam, 52, 58, 59
Houston, Tex., 152, 161, 165
Houston Astros, 165
Houston Buffaloes, 152, 161
Hurston, Zora Neale, 116

Iberia/Iberians, 90, 128
Ibos, 24

immigration, 14
Independent Party of Color, 49, 53, 60,
    61, 67, 69, 72, 74, 75, 81, 84, 85
Indian Removal Act, 9
Indians (indigenous), 9, 103, 127, 132
indigo, 101, 130
Industrial Revolution, xi, 128, 130, 147,
    148
Irish, 145
Islam, 24, 28–29, 32
Ivory Coast, 37

Jackson, Miss., 165
Jamaica, 9, 16, 33, 47, 130, 133, 146;
    culture of, 17, 25, 27, 31, 35, 37, 40,
    105, 120, 122, 123
Jamestown, 9
jamming, 109
Japan, 100
jazz, 23, 100, 109, 124, 125
Jews, 32
jigs, 107, 122
Jim Crow, 57, 67, 68, 74, 75, 87
jitterbug, 102
John Henry (John the Conqueror; High
    John; Pére Jean), 37
Jones, Bessie, 102–03, 108
jonkonnu, 122, 124
Jordan, Terry, 4
Joseph, Gilbert, 154
josey, 108

Kansas City, Mo., 157
Kemble, Fanny, 35–36
Kincaid, Jamaica, 17
Kingston, Jamaica, 99, 125
Kiple, Kenneth, 9
Knights of the Golden Circle, 4
Koran, 29
Kromanti Play, 123
Ku Klux Klan, 71
kumanti drumming, 117
kyazam, 121

La Désirade, 16
La Discusión, 62–63
La Escalera, 55
La Junta de Nuevo Laredo, 160
Lake Charles, La., 163
Lang, John, 31

language, 42, 43, 120
latifundismo, 4
latinos, xi; and baseball, 153, 155, 156,
  163, 164, 165
Les Saintes, 18
Leslie, Charles, 35
Lesser Antilles, 8, 9
Levine, Lawrence, 44
Lewis, Gordon K., 8
Lewis, M. G. ("Monk"), 33
liberalism, 144
Liberals, 70, 85
Ligon, Richard, 38
Limba, 37
Limbo, 109
Lindy, 103
Little Rock, Ark., ix, 4, 157
Lomax, Alan, 116
London, 42, 100, 147
Louisiana, 25, 45, 140
Loving, Richard and Mildred, 96
lowcountry, 39
Luba, 37
lucumí, 117, 191 n 5
Luo, 37
Lutheran, 27
lynching, 56–60, 63, 66, 68, 83, 88, 90,
  95, 187 n 92

macarena, 109
Madden, Richard, 38
Major League Baseball, ix, 166
Malcolm X, mother of, 17
Malone, Jacqui, 108–09, 110
mambo, 23, 103, 109
Mandinka, 23, 28, 29
Maraccas Bay, 6
Marichal, Juan, xi, 153, 155, 162
Marks, Morton, 99, 110, 116
maroon, 45, 116, 120–21, 123
Martinez-Alier, Verena, 95
Martinique, 8, 119, 124, 134
Maryland, 131, 144
Matanzas, Cuba, 62, 63, 117, 119
Mathew, Governor William, 12
mauritus, 13
mazurka, 122
McCullough, David, 8
Mediterranean, ix
Meinig, Donald, 4

Mende, 23
mento, 23
mercantilism, 128
Merida, Yucatan, 154
Merengue, 109
Methodists, 27–28
Mexican League, 160
Mexico, 100, 128, 151, 152, 153, 160
Middle America, 144
migration, 14–15
Millington, Tenn., 165
Miñoso, Orestes Minnie, 155, 156
Mintz, Sidney, 5, 13, 23, 33, 48, 97, 98,
  119
miscegenation, 81, 94
Mississippi, 5, 9, 16, 81
Montreal Expos, 164
Montserrat, 8, 38, 121, 134
Moore Town, 123
Moravians, 27–28, 31
Motown singers, 109
mulatto, 10, 68
Musial, Stan, 159
music, x, 34, 43, 100–01, 116, 120;
  musicianers, 36
Muslim. See Islam
Myalism, 28, 33–34

NAACP, 86–87, 91
Naipaul, V. S., 17
Napoleonic Wars, 135
Natal, 13
Ndjuka, 120, 123
Negro leagues, 153, 160
Netherlands (Holland), 13–14, 18, 24,
  128–29, 131, 133
Nevis, 16, 17, 18, 37, 105, 107, 134
New England, 129, 131
New Orleans, La., ix, 4, 91, 92, 124, 140
New South Wales, 41–42
New York City, 15, 163
New York Giants, 162–63
New York Yankees, 156, 157
Nicaragua, 3, 8
Niger Delta, 24
Nigeria, 39
North America, 8, 18, 111, 130, 131
North Carolina, 11, 124
North Dakota, 160
Nuevo Laredo, 160

Oakland Athletics, 162
Oaxaca, Mexico, 151
Obeah, 28, 33–34, 175 n 26
Oriente, Cuba, 50, 53, 60–61, 69, 74, 84
Ortiz, Fernando, 53, 86
Ostend Manifesto, 4

Page, Thomas Nelson, 93–94
Paige, Satchel, 160
Pan American Games, 160
Panama Canal, 4, 8, 14
Patterson, Orlando, 17, 33
Peon Cáseres, Miguel, 154–55
Peru, 128
Petit, St. Vincent, 18
Philadelphia, Penn., 120
Philadelphia Phillies, 158, 161
picong, 121
Pike, Ruth, 91
plantations, xi, 127, 131, 133, 134, 145
plat-eyes, 32–33
Platt Amendment, 82, 85
Plymouth Rock, 9
Poitier, Sidney, 17
populism/populists, 75, 83
Portugal, 24
Powell, Colin, 17
Power, Victor "Vic" Pellot, xi, 153, 155,
    156, 157–58
Price, Richard, 5, 36, 44, 48, 98, 119
Price, Sally, 119
Puerto Rico, 6, 13, 15, 25, 130, 135, 153,
    154, 156, 157
punk, 100

quadrille, 106–07, 122, 123
Quakers, 27
Quammen, David, 19
Quashee, 7

Raboteau, Albert, 48
race war, 60, 64, 67, 72, 76, 84–85
racial stereotypes, 71, 76
racism, xi, 11, 50–87, 137, 145, 162, 165
railroads, 142
Ramsey, Frederic, 116
rap culture, xi, 109, 110
rapist. See stereotyping
Reagan, Ronald, 3
rebellion, 147

Reconstruction, 57, 74, 80, 82, 83, 94
reel, 106–07, 122
reggae, ix, 17, 23, 99, 124
Regla, Cuba, 60, 86, 90
religion, 33, 42, 43, 117, 120; Africa, 28,
    69, 92; African American, 26, 30, 34
repartimiento, 132
Republican Party, 75
Republicans, 70
resistance, 23, 44
revolution, 54
Rhumba, ix, 109
rice, 29, 46, 101, 130
Richmond, Va., 153
Rickey, Branch, 156
ringplays, 111
Rio de Janeiro, Brazil, 99
Roberts, John Storm, 116
Robinson, Jackie, 155–56
Rochester, N.Y., 161
rock, 23, 100
rocksteady, 23
Rodney, Walter, 13
Rodríguez Mayoral, Luis, 156–57
Rohlehr, Gordon, 109
Rome, 21
Ruck, Rob, The Tropic of Baseball, 11
rum, 130

Saco, Antonio, 95
Saguas, 105
Saint Domingue. See Haiti
Salazar, Lázaro, 160
Salem, Mass., 93
salsa, 100
Samaná Bay, 4
samba, 23, 99, 109
San Francisco Giants, 164
San Juan, Puerto Rico, 158
Sanford, Fla., 162
santería, 69
Santo Domingo, 130
Saramaka, 120, 123; maroons of, 116,
    119
Savannah, Ga., 159
Schuler, Monica, 29
Scott, Rebecca, 5
segregation, 166
Seven Years' War, 130, 135
Shango, 33

Sheridan, Richard, 130–31
shouting, 30–31, 110, 173 n 20
Shreveport, La., 153
shuffling, 110
Sierra Leone, 37
Singing the Master (1992), 104
siyak, 122
ska, 23, 124
skiffle, 100
slavery/slaves, xi, 7, 54–56, 168 n 1;
    slave trade, 130, 139, 148. *See also*
    abolition; Africa; Brazil; Caribbean;
    Cuba; Great Britain; United States,
    the; U.S. South
smuggling, 143
Sobel, Mechal, 48
Social Darwinism, 56
Sommerville, Diane M., 55
sorcery, 33
South. *See* U.S. South
South America, 7, 100, 103, 133
South Carolina, 25, 29, 30, 32–33, 38,
    39, 40, 47
Spain, 24, 55, 78, 85, 91, 127–29, 130,
    133, 135–36, 140–41, 147
Spanish America, 54
Spanish-American war, 4, 90
Spanish Armada, 129
spirituals, 23
square dance, 107
St. Croix, 35
St. Domingue. *See* Haiti
St. Kitts, 9, 12, 16, 27, 134
St. Louis Cardinals, 158, 159, 160, 161
St. Lucia, 134
St. Martin, 8, 11, 18, 134
St. Vincent, 16, 37, 134
Stack, Carol, 15
Stearns, Marshall, 116
steel bands, 23
stepping, 108
stereotyping, 84–87, 179 n 6; of Black
    rapist and male witch, 49–89
Stinchcombe, Arthur, 134, 137
strutting, 109
sugar, 13, 22, 101, 128–31, 133, 135–38,
    140, 141, 144, 146–48
sugar beets, 13, 141
sugar cane, 5, 18, 14
sugar mills, 142

Suriname, 25, 116, 117, 119, 120
Sweden, 100
Szwed, John, 98, 108, 110, 120

Taino Arawaks, 9
tapping, 110
Tartabull, Danny, 162
Tartabull, José, 162
tea, 130
Ten Years' War, 141
Texas, 160
Thistlewood, Thomas, 47
Thomas, R. P., 131
Thompson, Robert Farris, 98, 110, 116
tobacco, 21, 46, 101, 128, 129, 130, 135,
    136, 141, 144
Tobago, 16, 37, 121, 131, 134
Topping, Dan, 157
Toronto, 100
Treaty of Paris, 135
trickster, 37–38
Trinibago, 105
Trinidad, 6, 8, 14, 16, 17, 27, 38, 100,
    109, 117, 130, 134
turkey trot, 103

United Fruit Company, 137
United States, the, 108, 154; economy
    of, 13, 140, 141, 142; and slavery, 44,
    46–47, 89. *See also* African American;
    blacks; U.S. South
U.S. Department of Labor, 165
U.S. Revolution, 45, 130
U.S. Senate, 8
U.S. South: African culture in, 105, 112,
    116, 120; and Cuba, 49–96; defined,
    ix–x, 3–20, 97; economy of, 135, 136,
    140, 146, 148; and slavery, 21–48,
    147. *See also* African American;
    baseball
U.S. Supreme Court, 74, 158
USA Today Baseball Weekly, 153

Vance, Rupert, 5, 7
Venezuela, 6, 14, 154, 155, 160
Veracruz, ix, 154, 160
Virgil, Ozzie, 156, 163
Virgin Islands, 15, 25, 105
Virginia, 128, 129, 159
voodoo/hoodoo, 33

Walcott, Derek, 17, 19
Walcott, Louis, 11
Walker, Dixie, 156
waltz, 102
War for Independence (Cuba), 56, 69,
  70, 72, 82, 85, 142
Waterman, Richard, 116
Wells, Willie, 153, 160
Wesley, John, 28
West Indians, 11, 120
wheat, 148
White, Walter, 91
whites. *See* baseball; blacks;
  Christianity; Cuba; U.S. South
Whitney, Eli, 136
Williams, Eric, 21, 130, 147, 168 n 1

Williamsport, Penn., 161
Wilmington, N.C., 124
witchcraft. *See* stereotyping
withness, 102
Wolof, 28, 29
World Series, 161

xenophobia, 90

Yoruba, 38, 39, 117
Yucatan, 154

Zande, 37
Zip Coon, 105
Zoila, 52–53, 61, 62
zumbi, 32